From right to left: "You're quiet ... what's wrong?" "This morning the chief of the Singapore branch committed suicide." "So what!?".
From 1991 adult manga *Shangrila*. Cover illustration and foreword used with kind permission of the artist, Nōjō Junichi. © Nōjō Junichi/Takeshobō Ltd., Tokyo.

ADULT MANGA
*Culture and Power in Contemporary
Japanese Society*

ConsumAsiaN Book Series
edited by
Brian Moeran and Lise Skov
The Curzon Press and The University of Hawai'i Press

Women, Media and Consumption in Japan
Edited by Lise Skov and Brian Moeran
Published 1995

A Japanese Advertising Agency
An Anthropology of Media and Markets
Brian Moeran
Published 1996

Contemporary Japan and Popular Culture
Edited by John Whittier Treat
Published 1996

Packaged Japaneseness
Weddings, Business and Brides
Ofra Goldstein-Gidoni
Published 1997

Australia and Asia
Cultural Transactions
Edited by Maryanne Dever
Published 1997

Staging Hong Kong
Gender and Performance in Transition
Rozanna Lilley
Published 1998

Asian Department Stores
Edited by Kerrie L. MacPherson
Published 1998

Consuming Ethnicity and Nationalism
Edited by Kosaku Yoshino
Published 1999

The Commercialized Crafts of Thailand
Hill Tribes and Lowland Villages
Erik Cohen
Published 2000

Japanese Consumer Behavior
From Worker Bees to Wary Shoppers
John L. McCreery
Published 2000

Adult Manga
Culture and Power in Contemporary Japanese Society
Sharon Kinsella
Published 2000

ADULT MANGA
*Culture and Power in Contemporary
Japanese Society*

Sharon Kinsella

UNIVERSITY OF HAWAI'I PRESS
HONOLULU

Published in North America by
University of Hawai'i Press
2840 Kolowalu Street
Honolulu, Hawai'i 96822

First published in the United Kingdom by
Curzon Press
Richmond, Surrey

Printed in Great Britain

Library of Congress Cataloging-in-Publication Data

Kinsella, Sharon, 1969-
    Adult manga : culture and power in contemporary Japanese society / Sharon Kinsella.
      p. cm. – (ConsumAsiaN book series)
    Includes bibliographical references and index.
    ISBN 0–8248–2317–6 (cloth : alk. paper) – ISBN 0–8248–2318–4 (paper : alk. paper)
      1. Comic books, strips, etc.–Japan–History and criticism. 2. Comic books, strips,
etc.–Social aspects–Japan. 3. Power (Social sciences)–Japan–History–20th century. 4.
Japan–Social life and customs–20th century. I. Title. II. Series.

PN6790.J3 K56 2000
741.5'952–dc21   99-049284

CONTENTS

Acknowledgements   ix

List of Figures   xi

Introduction   1

1 A Short History of Manga   19

2 The Manga Production Cycle   50

3 Adult Manga and the Regeneration of National Culture   70

4 Amateur Manga Subculture and the *otaku* panic   102

5 The Movement Against Manga   139

6 Creative Editors and Unusable Artists   162

7 Conclusion: The Source of Intellectual Power in a Late
   Twentieth-Century Society   202

Notes   208

References   213

Index   224

ACKNOWLEDGEMENTS

It is not possible to express gratitude in words. If gratitude could be distributed like bread, then those who would get the first wafers would be Roger Goodman and Arthur Stockwin: the supervisors of my doctorate at Oxford University. They gave me reliable and unflagging support. The next wafer would be Fed-exed to Brian Moeran, who gave me new directions and intensive encouragement long-distance from Hong Kong.

Naturally I would then submit a wafer each to the ESRC (Economic and Social Research Council), and the JFEC (Japan Foundation Endowment Committee), in time to meet their deadlines. The ESRC provided consistent, long-term financial support between 1991 and 1995, and the JFEC provided similar and timely funds in 1995. Together they made researching this book possible.

A wafer on a silver plate would then be presented at the end of the College Meeting at Pembroke College, Cambridge, in recognition of the College's hopefully far-sighted decision to select me as the Daiwa-Calbee Research Fellow of Japanese Studies. Pembroke College has been extremely kind and open-minded about this book project.

Manna would rain from the sky on the many friends, colleagues, and associates who donated significant portions of their time and intelligence to helping me write this book. Anne Allison, Martin Barker, Stuart Hall, Susan Napier, Toshio Watanabe, Kurihara Yoshiyuki, Suga Tomoko, Ichihara Shinji, Ōgawa Haruki, Kure Tomofusa, Shigeru Mukasa, Sagara Yūmi, Pierre-Alan Szigeti, Doi Takashi, Torigae Takushi, Kōiwa Shinobu, Hayakawa Takeshi, the late Nagai Katsuichi, Ishikawa Takeshi, Iishi Tohru, Hiranuma

Atsushi, the late Okamoto Makoto, Hiranuma Yoshiko, Tomioka Hidenori, Taka Yumi, Matsumoto Tomohiko, Lise Skov, Jaqueline Berndt, Paul Hulbert, Uchida Masaru, Ikegami Yoshihiko, Ryōtani Sai, Kan Miyoshi, Nagashima Shinji, Menjō Mitsuro, Takahashi Norio, Tachikawa Yoshitake, Nōjō Junichi, Morizono Milk, Yonezawa Yoshihiro, Alessandro Gomarasca, Hiroshi Narumi, Yuri Kōichi, Robert Kinsella, Ron Stewart, Paul Goodwin, Peter Rhoades, Emmanuel Ohajah, Tom Feiling, Rod Tweedy, Satoru Yoshida, Daniel Lloyd, and Anthony Gerald Hopkins, would all take a trip to the dry-cleaners.

FIGURES

1	Manga magazine editorial meeting	9
1.1	Change in the total annual circulation figures of ALL manga magazines between 1979 and 1997	21
1.2	Mizuki Shigeru's *Ge Ge Ge Kitarō* in 1965	25
1.3	Shirato Sanpei on the cover of *GARO* in 1970	26
1.4	Tsuge Tadao's *Seigan Ryokichi ni Shi* in 1972	27
1.5	Tsuge Yoshiharu's *Screwceremony* in 1968	28
1.6	Tezuka Osamu's *Lost World* in 1947	29
1.7	Fujio-Fujiko's *Mao Tse Tung* in 1969	33
1.8	Abe Kenji's *The Human Condition* in 1971	34
1.9	Chiba Tetsuya's *Tomorrow's Joe* in 1968	35
1.10	*Manga AMPO* union pamphlet in 1970	36
1.11	Yokoo Tadanori's *Magazine* covers in 1970	38–9
1.12	Shinohara Katsuyuki's *Nioi Yokochō* in 1976	40
1.13	Comparative circulation figures of *Jump*, *Magazine* and *Sunday* between 1981 and 1997	41
1.14	A comparison of the popularity of film, television, and manga between 1959 and 1981	42
1.15	The development of manga publishing categories	45
1.16	Comparative total annual circulation figures of all manga and adult manga between 1979 and 1997	47
2.1	Advertisement for a manga competition	53
2.2	Conference between an artist and an editor	56
2.3	Tsuchida Seiji's *Editor!* in 1992	57
2.4	Checking the spelling on manga manuscripts	60
2.5	Sticking typeset lettering into speech bubbles	61
2.6	Manga typesetting room	64
2.7	Art-work and page layout	65

2.8 Making manga negatives with an industrial camera 65
2.9 Touching up negatives of manga manuscripts 66
2.10 Manga on the roller of a printing machine 67
3.1 Ishinomori Shōtarō's *Japan Inc.* (English version) in 1988 72
3.2 Saito Takao and Morita Akio's *Made in Japan* in 1987 74–5
3.3 Ishinomori Shōtarō's *Manga History of Japan* in 1989 76
3.4 Hirokane Kenshi's Department Chief Shima Kōsaku in 1995 80
3.5 Kawaguchi Kaiji's *Silent Service* in 1995 81
3.6 Hirokane Kenshi's *Kaji Ryūsuke's Principles* in 1997 85
3.7 Kobayashi Yoshinori's *Arrogance Manifesto* 88
3.8 Ministry officials plan an *Environment White Paper in Manga* form in 1993 96
4.1 Increase in the number of individuals attending December *Comic Market* 1975–1997 107
4.2 Increase in the number of manga circles participating December *Comic Market* 1975–1995 108
4.3 Girls' manga by Miuchi Sakue in 1994 114–5
4.4 Amateur *parody* manga of *Silent Service* in 1991 116
4.5 Amateur *original yaoi* Yahagi Takako 1989 118
4.6 Sonoda Kenichi's *Gun Smith Cats* in 1994 123
4.7 A humorous caricature of a *manga otaku* in 1992 130
5.1 Change in the number of number of manga books categorized as 'harmful' 1990–1992 147
6.1 Photo-realism in *Kaji Ryūsuke's Principles* in 1997 177
6.2 Yamanaka Osamu's *Pendako Paradise* in 1994 187
6.3 Iwaaki Hiroshi's *Parasite!* in 1992 190
6.4 Kuroda Iō's *Pictures and Words of the Great Japanese Troll* in 1994 191
6.5 Fukumoto Yōji's *Gamurakan* in 1994 192
6.6 Chen Uen's *Heroic Stories of the Eastern Chō Dynasty* in 1993 194–5

INTRODUCTION

At the end of the Cold War a transformation took place in the nature of popular culture produced in Japan. In the last decade of the twentieth century publishing company employees began to take over the production of a cultural medium which was first created by self-appointed artists from low social origins. This is a book about the rise and fall of intellectual participation in society, through popular culture, during the span of post-war democracy.

Though the words 'working class' or 'pro-establishment' may be used, this is not a left-wing analysis of pop-culture. Amateur manga will not be defended over commercial manga, the underground over the industry, or girls' manga over conservative adult manga. These divisions no longer mean what they meant previously: underground culture may be more derivative than commercial culture, amateur manga may contain less individual expression than manga made through large-scale cultural production, conservative manga may have more in the way of progressive cultural themes than alternative manga. This is a book about the transformation of popular culture into a new cultural form, made by the employees of culture industries with the support of government agencies and national institutions, at the end of one political era and the beginning of another. The manga artist quoted below exemplifies the nature of the previous relationship between manga and society:

> Until high school I was a good boy, but at university I changed a lot. I lived alone and found new values. I didn't wanna join a big company and become a salaryman. It didn't seem like it was going to be a great deal of fun. My family, right back to

1

my grandad, worked at the Toyota car plant. Its the biggest and most profitable company in Japan and their values were always the values of Toyota: 'there is only one great power in the world that controls everything'. Originally they were blue-collar but my Dad rose up through the union at Toyota, he became the union leader, and from their a local councillor in Nagoya. They were mainstream, being average was considered the best thing you could possibly achieve. I joined the company anyway for 11 months till I quit coz it was so boring and started wondering what else I could do. I did not become a manga artist right away, rather I recalled that I was in the manga club at university, and wondered if I could make money out of it.

I went to Meiji University in 1970 at the peak of the student movement. Meiji and Waseda have the biggest university manga clubs coz they are *bankara* universities which attract poorer than average students from the countryside and provinces. They get lots of students that get there by their own devices, whose parents are not paying the fees for them. I wasn't particularly interested in the politics, I went to a few demos, something about rent strikes, that was it.

I went round to companies with things I had drawn and gradually I started getting work. I was really poor for the first two years. I worked for small companies, one man companies, especially porn magazines, of which there were a great many in the seventies.

After the AMPO movement a lot of students went into small companies and became owner-editors of erotic magazines or manga magazines. The students most involved in the demonstrations couldn't get jobs in big companies, or anywhere at all, but they had to make a living, so erotic magazines were the one thing they could be fairly sure of selling – no matter how crap they were at making them. Others just couldn't be company men. Usually the magazines would really be run by only one person who edited everything in it. Ninety per cent would be porn, and ten per cent would be what the editor wanted to put in that wouldn't otherwise sell on its own, like avant garde manga. Students used to buy those magazines. Artists with all kinds of talents would get into

2

those magazines, and I was one of them. Editors were slap happy. You could draw whatever you wanted.

I started at *Manga Erogenica* first, which is a porn magazine, though the stuff I drew wasn't. At that time the artists working there had been there for years without moving anywhere, but quite soon, starting with me, we started going all over. In about 1978 I was getting loads of money and loads of work all of a sudden. Nōjō Junichi and Otomo Katsuhiro (*Akira*) and me, we all suddenly broke through.

(Pers. Interview, Ishikawa Jun, 1994)

Until the mid-1990s manga represented one of the most extensive forms of culture in post-war Japan. It is a contemporary medium and it is pop culture. Manga is the name given to Japanese comics. Since the 1960s manga has been sold mainly in the form of weekly and monthly magazines. These magazines are inexpensive and bulky – they are made of several hundred pages of coarse lightweight paper, tinted in pastel shades. Each issue contains the latest episodes of between 10 to 20 separate series, all of which can be read in around an hour. Magazines are usually thrown away, like newspapers, after they have been read, but individual series are later re-published in smaller single-author volumes, which are collected like CDs or books by the readers. The expansion of the manga industry and medium has rested on the financial efficacy of this dual system of publishing. Manga magazines alone do not create large returns, but manga magazines and books published in tandem, have made big profits. In the mid-1990s the overall profit rates of the manga industry began to decline.

Though often thought of by foreign observers, as a specialized cultural trope with strongly defined themes such as pornography and science fiction fantasy, manga is primarily a medium. Like television, literature or film, the manga medium carries an immense range of cultural material. The bread and butter of the manga industry has been a large number of long-running series which can be loosely compared to the soap operas, dramas, sitcoms, comedies, and docu-dramas aired on British television. However, manga generally has a greater thematic range than Japanese television broadcasting, a medium which has been dominated by low-budget celebrity game shows, chat shows, audience and panel discussions, and food and travel guides. The themes of series have been defined mainly by their location, for example, in and around a sports club, school, college campus, workplace, household, historical set, or criminal underworld. In addition to drama about everyday life, manga has also absorbed a range of material, too raw, bawdy, satirical, politically subversive, delinquent, artistic, fantastic, or simply obscure, to get distribution in any other mass media. As with literature, the nature of manga publishing: the potentially infinite variability of the size of print runs, has blurred some of the practical, industrial foundations of the distinction between mass media and a minor media or art.

One of the most common synonyms used to describe manga is 'air', something that has permeated every crevice of the contemporary environment. Manga can be purchased from train platform kiosks, in book shops near railway stations and on shopping malls and streets, as well as in art book shops and luxury department stores; it can be bought from any 24-hour convenience store, a snack bar in a car park at a tourist resort, at a grocery store serving the needs of a remote village, or from a vending machine chained to the corner of a street. It can also be bought from second-hand manga superstores and specialist book shops, or from homeless men vending already discarded manga, arranged on blankets in underground pedestrian passes. It can be discovered left behind on seats in trains, or borrowed from collections made available for browsing in love hotel bedrooms, manga cafes (*manga kissaten*) or diners.

The skeleton history of manga is similar to that of pop music in the Anglo-American cultural sphere. Like pop music, manga has some aesthetic roots in a pre-war folk culture, but was itself developed by early pioneers of the contemporary form, *story manga,* during the 1950s. *Story manga* expanded rapidly during the 1960s, when it also became linked to political radicalism and counter-cultural experimentation. Commercial manga continued to expand and diversify throughout the 1970s and 1980s, during which period its contents also matured to meet the changing tastes of its original readership based in the baby-boom generation and the more 'everyday interests' of its newer readers. In the 1990s the broad popularity of manga was challenged by the rapid expansion of computer games, personal computers and the internet. While mass events flourished around the amateur manga medium, finding its European equivalent, perhaps, in rave the professional manga world

4

tended towards a self-conscious crisis of form and direction. Like pop music, manga has been a fantastically creative and diverse phenomenon. The colossal quantity and variety of manga reflects a little of the massive sociological power and energy of the post-war era.

Manga has always been a contentious medium prone to the 'practice [of] politics' (Benjamin [1936] 1992:218) as much as that of aesthetics. In 1967 it was defined as a 'border art', a new type of democratic medium accessible by cultural amateurs which could transgress the boundaries of low and high culture (Tsurumi 1967). While one of the points which will be made in this book is that the level of control exercised over the production of manga by governing organizations has increased by various means during the 1990s, neither the production nor the distribution of manga has ever been a stable and uncontested process. In other words the manga industry has never yet been a fully mechanized 'iron system' (Adorno and Horkheimer [1944] 1972:120) for producing culture, operating within a 'managed society' (Kurihara 1982: 133). To the contrary the instability of adult manga production reflects exceedingly well some of the power contests which have taken place between different sections of post-war society.

The focus of post-war Japanese *cultural politics* has been which manga ought to be distributed and where. From the beginning of the contemporary manga industry in the 1960s, fanaticism, violence, politics, and sex, *mediated through manga*, have been driven in and out of national political discourse. According to the intentions of different cultural policies manga has been wishfully defined and redefined as non-culture, children's culture, working-class culture, avant-garde culture, counter culture, youth culture, pop culture, corporate culture, Japanese culture, national culture, Asian culture and even international culture. Generally manga has been described by its opponents as a vulgar or low-class (*gehin*) media which undermines education, public morality, and national intelligence. Left-wing intellectuals, and class-conscious workers and students have simultaneously regarded manga as a progressive medium which flouts repressive social taboos. An additional attraction of manga in the eyes of many intellectuals is the fact that it is an authentic, home-grown, modern Japanese culture with its roots in Japanese social experience, rather than being an American or European political or cultural import.

5

Manga has displayed a special responsiveness to the changing political currents of society. One reason for this sensitivity to political ideology is the physical basis of the manga industry in publishing companies. Other mass media, including newspapers, radio and television have been produced by large media conglomerates which have more binding relations with the government. Most of these media corporations started as newspaper companies which later diversified into first radio, and then television broadcasting during the post-war period. Fuji Sankei Communications Group, for example, comprises Fuji Television which broadcasts Channel 8, and the *Sankei Shinbun* newspaper company, established in 1933. Tokyo Broadcasting System (TBS), which began transmitting black and white television in 1955 and colour television in 1960, was launched by the Mainichi Shimbun newspaper company, which was founded in 1876. Asahi Television was originally founded as Nihon Education Television (NET) in 1959, before being bought in 1977 by Asahi Shimbun newspaper company, itself founded in 1879. As these large media conglomerates are obliged to apply for television broadcasting licenses from the government in order to broadcast, effective political control has been maintained, over not only the contents of television, but also over a range of other mass-media produced by the same corporations. In contrast, publishing companies need never apply for government licenses and have had more freedom than other media corporations.

The typical readership of high-circulation manga magazines, moreover, are boys and men with low disposable incomes and restricted education. As a negative correlation exists between high levels of personal consumption and the habit of reading manga, it contains very little advertising (Moeran 1991:7). High-circulation boys' and adult manga magazines of 270 to 350 pages in length generally contain little more than 8 pages of advertisments. Advertisers have avoided placing adverts in manga because of the detrimental effect that association with a low-class male culture like manga would have on the image of most products. The positive result of this is that the considerable influence that advertisers can exert on the editorial decisions of ordinary magazines (Moeran 1996:223–229) does not have any effect on manga.

While manga has not been filled with the images of products for sale it has been filled with images of people. It has been a very sociable medium. Its pages literally teem with characters, whose

6

aspirations, frustrations, and adventures form the substance of manga series. Manga characters tend to embody aspects of caricature, they have exaggerated facial expressions, they swoon, they sweat, they cry, they bleed, they are visibly excited, shocked, distraught, embarrassed, and annoyed. It is possible that highly expressive and emotionally readable manga characters have held a particular attraction in a contemporary environment which has encouraged high levels of self-discipline and a relatively controlled mode of physical and facial expression.

The superfluity of expression in manga makes it a superb point of entry into the subjective mood of post-war Japan. Through manga it is possible to trace the deep veins of yearning, dejection, frustration, obsession, desire, euphoria, disappointment and fantasy not so apparent in other media. In an advanced industrial society in which the volume of information, intellectual attention, and culture focused on national ideology, national psychology, corporate organization, technology, and aesthetics, has overwhelmed any serious interest in actual people and contemporary creativity, manga culture has been an important extra dimension for communicating new attitudes and dealing with subjective issues. In this context the focus on *how people feel* has given manga a clear humanistic value.

While the focus of manga has been people the focus of the manga industry has been profits:

> When an editor meets a manga artist he has to be very enthusiastic about the artists' manga and the work at hand. He has to say ... 'Look! I've got this plan for a great manga story and only you could draw the pictures for it, it suits you perfectly ...' Editors get famous for their displays of enthusiasm. Talking is their trade, they are like car salesmen. As you know, there is no guidebook to perfect editing, but there is a famous car salesmans' guidebook about how to sell cars. I read it! It is really good! What the author says is that every time he goes to the door of a customer, no matter what he says to them, they turn him down. The customers give him excuses. What the author does then is listen to them, he listens to everything they say and when they have finished, he goes away. But then he goes back to the same door later, and again, perhaps, they give him excuses, and he listens to them all again, and goes away. Eventually the customers run out of

excuses when he calls for them and they actually have to consider buying the car. It is really true, that technique does work! I do it with manga artists. Every time I ask them to draw something, they refuse. I listen to all their complaints, and then I ask them again later. If you repeat your request and listen to everything they complain about, eventually, with time, they will actually consider drafting a few pages of manga. They begin to worry that perhaps you'll stop offering them work, or that maybe they ought to do a few pages just to keep up the relationship. I use that method with older shrewder manga artists. In the case of young, inexperienced artists I encourage and flatter them a lot – and that usually starts a good relationship.

The words of this manga editor, spoken in 1994, underscore the fact that before manga is a cultural object it is an industry. Manga is produced. Each and every minute stage of its production, from the consideration of new characters – to selecting print fonts, is subject to planning and forethought (see Figure 1). Most of this planning falls into the hands of editors employed by large publishing companies. Editors sit at the centre of an eccentric and rumbustious social network known as the *manga industry world* (*manga gyōkai*). In fact manga editors are cultural managers. The majority of the physical processes of producing manga are sub-contracted out from publishers to other companies. Manga artists and artists' assistants, the employees of photoset, printing, and binding companies, book distributors and truck drivers, and manga book shop sales assistants, are all part of the extended economic network of the manga industry world. The industry, dedicated only to manufacturing manga for profits, is synchronized by editors and publishers based in offices around central Tokyo.

From the moment that editors became the managers of manga magazines in 1959 they have been engaged in a continual struggle with manga artists. Editors have had to persuade artists to draw series in which they have typically lacked much personal interest. The degree to which editors have been able to persuade artists has been variable. A large number of well-known manga dramas, particularly those drawn by male artists for boys and adult manga magazines, have been serialized in spite of astounding levels of animosity between artists and editors. The manga world vibrates

Figure 1 Soul searching in a weekly manga editorial meeting (1994).

with secrets and rumours about artists abducted by their editors, artists who escaped through toilet windows, artists who fled their studios overnight, artists who beat-up their editors leaving them with facial scars, and artists who committed suicide.

Editor–artist tension has been generated from three main sources: it is the most basic task of editors to impose work discipline on artists; editors enforce deadlines and standards of quality; like many other workers artists have resisted employment discipline. The second source of tension has been a struggle over the contents of manga: while editors have seen manga as a product *they* are manufacturing for profit, artists have seen manga as a form of culture which belongs to them, and in which they have the right to express their own ideas. The third element, which also incorporates the issue of work discipline, and the question of the ownership of culture, is that of social class. Since the 1920s manga has been seen as a special form of expression of the Japanese working class. Since the 1960s editors employed by large publishing companies have been accused of being a middle-class, middle-management who exploit and manipulate the medium. The relationship between artists and editors has been the contemporary focus of ever more isolated, and outmoded strands of anti-bourgeois consciousness.

Manga artists however have become easier to persuade. In adult and boys' manga it is increasingly editors who presume ownership of the manga medium, and the right to determine precisely what will be drawn in manga series. Editors have begun to carry out new layers of intellectual and creative work, pushing manga artists to the periphery of the creative process. Adult manga has become a more middle-class medium which expresses the consciousness of both editors and bureaucrats employed in government agencies. From the mid-1980s adult manga has effectively changed from being an anti-establishment medium to being a pro-establishment medium. The following chapters of this book will examine in detail how this realignment has taken place. It is the story of adult manga, but it is also the story of late twentieth century socio-political change.

Each of the following chapters of this book details a different aspect of the production, content, and distribution of manga. In particular it is *adult manga*, and to some extent *boys' manga*, that together form the core of the manga industry and readership, which are the main subject of this analysis.

Chapter one outlines the history of the manga medium and industry, which is short. The connection between manga and political radicalism during the 1960s was one which created the audience and the circumstances for the initial take-off of the adult manga industry. In the next three decades manga reading spread through society and the different styles and genres of manga multiplied, creating the partial basis for new categories of manga publishing targeted at different sections of the population.

Chapter two looks at the physical cycle of production used to make manga. Contemporary production begins with formally self-employed artists in independent studios and with editors in publishing companies. Thereafter photoset lettering and 'art work' employees, printers, book binders, and magazine and book distributors are enjoined. The creative and the entirely mechanical aspects of making and reproducing manga are knitted together in a systemetized yet infinitely variable sequence.

Chapter three examines the new interest in manga displayed by government agencies and large corporations from the middle of the 1980s. In this period certain types of adult and boys' manga received recognition for the first time from museums, academics, and politicians in Japan. In this period a new cannon of realistic adult manga with (neo)conservative political themes was created and distributed, both in the form of a new publishing category of *information manga* books, and in existing adult and boys' manga magazines. Manga for adults and adolescents, which had previously been perceived as a cheap, tasteless and embarrassing blind-spot within Japanese culture, was discussed with pride by critics in literary journals and national newspapers. The new wave of pro-establishment series helped the manga industry to claim a more respectable and stable position in society and helped key companies and national institutions that adopted this manga to rejuvenate and modernize their cultural identity.

Chapter four looks at alternative manga made on the boundaries of the commercial manga industry during the 1960s and 1970s, and the growth, from the late 1980s, of a gargantuan amateur manga subculture, quite separate from the manga publishing industry. The distinctive genres of amateur manga – *parody, yaoi*, and *Lolicom* – have betrayed a widespread fixation with male and female gender types and sexuality. Sexual themes, which dominate amateur manga, are both a specific response to the highly gendered structure of commercial boys' and girls' manga magazines, and a creative outlet for new trends in social psychology linked to changes in the gender politics of society.

From the end of 1989 amateur manga subculture, in direct contrast to the positive appraisal of the new style of information manga, began to attract a great deal of negative publicity in the news media. This centred on the argument that there was a causative link between amateur manga subculture and a serial-child-murder case known as the 'Miyazaki incident'. Amateur manga fans were characterized as lonely and psychologically disturbed young men, and became the targets of a nation-wide panic about the murderous anti-social effects of involvement with violent and erotic *Lolicom* manga and animation. The Miyazaki incident bore similarities to the British 'James Bulger' case of 1993, and the American 'Colorado' schoolroom shootings incident of 1999.

Chapter five probes the legal structure of manga censorship and the sharp increase of bureaucratic activities regulating the distribution and production of manga from 1990. Organizations as diverse as women's groups, local citizen's associations, the PTA (Parent Teacher Association), local government officers, the police and large quasi-governmental organizations became involved in the project of controlling the output of certain genres of manga. The impulse towards manga censorship was based on the political thought of the post-war era, a period in which manga was negatively associated with both the lower classes and with the radical Left. The new trend towards the promotion of adult manga hinted at a new way of integrating political opposition into the institutional mainstream of society.

In Chapter six the focus of analysis moves away from society and into the editorial office to look at hidden changes in the ways in which adult and boys' manga were being produced. In the 1990s manga editors in large companies had a vision of a new type of adult manga. To realize it they took control of the creative aspect of making manga. New criterion determining which artists would be selected to draw series came into vogue, freelance writers, researchers and contract editors were contracted to work for manga editors, carrying out new layers of creative and intellectual work, and editors themselves attempted to carry out some of the creative and intellectual work involved in manga production. Increasingly the intellectual structure of most major adult manga series originated amongst the editors of publishing companies. Not only were these editors white-collar company employees rather than *artists*, they were also relatively wealthy, highly-educated and privileged individuals whose tastes and social consciousness were channelled into re-forming adult manga into a new cultural medium.

In the concluding chapter, the separate influences shaping adult manga which are discussed in detail in each chapter are linked together. From the end of the 1980s adult manga has been a dynamic medium reflecting a social order in flux.

If manga made a sudden debut in museums and literary reviews in Japan in the 1990s, it received no less attention throughout the rest of the world. Contemporary Japanese design, fashion and pop culture, *and* manga, have become steadily more visible in Europe and America in the last decade of the twentieth century. Fascination with contemporary culture from Asia has united the media and academia. An unorthodox interest in pop-culture and the mass media emerged from within the Japanese Studies discipline in the late 1980s. From the mid-1990s the British Cultural Studies group began another strand of scholarly engagement with Japanese and Asian youth culture. This steadily growing research interest in contemporary culture in Japan and Asia in the academy has joined the close attention given to Japan by European designers, artists, producers, retailers, publishers, and editors, working in the culture and entertainment industries. The Institute of Contemporary Art (ICA) in London which plays a special role in introducing new trends into British culture has nurtured film and animation from Japan. The ICA showed first overseas releases of animated films including *Akira, Nausicaa,* and *Ghost in the Shell,* Japanese pornography, and low-budget cyberpunk films through the 1990s. The British terrestrial television station, Channel 4, also broadcast an intermittent series of Japanese animated films, including *Cyber City, Megalopolis, Doomed, Devil Man,* and *Tokyo Babylon,* through 1995 and 1996.

At the end of the twentieth century the Orient is once more the focus of European desire and fantasy. This time it is the turn of advertising, fashion and youth culture to imagine in Japan or China that which they can no longer believe in, in Europe and America. One of the few forms in which European youth have been able to imagine the future is to imagine one in neo-Tokyo. In a relationship which began with the release of Ridley Scotts' film *Bladerunner* in 1982, and was refreshed a decade later with the release of Otomo Katsuhiro's animation *Akira* in 1990, images of the future and images of Japanese popular culture, design and technology, have been fused into one genre. Japanese animation and motifs taken from manga, such as the Atom Boy character, have inspired new style ideas in international design and fashion in the late 1990s.

Nevertheless, the popularity of manga and animation in Europe and America has not been the unplanned result of a merely active interest in Japan. The initial circulation of manga outside Japan has also been attributable to a more official and managed initiative to export Japanese culture abroad on the part of governmental agencies, institutions, and companies in Japan, working with European and American institutions and professional individuals. In 1988 the University of California Press published an English edition of the manga series *Japan Inc. An Introduction to Japanese Economics in Manga.* In 1992 one of the largest ever manga exhibitions was held in the San Francisco Cartoon Art Museum sponsored by two major manga publishers, the Japan Foundation, and the US Consulate General in Japan. In 1999 a Manga Exhibition sponsored, once again, by the Japan Foundation, was held at the Maison de la Culture du Japon in Paris, and Kunsthal in Rotterdam.

This book too is the result of a plan to introduce manga to Europe and America, originally initiated by manga editors in Japan, as much as by myself. As a graduate student in 1994 I became the fortunate recipient of a monthly sum of 160,000 yen given to me for 6 months through the auspices of an International Manga Fellowship Program funded by a manga publishing company, Kōdansha. The Fellowship Program could never guarantee what its visiting fellows, mainly professional comic experts from Europe, chose to say about manga. However funding did guarantee that we would say something.

Images from Japanese animation and manga presented in television shows and magazine reports on the phenomenon in Europe and America, however, have generally been edited to emphasize violence, sex and strangeness. This type of manga review in the media has fitted snugly into pre-existing notions of Japan as a cruel, sexist, strange and repressed society. So long as manga is perceived only as a finished work, as a discreet cultural object, the temptation to categorize it as another example of self-explanatory cultural exotica will be strong. But manga is not the gauche imprint of a collective Japanese unconscious caught unawares, anymore than are Toyota motorcars or Evisu jeans. Rather than being an accidental reflection of a national, or racial (Japanese) psyche, that just *somehow* surfaced, manga is the end product of a series of complicated conscious social exchanges and intelligent cultural management. The closer we look at the making of manga the more we see that it is not so much 'Japanese culture' as contemporary culture in a modern industrial society.

Another way of making an enquiry into manga, other than observing its production, would be to read it. A careful reading could amount to a content analysis. Impressions developed through reading manga might be theorized with ideas derived from Bakhtin, Freud, Jung, Lacan, Althusser, feminist literary theory, or Japanology, and then related back, if at all possible, to general aspects of the society from which the manga had *somehow* arisen. It is quite possible to analyse manga in that way: manga books and magazines are far more accessible than the people who make them. But, on the whole, this book does not employ that approach. Rather than *taking apart* the constituent elements of manga stories on an abstract level, this book is based on research into how the different elements which make manga are *put together* in the first place. It is an ethnographic study of *cultural production*. The understanding of manga that this approach generates is quite different to the type of understanding achievable from the assessment of manga texts alone. The analysis laid out in this book is in many ways better evidenced, more precise, and more clearly situated within social history. The starting position of this book is not a defence of manga (which is already well defended) but a defence of the modernity, creativity, and complexity of society in Japan in the post-war period.

In the process of carrying out this research I became acquainted with a large number of people who came together between the mid-1960s and the mid-1990s to make manga. When I met them, between 1993 and 1997, they were involved with manga at a particular time; at a time when a sense of imminent historical closure pervaded society. Many of these people – editors, publishers, artists and managers, were uncertain about the future of the culture they made, and they responded to this uncertainty by attempting to take an open approach to their work. This not only had an effect on the manga itself (to be discussed in Chapter six), but also made them relatively willing to try out talking to a foreign researcher. No doubt part of their motivation for talking to me was to use me as a sounding board to help them develop a new perspective on their own work.

I do not believe that it would be possible to enter the manga industry and the amateur manga world again today in quite the way that circumstances made it possible to access them in the early 1990s. The culture industries as a whole are notorious for their secretive tendencies. The manga industry has shown the same reticence exhibited by the culture industries in general, about providing interviews and information about its internal affairs.

A central plank of my research was sponsored by a manga magazine, *Morning*, published by Kōdansha. For a period of nine months, I sat at a desk situated amongst a bank of identical desks, in the editorial offices of *Morning* and *Afternoon* manga magazines. A few weeks of this time engaged in *participant observation* style research were also spent in the editorial offices of *Magazine* boys' magazine. In *Morning* and *Afternoon* editorial I attended most weekly editorial meetings, 'world' meetings, new magazine creation (*zōkan*) meetings, manga award ceremonies, and editorial parties. Occasionally I was asked to earn my bread and butter (or at least look as if I was) and so engaged with trolley-loads of amateur manga scripts sent into the editorials' own manga competition. This manga was circulated laboriously from desk to desk before being graded and verbally assessed by every editor in a lengthy assessment and voting meeting. A plethora of introductions, feedback, snippets of useful information, and unintentionally disclosed illustrations of how editors and artists think, was collected through casual chatter in and around editorial offices, and through observations of editors at work, during editorial meetings, on the phone, or engaged in discussions with visiting manga artists.

Due to the fact that this part of my research was supported by *Morning* editorial and indirectly by Kōdansha, it contains an informational bias towards manga published by Kōdansha. This is partially offset by supplementary material gathered on day-trips and even week-long excursions to 'play' in the editorial offices of *Young Sunday, Big Comic Spirits, Hime, Hana to Yume, GARO, Magazine*, and *Manga Boys*, manga magazines produced by six quite different publishing companies. However some degree of irreducible bias towards manga produced by Kōdansha remains, with the overall effect of focusing our attention on activities taking place in one of the three biggest manga publishers in Japan, and on major rather than minor cultural trends.

A second plank of the research was based on interviewing. During the time spent in manga editorials I invited editors to be interviewed about their work. Usually the interviews took place in cafes, bars, and restaurants in the vicinity of the editorial office. No sooner had we left the editorial office than editors would tend to see an interview with me as an excuse to do their part for corporate hospitality. At this point I promptly lost control over the location of the interview session. While some were mercifully enacted in diners or cafes, others took place through clouds of alcoholic inebriation. During these latter sessions, sometimes lasting until the early hours of the morning, my already imprecise identity as a (young, white, female) researcher tended to become blurred with that of a badly trained bar hostess, in the hazed judgements of some editors. As the night drew on, some of them become personal, amorous or abusive, as well as informative.

Despite becoming the occasional subject of sarcastic racial resentment, unwanted advances, and formulaic sexist humiliation, editors were generous and ostentatious during these extended interviews. Some of the more senior editors introduced me to their private thoughts in a pocketful of the most exquisitely run-down

16

(*jime*), and exclusive drinking establishments in central Tokyo. The interiors of these unreal establishments, almost entirely dependent on the entertainment allowances of big business for their continued existence, corresponded in many ways to the mysterious atmosphere and aesthetic precision of more dark (*kurai*), avante gard manga and *gekiga*. The most flamboyant interview appointment of all was to take place during an orgy organized by the convivial manga artist, Narita Akira, on the 45th floor of the Keio Plaza Hotel. After an hour snatching little pieces of worthless information over the heads of emaciated women in black leather thongs and bodices posturing for podgy middle-aged men in boxer shorts, we were all gratefully released from our various postures by a visit from the police.

Excluding the time during which structured interviews broke down into mannered social mayhem, I collected approximately 300 hours of interviews from 65 manga artists, editors, critics, and publishers from across the spectrum of the manga industry and medium. Some of the manga artists – Yokoyama Ryūichi, Maruo Suehiro, Sonoda Kenichi, Fujishima Kōsuke, Ishikawa Jun, Nagashima Shinji, Kobayashi Yoshinori, Hatanaka Jun, Sonoda Kenichi, Hirokane Kenshi, Kawaguchi Kaiji, Narita Akira, Nōjō Junichi, Morizono Milk – that I interviewed at length, were household names, as famous in the Asian cultural sphere as pop stars are in Britain and America. Chief editors and critics that I interviewed at length include Uchida Masaru, Kure Tomofusa, Yonezawa Yoshihiro, Menjō Mitsurō, (the late) Nagai Katsuichi, Nishimura Shigeo, (the late) Okamoto Makoto, and Saitani Ryō. The personalities and ideas of these individuals, all of whom are well-known figures within the manga world, have become fused with post-war culture. Others that I also spent considerable time with – including Yuri Koichi, Kurihara Yoshiyuki, Torigae Takushi, Hara Takao, Doi Takashi, Ogawa Haruki, Ichihara Shinji, Iishi Tohru, Shin Kasayuki, Tsutsumi Yasumitsu, Watanabe Kyō, Igarashi Takao, Konagai Nobumasa, Tachikawa Yoshitake, Nishimura Hiromi, Hayashi Tarō – were largely unknown manga editors, contract editors, and cultural promoters, who are the unseen 'puppeteers' of the manga industry.[1]

The openness of manga publishers to scrutiny had a few limitations. While interviews with editors, publishers, promoters and other professionals representing organizations such as Manga Japan, The Society for the Freedom of Expression in Manga, or the

Publishing Industry Association, were reasonably easily acquired, obtaining useful interviews with working manga artists and artists' assistants was more difficult. The main reason for this difficulty was that one of the more important jobs which editors perform is 'canning' (*kan-zume*) – literally sealing off manga artists from the outside world, like tinned fruit. Artists are 'canned' or isolated as far as possible by editors to prevent them from becoming distracted from their work and failing to meet their weekly deadlines, or else to prevent them from being persuaded by editors from other companies to switch their contracts.

While the practical obstacle to contacting unknown manga artists directly is the lack of information about their whereabouts, famous working manga artists were often accompanied by editors who carefully supervised and managed interviews with manga artists in their charge. I was able to interview a handful of famous artists at length in their homes or studios, and to observe many more 'conferences' (*uchiawase*) between editors and artists. On all such pre-arranged occasions the artists were accompanied by editors attached to the magazines for which they were working, and in those circumstances were guarded in their comments and reluctant to discuss their experiences of the manga industry and medium.

Artists were aware that while any type of interview about the contents of manga and their manga series, was permissible and actually encouraged, at no time should they disclose information about the conditions of their contracts, or personal experiences of the social relationships which pertained between artists and editors. As I developed a more extensive contact network in the manga world I was able to approach and make independent appointments for interviews with manga artists. However my association with Kōdansha – one of the most desirable places of employment for manga artists – meant that artists, unless they had already retired, preferred to be silent about the role of editors and publishing companies in their lives. Manga artists quoted in this book tend to be individuals known for their 'attitude' and refusal to conform properly to the demands of the manga publishing industry.

1

A SHORT HISTORY
OF MANGA

The immense manga medium has flowered in the space of only four decades and like springtime in a desert it may disappear entirely from the face of society as rapidly as it appeared. Like the democratic political systems of the post-war period in which they flourished, pop cultures like manga represent a highly specific form of culture based on the institution of political opposition and open social organization.

The impressive spectrum of graphic styles and genres which comprise the manga medium emerged only after the Pacific war, and most in the briefer period since 1960. Nevertheless, the majority of cultural criticism has so far associated manga not with the international phenomenon of popular culture, but with far earlier forms of Japanese graphic art. Manga has been compared repeatedly to the twelfth century illustrations of Bishop Toba (*Toba-e*), or the wood block print (*ukiyoe*) culture of the eighteenth and nineteenth centuries. About this tendency to compare manga with earlier examples of Japanese illustration, manga critic Kure Tomofusa observes: 'This kind of discussion about the origins of manga is intended to compete with the hysterical denial of the manga as a form of Japanese culture by educationalists.' (Kure 1990: 191) The opposition to the manga and animation industries by conservative elements in post-war society has encouraged the defenders of manga, namely professional manga critics, to emphasize or even invent stylistic origins for manga in ancient Japanese history. Its critics have hoped that if they could prove that manga is, somehow, a part of *traditional* Japan, then it cannot possibly be uprooted and repressed by the government. This defensive argument has drawn

19

attention away from the fact that manga is a strikingly *contemporary* cultural phenomenon.

The earliest recorded usage of the *term* 'manga' has been dated to the 1770s (Shimizu 1991:18–20). During the nineteenth century the word manga entered occasional, specialist usage, principally to describe wood block prints with comic themes, such as Katsushika Hokusai's series of wood block caricatures (*Hyakumensō*) published in 1819. Neither the term *manga* nor the term *manga* artist (*mangaka*) became part of everyday Japanese until the early Shōwa period [1926–1989] (Shimizu 1991:15). The spread of the term manga into everyday Japanese in the 1930s complemented the publication of the first serialized comic strips published in newspapers.

Since the 1980s the Tokyo Metropolitan region has acquired what is almost certainly the highest density of cultural production and distribution in the modern world (Ivy 1993:242). The manga publishing industry, which sits at the base of this pyramid of cultural production, often acts as a rich bed of ideas and characters later adapted for use in other media. Between 1959, when the first weekly manga magazines were launched, and 1994, when the circulation figures of manga peaked in size, the manga industry expanded continuously. Though the first systematic records of the circulation figures of manga magazines were not recorded until 1979 by the Centre for Publishing Research (*Shūppan Kenkyūjō*). The growth of manga production, measured according to the annual circulation figures of all manga magazines, is shown in Figure 1.1.

The 1920s

Two types of comic strip began production during the 1920s. One of these was comic strips for small children published in newspapers and journals bought by their parents, and strongly influenced by similar comic strips appearing in American newspapers. American comic strips such as George McManus's *Bringing up Father*, Bud Fisher's *Mutt and Jeff*, and Pat Sullivan's *Felix the Cat* were translated into Japanese and printed in newspapers such as the *Hōchi* and *Asahi Graph* in the 1920s. American cartoons published in newspapers became popular with Japanese readers. In the early 1920s the chief editor of the *Asahi Graph*, Suzuki Bunshiro, conceived an idea for a children's comic strip whilst touring Europe and America. On returning to Japan with samples of American

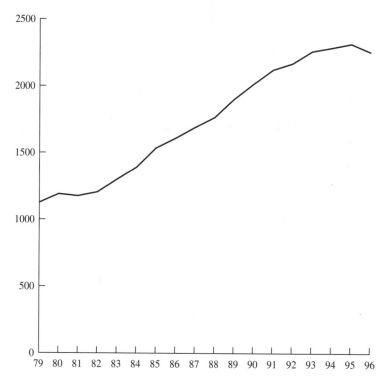

Figure 1.1 Change in the total annual circulation figures of ALL manga magazines between 1979 and 1997 in units of 1 million [Source of Data *Shuppan Nenpō* 1983, 1994, 1997]

comics, Suzuki arranged for his story, about a little boy and a squirrel, to be scripted and drawn by two members of his staff. *The Adventures of Little Shō* (*Shō Chan no Bōken*) became the first successful children's comic strip (Tsurumi 1987:28–29). From 1914 Kōdansha publishing company produced children's magazines which featured stories, photographs and illustrations, as well as serialized comic strips which gradually extended in length throughout the 1920s.

At the same time short political cartoon strips for adult readers became popular. The 1920s were a decade when unprecedented social and political activity under the Taishō democracy led to experimentation with ideology and lifestyle. New popular culture and serious literature, and working class and feminist movements

21

influenced by Marxism emerged in the cities. Economic inequality and political injustice became the target of bitter criticism. In the minds of Marxist manga artists such as Shimokawa Bokoten, manga was connected to revolution. In his treatise on 'ideal manga' Shimokawa theorized that 'Now is a transitory period in which bourgeois art is in decline and the art of the people, such as illustration and manga are in ascendance.'(Ishiko 1980:21) A range of independent cartoon and comic strip artists' associations were established, including the Japan Manga Artists' Federation (*Nihon Mangaka Renmei*). Some Marxist cartoonists allied themselves with the pro-working class political and cultural program of the Proletarian Artists League (*Proletarian Geijutsu Kai*). The leader of this organization, Kobayashi Tokiji, was tortured to death in a police station in 1933 (Tsurumi 1987:36).

A range of publications containing political cartoons and comic strips, including *Workers' News* (*Musansha Shimbun*), *War Banner* (*Senki*), *Labourers' Manga* (*Rōdō* Manga), and *Farmers' Manga* (*Nōmin* Manga), were produced by artists with a Marxist leaning during the 1920s (Lent 1989:227). For a brief period anti-capitalist comic strips, such as Masamu Yanase's *A Capitalist's Education* (*Kanemochi Kyōiku*), serialized in the *Sunday Yomiuri* newspaper, appeared even in major publications (Schodt 1988:50).

The 1930s and Wartime Japan

The passage of the Peace Preservation Law in 1925 marked the beginning of the long reversal of the democratic political culture of the Taishō period. Following the Manchuria incident of 1931, the 1930s became a decade of increasingly severe and centralized media regulation and social control. Intellectuals, writers, artists, publishers and cartoonists were pressured to conform to national political objectives (Havens 1986:22–23). A number of comic strip artists were imprisoned, tortured, and in some cases killed, by the police (Lent 1989:227). In August 1940 all independent cartoon and manga artists' associations, including the New Manga Society (*Shin Manga Shūdan*) founded in 1932, were dissolved into one official association, the New Japan Manga Association (*Shin Nippon Manga Kyōkai*) organized by the government.

Under the New Order of 1941 censorship and media control escalated further. Between 1937 and 1944 the number of magazines circulating fell from 16,788 to 942 (Kasza 1988:223–224). At the same time remaining members of the New Association were drawn into the project of producing wartime propaganda for the military authorities. *Manga*, a cartoon magazine produced by members of the New Japan Manga Association, featured nationalist propaganda in which, amongst other things, British and American leaders were portrayed as vampires and devils (Tsurumi 1970:1). After the war the New Japan Manga Association renamed itself the Japan Cartoonists' Association (*Nippon Mangaka Kyōkai*), which has continued to be the best organized independent manga artists' organization of the post-war period.

While critical publications and radical manga artists came under increasingly direct government suppression, innovation in the narrower field of children's comic strips and non-political manga continued. Much of the latter fell into the category of *nansensu* ('nonsense') manga. In 1931 Kodansha launched a colour children's magazine titled *Boy's Club* (*Shōnen Gorakubu*). Collected editions of serialized manga stories such as Tagawa Suiho's popular series *Black Stray* (*Norakuro*) and Shimada Keizō's *Dankichi the Adventurer* (*Bōken Dankichi*) serialized in *Boys' Club* (*Shōnen Gorakubu*), reached up to 150 pages in length. Reprints of these eternally popular series were still going to press in the 1980s. Manga stories published in monthly children's magazines, and collected editions arising from them, constituted in a nascent form the post-war manga industry.

From the mid-1930s children's colour magazines were obliged to contain progressively less manga and a great deal more proselytizing military adventure stories. Newspaper comic strips were restricted by the military authorities as one part of the policy of strict centralization and censorship of all forms of national cultural production (Ben-Ami 1981:121–122). During the Pacific war children's magazines became subject to particularly strict censorship (Havens 1986:23) and only manga artists who were members of the single government sanctioned manga artists' organization, the New Japan Manga Association (*Shin Nippon Manga Kyōkai*), were able to draw manga stories for a few children's magazines still being published by Kōdansha (Ishiko 1994:19).

In 1942 magazines and newspapers were merged. Paper shortages caused by the breakdown of trade and transport also forced publishers to produce increasingly slender editions of their publications. All paper distribution was placed under direct government control in 1943. Comic strips were banned from newspapers entirely from the middle of 1944 (Tsurumi 1987:32). The sole officially sanctioned cartoon magazine, the generically titled *Manga*, remained in circulation until 1944, when an Allied bombing raid destroyed its printing plant (Shimizu 1993:15).

Picture Card Shows and Rental Manga in the Early Post-war Period

In the immediate post-war years a destitute new audience for cheap instant entertainment crawled out of the ruins, agitating a rapid revival of previously declining local cultural activities (Tsurumi 1987:34). In the brief period between 1946 and 1948 storytelling (*rakugo*) and picture card shows (*kamishibai*) flourished (Morioka 1990:264). Picture cards were drawn by ill-paid artists working up to 15 hours a day for picture card companies, which then distributed sets of cards to storytellers. Picture card storytellers performed a version of primitive animation on the street using picture cards and a miniature theatre. Each set of colour picture cards illustrating a single story were slid in and out of the side of the wooden theatre, and brought to life with synchronized oral narration.

As late as 1953 up to five million people a day watched a picture card show. Picture card artists also began to work for specialist publishing companies producing hard-bound books and magazines for sale to book rental shops (*kashihonya*), which also multiplied for a second time during the 1950s. Some manga artists, including Mizuki Shigeru (see Figure 1.2) and Shirato Sanpei (see Figure 1.3), graduated from picture cards, to rental manga, to the manga magazine industry, through the course of their early careers in the 1950s and 1960s (Sato 1996:155). Many young and unknown manga artists eked out an existence writing manga for rental manga publishers which distributed limited runs of manga books (typically 5000 copies), and magazines (typically 8000 copies), for distribution to book rental shops. During the mid-1950s the number of book rental shops grew exponentially until around 30,000 outlets, situated at train terminals and street corners, were renting books and magazines at a rate of ¥10 for two-days' borrowing. *Shadow* (*Kage*) and *Street* (*Machi*) launched in 1956, became the two leading rental manga magazines, each reaching a monthly readership of

Figure 1.2 Kitarō the hapless school boy vanquishes a scarey monster and gets more advice from his dead father's eye, which accompanies him on all his adventures. (1965) [*Ge Ge Ge Kitarō* . Vol. 7. 1994 edition. © Chikuma Bunko/ Mizuki Shigeru]

approximately 160,000 young men at the peak of the rental manga boom between 1956 and 1959 (Nosaka 1979:115).

During the 1950s the population of the reconstructed cities was swollen with young migrant workers from rural areas. The majority had become ill-paid factory workers for whom rental manga was one of the only available sources of cheap entertainment (Tsurumi 1987:32–33). Rental manga artists, all of them amateurs and most of them no more than teenagers, began to develop a more realistic and political form of manga, oriented towards young adults like themselves. Later, in 1957, a teenage artist, Tatsumi Yoshihiro invented the term *gekiga*, meaning 'dramatic pictures', to describe this new genre of serious adult manga dramas.

Early *gekiga* was characterized by a new degree of graphic realism and themes related to society and politics. It captured a youthful passion which contributed, in the view of some critics, to its striking 'authenticity' as a cultural form (Ishiko 1994:12). Young artists in arms, including, Tsuge Tadao (see Figure 1.4), Tsuge Yoshiharu (see Figure 1.5), Takahashi Shinji, Saito Takao (see Chapter 3, Figure 3.2),

Figure 1.3 Shirato Sanpei's peasant uprisings echoed the scenes of students demonstrating, on the streets of Tokyo, against the renewal of the Japan-America Security Treaty. [*Kamuiden*, *GARO* front cover, December 1970, © Seirindō/Shirato Sanpei]

Figure 1.4 The mad man and the sea. (1972) [*Seigan Ryōkichi no Shi* in *GARO* Vol. 112, December 1972. © Seirindō/Tsuge Tadao]

Yamamori Susumu, and Iwai Shige, named themselves the *Gekiga Factory* (*gekiga kōjō*), but it was Shirato Sanpei's eight-volume rental *gekiga* story, *Secret Martial Arts of the Ninja* (*Ninja Bungeichō*), serialized between 1959 and 1962, which defined the height of the rental *gekiga* era. *Secret Martial Arts of the Ninja* featured 'invisible organizers who fight to the death against the oppressive rule of the fief lords' and 'take the standpoint of the peasants, the beggars, and the still more discriminated against Buraku people'(Tsurumi 1987:34). It was immensely popular amongst young male readers.

Alongside picture card shows and rental manga various minor forms of published manga flourished on the streets. In Osaka small books of manga printed in red ink and known as *akabon* ('red books') were sold by street vendors. In 1947 Tezuka Osamu published *New Treasure Island* (*Shin Takarajima*) in *akabon* format. This title sold 400,000 copies stimulating a national craze for *akabon* manga books and the Tezuka manga stories (Nagatani 1994:31). Another of Tezuka Osamu's early stories, *Lost World*, can be seen in Figure 1.6.

Figure 1.5 The *Screwceremony*: a topless Tsuge wanders through a field of shirts and searches for a doctor who can stop the incessant bleeding in his left arm in 1968. [*Nejishiki to Akaihana*, 1988 reprint © Shōgakukan/Tsuge Yoshiharu]

The first colour children's magazine containing manga to re-emerge after the war was published by Kōdansha from 1947 onwards (Ishiko 1994:59–64). *Manga Boy* (*Manga Shōnen*) was a monthly magazine which began to serialize the work of a group of young manga artists, including Fujio-Fujiko, Ishinomori Shōtarō (see Chapter 3, Figures 3.1 and 3.3) and Matsumoto Reiji. It quickly became extremely famous. The exciting graphic style and extended form of *story manga* developed within *akabon* manga booklets was captured by the editors of *Manga Boy* (Takeuchi 1995:18–19). The most important series of this magazine, *Jungle Emperor* (*Jungle Taitei*), was drawn by Tezuka Osamu, already successful as an *akabon* manga artist (see Figure 1.6).

In contrast to the *gekiga* style, manga stories serialized in high-quality children's magazines remained child-oriented and were rendered in a cute graphic style. This style of manga was influenced by the large 'pie eyes' and distorted physical features of the characters featured in American Disney animation. Disney comics

Figure 1.6 Discovering Masutodon: the planetary capital of Tezuka Osamu's *Lost World* in 1947. [1994 reprint © Kadokawa Bunko/Mushi Pro]

and animated films were distributed in Japanese bookshops and cinemas during the Allied Occupation between 1945 and 1951 (Ono 1983). Their influence could be felt through the work of that early pioneer of post-war *story manga*, Tezuka Osamu.

While the main contemporary usage of the term 'manga' is a general one, used to describe all types of Japanese cartoons, comic strips, and manga books and magazines, from the 1950s manga also attained a second and more specialized usage which distinguished *manga* from the emergent *gekiga* tradition. In this secondary usage *manga* refers to child-oriented, cute, fantastical, and sometimes educational *manga*, associated with Tezuka Osamu. While *manga*, in this sense, has been perceived as a clean and healthy form of children's entertainment, *gekiga* has been associated with poorly educated young urban workers and anti-establishment politics. Not surprisingly artists linked to the *gekiga* movement and artists linked to the *manga* movement occupy two different social and political territories and have often perceived each other as 'old enemies' (GARO Mandara 1992:229).

During the 1950s another small manga industry produced manga booklets (*yokabon*) largely for sale in discount book shops (*zokki*) and children's toy shops. In 1955 there were approximately 1000 discount book stores and 5000 toy shops, where manga booklets, priced between ¥15 and ¥20, sold between 5000 and 30,000 copies per issue (Hatano 1959:104–105). Deluxe albums of manga printed in runs of 5000 to 10,000 copies were also sold in ordinary book stores, priced between ¥70 and ¥90 (Shimizu 1991:177). The growth of the rental manga industry has been linked to the extravagant retail prices of these manga books. In 1959 large publishers like Kōdansha and Shōgakukan launched the first cheap weekly manga magazines for direct retail, an innovation which rapidly undermined the rental manga industry while funnelling one half of rental manga artists into a new manga industry.

Weekly Manga Magazines in the 1960s

Between 1956 and 1961 a period of massive growth transformed the whole of the Japanese publishing world. The launch of weekly current affairs magazines and manga magazines anticipated the spread of television by several years. In March 1959, *Asahi Journal*, which quickly become 'the top magazine, with a modern-layout, for progressive and cultured individuals' (*Gendai Fūzoku Shi* 1986:118), was launched. In April 1959 *Shūkan Gendai* and *Shūkan Bunshun* news magazines were launched, and joined by *Shūkan Heibon* in May and *Shūkan Kōron* in November 1959. The first weekly manga magazine, titled *Magazine*, was launched in March 1959, followed rapidly by *Sunday*, launched by Shōgakukan in November of the same year. In 1963 *King,* a third weekly manga magazine, was launched by Shōnen Gahōsha publishers. Throughout the 1960s *Magazine*, *Sunday*, and *King* jockeyed for the position of the number one weekly manga magazine.[1]

The audience for television increased rapidly at the same time as the readership of manga. Public television began in 1953 when NHK started broadcasting in the Tokyo area. By 1959 Japan boasted four broadcasting stations: NHK, TBS, NET, and Fuji (the full titles are: Japan Broadcasting Association, Nippon Education Television, Tokyo Broadcasting System, and Fuji Television respectively). Television entered most Japanese homes from 1960 onwards, when both NHK and NTV television stations began to broadcast in colour.

The attraction of seeing the 1964 Tokyo Olympics on television helped to boost the number of TV sets in the country to 10 million. The spread of television continued to rise throughout the second half of the 1960s.

The acceleration of manga production from a monthly to a weekly cycle enabled manga publishers to keep up with the electronic pace of television broadcasting. Rather than finding a formidable competitor in television the manga and television industries expanded alongside each other and developed a symbiotic relationship. Serialized manga stories were adapted into televised animation, which served to advertise further the original manga stories and inflate manga book sales.

During the first years of its production *Magazine*, launched by Kōdansha was not the all-manga magazine it later became, but a children's magazine containing some manga series. Rather than continuing to publish straightforward children's manga stories, the editors producing *Magazine* also wanted to capture the burgeoning adolescent readership of rental *manga* and *gekiga*. From 1965 the then chief editor of *Magazine*, Uchida Masaru, invited *gekiga* artists to work for Kōdansha. This experimental fusing of children's manga magazines and adolescent *gekiga* was an extraordinary success and attracted a broad range of new readers to manga magazines. The readership of *Magazine* expanded rapidly and by the end of 1966 it approached one million. By 1974 there were 75 manga magazines with a total monthly circulation of 20 million.

From the mid-1960s on the themes of manga moved to the left. In 1964 an alternative manga magazine titled *GARO* was launched by Nagai Katsuichi in order to introduce the Marxist historical perspective of *kashihon gekiga* artist, Shirato Sanpei (see Figure 1.3), to school children. While the children were apparently uninterested in eighteenth-century peasant uprisings and class warfare, amongst college students *The Legend of Kamui (Kamuiden)*, serialized in *GARO*, became one of the most widely read manga series. *The Legend of Kamui* tells the story of a Buraku boy, *Kamui*, with an Ainu name, who fights against poverty and oppression. By the height of its popularity and circulation in 1970, *GARO* was closely involved with the political activities of students and the anti-AMPO movement. Though initially becoming popular amongst young blue-collar workers during the 1950s (Ishiko 1980:114), the historical themes of Shirato's series eventually converged with the themes of *Zengakuren,* the students' movement. Shirato's *gekiga* contributed greatly to shifting the readership of manga from children to young, educated adults.

During the late 1960s commercial publishers sought to include political and social themes in their manga. By introducing *gekiga* into commercial weekly magazines and encouraging artists to draw politically anti-establishment manga stories, the editors of *Magazine* became the talking point of the Japanese media. Between 1969 and 1971 *Sunday (Shūkan Shōnen Sunday),* published by Jitsugyōno Nihonsha, serialized a historical drama by the artist-team Fujio-Fujiko about the Chinese cultural revolution titled simply *Mao Tse Tung (Mo Taku Tō)* (see Figure 1.7). In 1971 *Jump (Shūkan Shōnen Jump),* published by Shūeisha, carried a story titled *The Human Condition (Ningen no Jōken),* which protested against oppression and the forced imposition of American army bases in Japan (see Figure 1.8).

Between 1968 and 1973 *Magazine (Shūkan Shōnen Magazine)* serialized *Tomorrow's Joe (Ashita no Joe),* a story by ex-*kashihon* artist Chiba Tetsuya and script writer Kajiwara Ikki (see Figure 1.9). *Tomorrow's Joe* tells the story of a poor boy who becomes a boxer and fights his way to fame and respect. *Tomorrow's Joe* was favoured by students occupying university campuses and was accused of inciting violence amongst students participating in street demonstrations. The words of the phrase coined by Waseda University student newspaper in 1970, 'In the Right hand we have *Asahi Journal* and in the Left hand we have *Magazine',* became a ubiquitous slogan sampled by cultural critics to explain the political role of manga in their time.

Jump also published encouraging photographs of political demonstrations, such as students campaigning for B52 bomber planes to leave Japan and go back to the USA. When in 1968 the Japanese urban terrorist organization, Red Army (*Sekigun*), hi-jacked a plane to North Korea, they made press releases which stated simply that 'We are *Tomorrow's Joe!'*. In doing so they attempted to capture the sympathies of young Japanese familiar with the manga character.

Many top manga artists of this period who were contracted to produce series for the leading weekly commercial magazines also lent their talents to producing political materials in manga form for organizations such as the Japan Labour Union (*Nihon Rōdō*

Figure 1.7 Chairman Mao leads a workers and peasants through the crop fields. [*Shūkan Manga Sunday*. 14 July 1969. © Jitsugyō no Nihon Sha/Fujio Fujiko]

Figure 1.8 American military bases on Japanese soil seem to make the *The Human Condition* unbearable in 1971. [*Shōnen Jump* © Abe Kenji & Gomikawa Junpei]

Kumiai). In one such pamphlet published in 1969, manga artists Ishinomori Shōtarō, Fujio Fujiko, Mizuki Shigeru, and Asaoka Kogi, identified themselves with the cause of workers fighting against factory exploitation, and students fighting against the US-Japan Security Treaty. See *Manga AMPO: An Introduction to the Japan Labour Union* in Figure 1.10.

Conservative sections of society, including local branches of the Parent Teacher Association (PTA), reacted strongly against the student demonstrations and against what was considered to be the perverse habit of young adults reading children's manga. Manga was blamed for inciting students to involvement with violent and anti-social activities. Between 1968 and 1970 attempts to ban the sale of manga, and in particular *gekiga* dramas, were orchestrated by a range of small right-wing religious and citizens' organizations. 'NO SALE' demonstrations (*fubai undō*) protesting against the commercial availability of manga, were orchestrated in the streets outside the offices of Tokyo manga publishing companies in Otowa and Jimbōchō.

Figure 1.9 Tomorrow's Joe doesn't let prison get him down in 1968. [*Ashita no Joe* Vol. 1, p. 177 © Kōdansha/Chiba Tetsuya & Kajiwara Ikki]

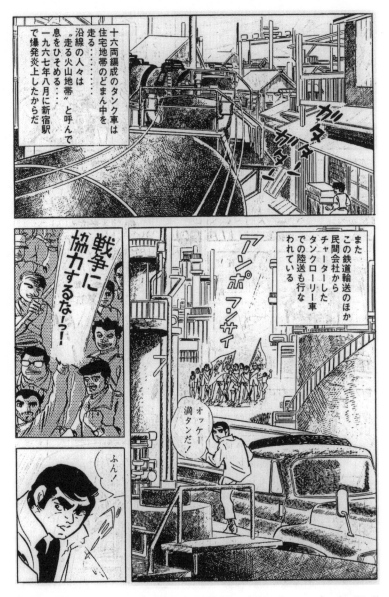

Figure 1.10 Workers should 'Smash AMPO' and 'No Support for the War!' according to an educational pamphlet drawn by Fujio-Fujiko, Ishinomori Shōtarō, Mizuki Shigeru and Asaoka Kogi for the Japan Labour Union in 1969. [*Rōdō Junpōsha: Manga AMPO*]

Avant garde Manga in the 1970s

During the 1960s realism in manga was associated with overcoming obstacles to personal progress, passionate attitudes towards society, and left-wing politics. In the period of calm and disillusionment following the student riots, which is sometimes referred to as the 'doldrums' (*shirake*), overtly political stories quickly disappeared from commercial manga magazines. New genres of girls' manga emerged which were influenced by the dream-like and naturalistic aesthetics of the hippie movement. Girls' manga with unrealistic drawing styles, incorporating characters with large eyes and cute faces, drawn in fragmented compositions lacking perspective, were linked to the themes of romance and the inner or spiritual world. The focus on individual psychology in early girls' manga of the early 1970s was perceived by some as a form of petty individualism and a reactionary retreat from more important political and social issues.

Commercial boys' manga also absorbed some of the experimentation in the fields of art and design, stimulated by the counter-cultural environment of the late 1960s. During 1970 the front cover of *Magazine* was designed by Yokoo Tadanori, a radical young poster designer, later to become an artist of international standing. This resulted in an exciting mix of manga and graphic design (see Figure 1.11).

In the early seventies the themes of the *gekiga* movement also began to focus on developing the artistic potential of the manga form. *Gekiga* began to explore the realm of dreams, collective memories, and social psychology. A highly distinctive new genre referred to as *angura* (underground) or avant garde emerged, typified by the pages of the alternative magazine, *GARO*. Avant garde was characterized by obscure and typically nihilistic vignettes about individuals living on the fringes of modern society. Tsuge Yoshiharu's *Screwceremony* (*Nejishiki*) is probably one of the most widely-known works of the avant garde oeuvre (see Figure 1.5). *Screwceremony* is a resonant account of a peculiar day-dream experienced by Tsuge, which alludes to industry, rural poverty, and the Pacific war. Avant garde was not incorporated into commercial manga magazines during the 1970s, but has been revisited many times from the late 1980s and has come to represent a minor but important juncture in the *gekiga* tradition, which continues to exert an aesthetic influence within the manga medium. Rather rare examples of avant garde by Shinohara Katsuyuki and Tsuge Tadao[2] can be seen in Figures 1.4 and 1.12.

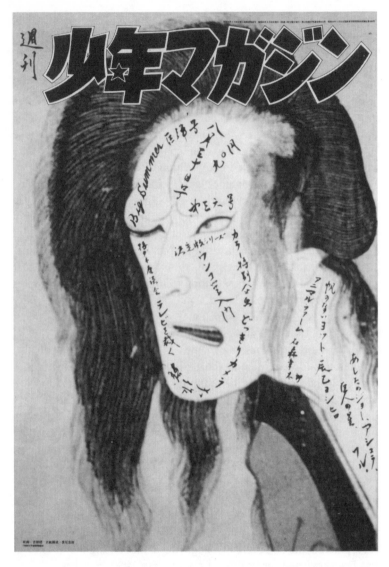

1.11 Experimenting with the cover of *Magazine* in 1970. [Used with the kind permission of the artist Yokoo Tadanori ©]

1.11 *(continued)*

The Structure of the Contemporary Manga Industry

Like television the contemporary manga industry is largely oligarchic. Five companies – Shūeisha, Shōgakukan, Kōdansha, Hakusensha, and Akita – dominate production. 75.3 per cent of the total manga market 75.3 per cent was controlled by the first four of these companies in 1993. Launching a new manga magazine has been a risky project typically involving capital losses spread over several years. These losses are not recovered if the magazine fails to eventually establish a niche in the market and is discontinued. The annual revenues of even well-established manga magazines are unstable. Average weekly circulation figures of the three best-selling manga magazines in the 1980s and 1990s, *Jump*, *Sunday* and *Magazine*, is shown in Figure 1.13.

In 1992 the total revenue of the manga industry was 539 billion yen. In 1993 the profits of large manga publishers were notched at an average of 68 per cent of their revenue, representing a higher profit margin than those of the two leading companies on the Tokyo stock exchange in the same year (*Nikkei Business* 1993). In 1997

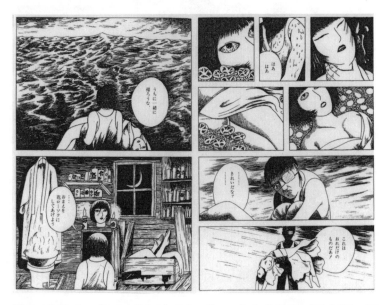

Figure 1.12 A smitten stall holder takes the pretty lady home. [Nioi Yokochō in *GARO* Vol. 155 August 1976 © Seirindō/Shinohara Katsuyuki]

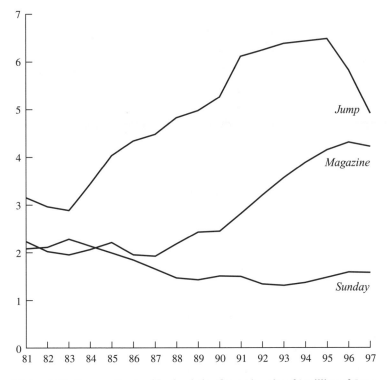

Figure 1.13 Comparative weekly circulation figures in units of 1 million of *Jump*, *Magazine* and *Sunday* between 1981 and 1997. [Source of Data: Kōdansha]

manga accounted for 38 per cent of all titles published and for 22 per cent of all publishing revenue. The lucrative nature of manga publishing has made it a tempting enterprise for even the most culturally refined of companies, and for companies lacking prior experience of manga publishing.

Japanese film, though popular in the early post-war period, lost the greater part of its audience to manga and television during the 1960s. By the 1990s the domestic manga market was procuring three times the revenue of the domestic film industry (*Nikkei Business* 1993:115–117). The rapid decline of the film industry in post-war Japan has often been linked to the rise of manga, which has in turn been described as a 'poor man's film industry'. The relative popularity of film, television and manga is illustrated in Figure 1.14.

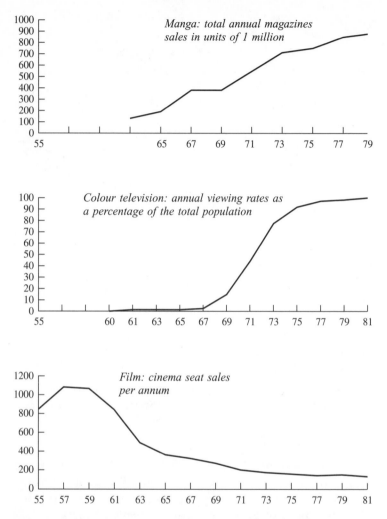

Figure 1.14 A graphic illustration of the relative popularity of film, television, and manga between 1959 and 1981. [Source of Data: Soeda 1983: 32]

Circulation

'Circulation figures' is the most important principal in the 'manga industry world' (*manga gyōkai*). These simultaneously measure both the sales and popularity of any book or magazine, and its revenue. First-rate magazines are loosely defined as those with circulation figures which exceed one million. In 1994 there were 12 of these 'one million sellers' (*hyakumanbu*), while a further 50 magazines had still considerable circulation figures of between 990,000 and 150,000. By comparison, the circulation figures of the highest selling weekly current affairs magazines hovered marginally below 1 million in the 1990s, of which the most popular, *Shūkan Bunshū*, had an average weekly circulation of 900,000 in 1992. Throughout the 1980s and 1990s the best-selling manga was *Jump*, a weekly boys' magazine which sold an average of 6.53 million copies a week at its peak in 1995.

The actual readership of manga magazines however is approximately three times as high as their circulation figures. Each magazine sold is read by an average of three people. *Jump,* which sold 6.5 million copies a week, may have been read by 20 million people, or one sixth of the total national population in 1995. Reading books and magazines on the hoof in book shops and convenience stores (*tachiyomi*) is a common pastime activity. Used manga magazines are often left on train seats, public benches, or paper recycling bins, where other commuters (and illegal vendors of second-hand magazines), can pick them up. Paper recycling bins located on train platforms double as free manga banks for passersby.[3] The most common form of 'multiple reading' (*mawashiyomi*) however is between classmates and household members.

Unlike the smaller comic industries which operated concurrently in the UK, France, Italy, Spain, and USA, the manga industry has based itself on the system of producing magazines and books in tandem. Standard weekly 'manga magazines' (*manga-shi, comic-shi*) are 256 × 185 mm in size, and priced between ¥230 and ¥250. Standard *shinshō* size, 180 × 127 mm, 'manga books' (*tankōbon, manga books, manga-hon, comics*), around 200 to 230 pages in length, typically cost ¥500 each during the 1990s. With rare exceptions popular stories are compiled into manga books of about 15 episodes in length. Manga book manufacture yields approximately two and a half times as much revenue as that of magazines. In 1997, for example, magazines accounted for 27 per cent of all published titles in Japan but only 11.5 per cent of publishing revenue; manga books on the other hand accounted for 11.5 per cent of all published titles but 9.5 per cent of publishing revenue. Manga book publishing is lucrative because books are relatively less bulky and less expensive to produce and distribute, and because there are no initial editorial production costs since books are essentially compilations of already serialized stories rather than new cultural material.

The serialization system has exerted an influence on the internal form of manga stories. Stories are written into short action sequences or cycles, which can be multiplied and extended almost infinitely.[4] Popular manga stories have frequently run for over a decade before finally being brought to an end. In 1997, Saitō Takao's *Golgo 13*, in serialization since 1969, accumulated its one hundredth volume.

Since 1995 the manga industry as a whole has experienced a slow-down in growth (this is illustrated in the graph shown in Figure 1.1). The rapid decline in sales of the most popular magazines has been interpreted by many senior editors in the manga industry as a watershed marking the beginning of the end of the industry. One reason given for the decline of manga sales is the greater interest in computer games amongst the children of the 1990s and the rapid spread of internet and home computer usage amongst adults from the mid-1990s.

A slight dip in manga circulation figures in 1986 following the introduction of home computer games (*famikon*) and *Nintendo*, another slight dip in early 1995 following the launch of Sony *Playstation* in December 1994, and another dip following the introduction of Microsoft *Windows95* in November 1995, suggest that there has indeed been some correlation between the spread of computers and the decline of manga. Another related factor has been the steady decline in the size of television audiences. Rather than watching animation on television, fuelling the purchase of more manga books, Japanese children were spending more time playing interactive animated computer games. Ironically the graphic styles and characters, such as the *Pokemon*, employed in computer game design are derived from manga.

Reader Categorization

As the manga industry, originally based around magazines for boys, expanded its production to magazines for adolescents and girls, publishing categories emerged which were delineated almost entirely by age and gender. In fact these categories have been particularly strong throughout post-war media, advertising and marketing (Skov and Moeran 1995:58–67). Excluding specialist magazines such as *GARO*, manga publishing has been divided into four main categories: boys' manga (*shōnen manga*); girls' manga (*shōjo manga*); adult manga (*seinen manga*); and ladies comics for adult women. A diagram sketching the historical development of these manga publishing categories can be found in Figure 1.15. In 1996, boys' manga accounted for 40.6 per cent; girls' manga 8.7 per cent; adult manga 35.5 per cent; ladies comics 6.5 per cent; and 'other' hobby, specialist, sports, erotic and pornographic manga magazines together accounted for 8.7 per cent, of all manga published (*Shuppan Nenpō 1996*).

In common with 'adult comics' in Europe (Sabin 1993:1–4) the actual categorisation and labelling of adult manga has been awkward from the beginning of the boom in adult manga publishing in the late 1960s. The Publishing Research Centre (*Shuppan Kagaku Kenkyūjō*) which has categorized and compiled statistics on the manga publishing industry since 1979,[5] separates 'adult magazines' (*seinen-shi*) into two sub-categories.

The largest of these sub-categories is titled 'youth magazines' (also pronounced *seinen-shi*) occasionally qualified with the

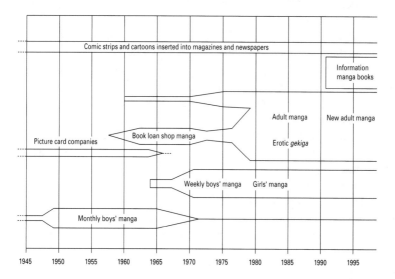

Figure 1.15 The development of manga publishing categories. [Used with the kind permission of Kure Tomofusa]

45

additional label 'adult' (*otona*). Pressure from government institutions opposed to a culture of adults reading manga, has encouraged large manga publishers to avoid formal recognition of their large body of adult readers, and to label their 'adult manga' according to the more ambiguous term 'youth manga' instead. The identical pronunciation of 'adult magazines' (*seinen-shi*) and 'youth magazines' (*seinen-shi*) has made 'youth manga' a particularly convenient linguistic camouflage for referring to manga for adult readers.

The smaller of the sub-categories is labelled 'mature magazines' (*narunen-shi*) and comprises pornographic and erotic manga as well as censored *gekiga* and Lolita complex stories. By means of these sub-categories, adult manga in general, is statistically divided into: adult manga deemed suitable for 'youth' to read, and adult manga deemed to be violent or pornographic and therefore unsuitable. In fact these are categories based on political and cultural judgements rather than the age of readers. However these distinctions have a reality in the structure of the manga publishing industry. Adult manga books produced from 'mature magazines' are referred to as *adult comics*, while adult manga books produced from 'youth magazines' are referred to as 'youth comics' (*seinen comics*). Adult manga falling into the 'youth' sub-category tends to be serialized in high-circulation weekly magazines published by large publishers such as Akita, Kōdansha, Shūeisha, Shōgakukan, and Futabasha, for a general adult male audience. Adult manga falling into the 'mature' or *adult comics* category tends to be serialized in low-circulation, specialist, semi-pornographic magazines and books published by small specialist soft-porn manga publishers such as Million Books, San Shuppan, and Fujimi Shuppan.

In general pornography has not been as strongly compartmentalized in post-war Japan as it has in post-war America or Britain (Abramson and Hayashi 1984:178–180). Pornographic images have tended to appear throughout the media as well as in specifically pornographic productions. Despite this more generalized distribution pattern, pornographic and non-pornographic manga are firmly distinguished within the manga publishing industry and high-circulation manga magazines falling into the 'youth' sub-category contain little in the way of hard-core pornography or explicit sexual material. This became particularly the case from the early 1990s as shall be discovered in Chapter five.

This book focuses on high-circulation, mainstream, non-specialist, non-pornographic adult manga, the great majority of which falls into the large statistical sub-category of 'youth magazines' and 'youth comics'. During the 1990s 'youth' manga comprised one third of all manga published. In terms of the volume of published material, the category of non-specialist adult manga is approximately seven times as large as that of specialist pornographic adult manga.[6] Figure 1.16 illustrates the growth of non-specialist adult manga publishing (adult manga in the 'youth manga' category) alongside the growth of the manga publishing industry as a whole.

Each of the large manga publishing companies has accumulated a stable of 'youth magazines' loosely targeted at different demo-

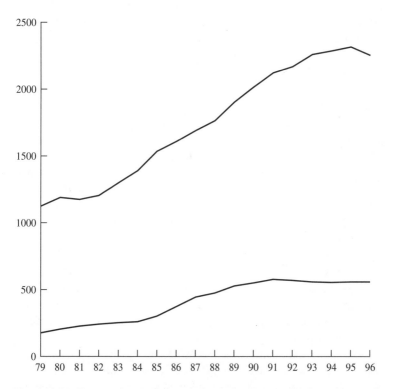

Figure 1.16 Comparative total annual circulation figures of ALL manga and all ADULT manga between 1979 and 1979 and 1997 in units of 1 million [Source: of Data: *Shuppan Nenpō* 1994, 1997]

graphic and cultural groups. Shūeisha produces *Jump, Monthly Jump, Young Jump*, and *Business Jump.* Shōgakukan produces *Big Comic, Big Comic Original, Big Comic Spirits,* and *Big Comic Special*, while Kōdansha produces *Magazine, Monthly Magazine, Young Magazine*, and *Mr Magazine.* Shōgakukan also produces another short series of manga for boys and young adults comprising *Sunday* and *Young Sunday*, while Kōdansha also produces a separate magazine couplet, *Morning* and *Afternoon.*

As the manga industry matured in the 1970s and 1980s, the age and gender of the readers became increasingly heterogeneous. Demographic categories, reflecting the actual gender and age of readers of specific magazines, partly transformed into stylistic categories, describing the style and content of the manga. Girls' manga, for example, became manga with a distinctive graphic style read by adult women and men, as well as adolescent girls, in the 1990s. An important factor contributing to this slippage between magazine readerships, has been the gradual ageing of the original generation of manga readers. As the first generation of young adults to read 'children's manga' magazines in the 1960s grew older, publishers followed them by producing stories of interest to successively older readers. In the late 1960s publishers launched 'youth' magazines (*seinen-shi*) for adults, including *Big Comic* and *Play Comic* published in 1968, and *Young Comic* published in 1969. In 1980 publishers launched 'young' magazines (*young-shi*) for a second generation of adult readers, including *Young Jump* published in 1979, and *Young Magazine* and *Big Comic Spirits* published in 1980. In a pattern similar to the emergence of Adult Oriented Rock (AOR) within the British music industry (Frith 1978:21), manga industry magazines have mellowed with their readers.

Evidence suggests that this process of cultural maturing has been driven less by the pull of manga readers and more by the push of publishing companies. Manga editors recognize that adult manga readerships are 'sticky', meaning that the readers of adult manga tend to be persistently younger than the middle-aged readers targeted by publishing companies.

One other explanation for this 'stickiness' of younger readers is the growing reality of the fact that in contemporary culture 'adult' has become a conceptual and aesthetic category, and one which has most resonance with biologically younger readers. In the language of contemporary culture the concept of 'adult' (*otona*) has become closely linked to the concept of 'serious' (*majime*), and by association 'responsible', 'realistic', 'official' and 'conservative'. For men, having 'adult' taste often implies a personal decision to reject the infantilism and frivolity of youth culture, and to become a serious, disciplined, and 'realistic' person instead. In 1994, the average age of all adult manga magazine readers was 30 years and 2 months. The average age of the readers of *Morning* magazine, which made a particular effort to create manga with an 'adult flavour' (*otona no aji*), was 30 years and 1 month. The readers of adult manga specifically targeted at a middle-aged male audience have in reality been quite young. Moreover a significant proportion of the readers of adult manga ostensibly targeted at older men, have been young women.

In 1994, housewives comprised 18 per cent of the readership of *Morning*. In terms of occupation 47.4 per cent of the readers of the same adult magazine were company employees, a further 9.8 per cent were low-grade civil servants, and a mere 4.1 per cent were professionals. During the 1990s the manga magazine reputed to have attracted the most heterogeneous readership was *Jump*, whose regular readers varied in age 'from the under-tens to the over-sixties'.

From the mid-1980s the number of adult manga magazines increased rapidly. As the market for children's manga began to shrink, publishers attempted to develop concept-based adult manga magazines further, such as *Morning* launched in 1982, *Afternoon* launched in 1987, and *Comic Are* launched in 1994. In the 1990s large publishers were keen to take advantage of a new political and cultural environment to develop appropriate new forms of adult manga. Negative associations between manga and poverty, manga and student radicalism, and manga and juvenile delinquency, which prevailed throughout the post-war period, creating a barrier to the expansion of adult manga readerships, had begun to weaken. A new genre of adult manga with a distinctive content and style emerged from adult manga magazines, enhancing the growth of adult manga publishing and encouraging the expansion of adult manga titles. This cultural renewal and transformation contributed towards the expansion of adult manga publishing from the late-1980s.

2

THE MANGA
PRODUCTION CYCLE

Between the 1950s and the 1990s manga did not just transform from the outside, in its relationship to society, it also changed on the inside. Change in the mode of production of a culture like manga is a more elusive and less quantifiable process, not as easily isolated for the purpose of analysis, than cultural change visible in society. And yet it is a vital aspect of how cultural change happens and one which is closely tied up with the question of freedom of expression, democratization, participation, and representation. For technology and resources are the bare bones of a cultural production cycle upon which small groups of people, representing different sections of society, exchange skills and interests with one another, driving the production cycle forward, to produce a single unified cultural product. Without some understanding of how the industrial production cycle itself operates and how, therefore, its various producers interact, it is not possible to fully understand the sociology of cultural producers, or how this sociology may change and with what significance. This chapter outlines the basic cycle of production developed by publishing companies to make manga magazines and books, and it prepares the ground for analysing the organization of amateur manga subculture in Chapter four, and the recent trends in manga production and editing in Chapter six.

Division of Labour

The take-over of the large numbers of small *kashihon* and *akahon* manga publishers by large publishing companies based in Tokyo during the 1960s also involved the simultaneous reorganization of

50

manga production. Large publishers introduced a new division of labour into manga production which speeded up the process of manga production and enabled manga to be published on a weekly basis. Newly established manga editorial offices developed systems for the ongoing recruitment and training of new artists and the management and control of artists producing popular serialized stories. Manga editors began to carry out separable tasks such as checking the first 'pencil manuscripts' (*shitagaki*) before they were drawn in ink, ordering typeset lettering for speech bubbles, sticking in typeset lettering, and checking the spelling of speech bubbles before and after typesetting. By reapportioning the more mechanical stages of manga production to editors, publishers were able to speed up manga production to meet weekly deadlines. Uchida Masaru, the ex-Chief editor of *Magazine*, describes the new 'bundle of tasks' for editors (Becker 1982:7–14) created by large publishing companies as 'editorial production' (*henshū saisan*), and 'editorial production' as one section of the wider 'manga division of labour' (*manga bungyo*).[1]

Rental manga and *akabon* artists accustomed to working to monthly publishing schedules, and determining for themselves how and by what timetable manga were made, were forced to work closely with editors to meet the deadlines for weekly manga magazines. The transition to producing weekly episodes for large companies has been described as a traumatic one. It was a hurdle which many famous manga artists of the 1960s, such as Tsuge Yoshiharu and Nagashima Shinji, could not or would not jump.

Artists' Production System

The majority of artists who succeeded in transferring to weekly production schedules did so by forming small production companies which mediated between themselves and editors employed in large publishing companies. Saitō Takao became 'Saitō Takao Pro', Tezuka Osamu became 'Mushi Pro', and Fujio-Fujiko became 'Akatsuka Fujiko and Fujio Pro'. Artists became self-employed: businessmen employing anything up to 20 assistants to work with them in their studio, which enabled them to increase their production capacity to meet weekly deadlines. Whereas a single manga artist could rarely produce more than 100 pages a month, under this 'production system' (*production seido*) best-selling artists increased their output by four or five times, and were able to produce one or even two major series simultaneously for different weekly magazines.[2]

Independent studios helped artists to maintain autonomy from publishing companies and to maintain control over their production techniques. As the manga publishing industry expanded, however, the prevalence of the studio production system decreased in relative terms. The great majority of the approximately 4000 professional manga artists working for the range of 273 manga magazines published in 1997, were not famous and were unable to guarantee receiving enough work to establish a company and hired assistants on a permanent basis. These artists, the great majority, generally hired just a few assistants on a casual basis, and they frequently requested friends – who are also low-ranking manga artists – to help them meet their occasional deadlines. The studio production system became particularly strongly rooted amongst the first generation of manga artists of the 1960s, now referred to as the 'veterans', and amongst contemporary best-selling female manga artists such as Morizono Milk and Ide Chikae, who have relatively stable and reliable readerships. The operation of a separate production system within the artist's studio is seen in a negative light by publishing companies. Manga drawn in this way is described as mechanical, 'formulaic', and 'lacking in artistic value'. Perhaps as importantly, the production system also enabled individual artists to increase their power and independence from publishing companies.

Artists' Contracts

Publishing companies make initial contact with new artists through a system of manga competitions operated by the editorials of magazines. High-circulation magazines, put out by large publishing companies, offer the winners large cash prizes. Each magazine advertises a competition with a range of cash prizes held several times a year. In 1994 prizes given by best-selling magazines ranged between 150,000 yen (£1000) and 2 million yen (£13,300). Figure 2.1 shows an advertisement for an adult manga competition held in 1995. Every year several hundred new manga manuscripts are sent in to the editorial offices of each magazine by new artists searching for recognition, work and money.

The competition system originated in readers' competitions run in *Manga Boy* (monthly children's magazine) between 1947 and

Figure 2.1 'I wanna terrify the manga establishment': an advertisement for an adult manga competition in 1995. [Printed in *Morning* magazine © Kōdansha]

1955, later used in Tezuka Osamu's manga magazine, *COM*. During the 1960s 'competition' became integral to the structure of the manga industry. *Magazine, Sunday* and *King*, launched between 1959 and 1960, had already requisitioned and secured the time and talent of the best-known *gekiga* and manga artists. Magazines launched after the first wave of recruitment, such as *Jump*, launched by Shūeisha in 1968, were forced to find, recruit and train a new generation of artists to draw manga for their magazines.

Through the competition system editors are able to attract and organize new layers of artists around their offices; make regular reviews of the range of new work being produced; and establish supervisory (*tantō*) relationships with artists that they believe show commercial potential. The cash prizes of competitions are indirectly used as a retainer fee to enable artists in whom editors have an interest to be temporarily unemployed in order to practise and improve their skills in drawing manga. Though the magazines are obliged to some degree to publish the work of prize winners, editors may decide to keep in contact with either the winners or the losers of manga competitions for indefinite periods of time after this initial point of contact. For artists, becoming a manga competition prize-winner or having work published in a magazine, preferably a high-circulation magazine, is their universally acknowledged professional début (*debyū*).[3]

Contracts between manga artists and publishing companies are variable. Most large publishing companies, including Kōdansha and Shōgakukan, have not generally issued written contracts to artists. Arrangements made with artists to produce series have been made on a discretionary one-to-one basis maintained by mutual trust and convenience. Artists are discouraged from breaking 'spoken agreements' (*iihan keiyaku*) by the knowledge that they could become known as an unreliable artist and damage their reputation within the industry. On the other hand, Shūeisha publishing company has operated a unique system of 'exclusive contracts' (*senzoku keiyaku*) which forbids artists contracted to Shūeisha from working for any other publishing company. In exchange for entering into an exclusive contract Shūeisha pays artists a fixed sum of money described as a 'trainees research allowance', whether or not they were currently employed to produce series. While the same pool of artists may work interchangeably and simultaneously for Kōdansha, Shōgakukan, Kadokawa Shoten, Futabasha, Akita

Shoten, Jitsugyōno Nihonsha, and any other smaller publishers, the work of artists contracted to Shūeisha is an exclusive cultural product which can be found only in magazines published by Shūeisha. During the 1990s artists, in new organizations such as Manga Japan (which will be discussed in more detail in Chapter five), have insisted that companies must respect their copyrights, and this pressure has made written contracts, stipulating fees, royalties, and copyright arrangements, more common.

In the mid-1990s the standard fees for manga manuscripts were 8000 yen per page for unknown and new artists, 25,000 yen per page for middle-ranking artists, and between 800,000 and 100,000 yen per page (£500 to £700) for famous, best-selling artists. Artists generally received 10 per cent of the revenue from the sales of manga books in royalties, though it is likely that best-selling artists claimed a higher percentage through private agreements. The copyright (*hanken*) of each manga series' is shared equally between the publishing company and artist. In practice publishing companies have tended to sell the copyrights of manga works without the agreement or even the knowledge of the artists, though the increasing fees charged to foreign publishers, film, animation and advertising companies for the right to use manga stories and characters has encouraged artists to demand that publishers protect their copyrights more effectively, in the 1990s.

Conference between Editors and Artists

Serialized manga made on a weekly, bi-weekly (every two weeks) or monthly production cycle revolves around the interaction of an artist and an editor at its core. While the artist is based almost entirely in his own home or studio, and the editor is based in an editorial office, both are engaged in producing the same episode of manga. Within this partnership editors carry out mechanical and administrative tasks, and maintain liaisons between the artist, publishing company and various typesetting and printing companies. In essence editors align artists with business: the cultural economy. Editors supervise artists and take responsibility for meeting deadlines with publishers and printers. The separate tasks which the editor and the artist carry out are brought together through a series of 'conferences' (*uchiawase*) and copious communication and exchange by fax, telephone, and scripts delivered by courier.

Conferences take place in a variety of locations. New artists (*shinjin*) and relatively unsuccessful artists are often obliged to go to editorial offices themselves to meet their editors. This visit symbolizes the subordinate position these artists have in relation to their editors. Figure 2.2 shows a conference between a new manga artist with a chief editor in an editorial office. A great number of briefer meetings take place in cafes and bars near the main publishing companies in Otowa (Kōdansha) and Hitotsubashi (Shōgakukan and Shūeisha). In the case of best-selling artists neither the editor nor the artist is likely to have time to meet outside of the artist's studio. Editors travel to the studios of the majority of these artists several times a week, and conferences often merge into general supervision which can last anything up to several days.

Extended supervision sessions, in which editors oversee artists and insulate their charges from any possible distractions to producing work in time to meet deadlines, also take place in hotels where editors can more effectively 'can'(*kan-zume*) artists and seal them off from the rest of the world. Other artists live away from the centre of manga publishing in Tokyo, in areas as distant as Aichi prefecture or Osaka city. Well-established manga artists tend to work in detached residences or studios, often located in the Western

Figure 2.2 Conference between an artist and an editor. (1994)

suburbs of Tokyo, such as Kichijōji, Hachiōji, Ogikubo, Asagaya, and Chōfu. These areas, now located around the Chūō railway line, had previously been populated by large numbers of craftsmen and artists.

Stories about the intense, dependent and conflicting relationships which often develop between artists and editors brought together in these circumstances form the most enduring topics of gossip within the manga industry world (Ohizumi 1996; Schodt 1988:144). Figure 2.3 shows an idealized depiction, (depicted in a manga series about editing manga), of how an artist should work under the supervision of an editor.

Weekly Production Cycle

The editorial offices of weekly magazines generally organize the work of the editorial around a monthly schedule which indicates to editorial staff the number of pages a series will be allocated in the following four issues of the magazine. Episodes are completed between two and three weeks in advance of the publication date – one week prior to the publication being the last possible date at which the most flexible contemporary printing plants are likely to accept late work.

The weekly production cycle generally begins on Sunday night or Monday morning with a meeting or telephone conversation in which

Figure 2.3 'All right, I'll do it! ... manga is not just an artists' thing.' A good manga editor experiences the passion of an artist vicariously. [*Henshūō! Ashita no Joe* 1992, Vol. 1: 145–147 © Shōgakukan/Tsuchida Seiji]

the artist and editor discuss what will take place in the next weekly episode. For series which are written by a script-writer this discussion will be relatively straightforward as the artist is given a script worked out in advance by a script writer and an editor.[4] In this conference the plot, layout of the boxes, and contents of the speech bubbles (*serifu*) are discussed.

Generally the artist quickly drafts a rough pencil preview of the manuscript, mapping out the size and position of the boxes, and simple circles depicting the size and position of speech bubbles and characters' faces. Sentences representing the thoughts and utterances of characters are also filled in pencil at this early stage.

This part of script production is referred to as *nēmu*, a term distantly derived from the English word 'name'. It is the point of production when an editor is most likely to intervene and block (*dame dashi o suru*) the manga artist's execution of the story. When the editor and artist are satisfied with the rough pencil outline, the artist will begin pencilling in the actual pictures and speech bubbles into the boxes in more detail, sketching out how they will appear in ink. This task takes between two and three days. During this stage of production, which engages the imagination and graphic skills of the artist, editors or assistants may provide artists with research materials such as books and photographs. Editors who do supervise artists to a great extent are likely to stay with artists at this stage while the 'pencil manuscript' (*shitagaki*) is being completed. By supervising this work editors can continue to engage with artists about the contents and at the same time as put pressure on the artists to keep to the deadline.

Manga artists employing a large number of assistants are likely to pencil in only the heads or heads and bodies of the lead characters before passing the manuscript on to assistants to complete. Assistants fill in the background detail of the pictures according to either their own interpretation of the plot or in accordance with explicit instructions set by the artist. The precise division of labour employed within artists' studios varies according to the attitude of each artist to the manga they draw.

The pencil manuscript (*shitagaki*) is generally completed by Wednesday evening when it is checked by the editor. Editors are likely to request that anything up to half of the pages of the pencilled manuscript are 're-drawn' (*kakenaosu*). When the editor is entirely satisfied with the quality and contents of the pencil manuscript, photocopies are retained by the editor, and the artist will return to their desk to begin the second major stage of their work, which consists of drawing in ink on top of the pencil manuscript. Artists' assistants are also engaged at this stage to ink in the background detail of the pictures and apply 'screentone'. 'Screentone' is the name given to large sheets of patterned transfer paper specifically produced for manga making, and often used to fill in large spaces with backdrops such as sky, sea, or hatching in areas of shadow. Inking in the manuscript takes about two days and is completed by about Friday evening.

Back in the office, the editor prepares an order of typeset lettering to place inside and outside of the speech bubbles, and on the title page of the episode. First of all editors check the spelling of the speech parts and correct mistaken or incorrectly written Chinese characters. Editors then measure the speech bubbles (*fukidashi*) and page-layout on their photocopy of the pencil manuscript (*shitagaki*) and estimate what print size and print font to order for each speech bubble or episode title. Editorial offices in large publishing companies such as Kōdansha and Shōgakukan may be wealthy enough to sub-contract this job (*moji heisei*) to manga editing companies such as Ginnansha, or else employ part-time staff, often young female college students, to carry out these tasks at desks situated within the editorial office itself – in which case these tasks may be referred to simply as 'desk'. Figure 2.4 shows part-time assistants working on manuscripts inside an editorial office.

One of the most commonly used print size and font combinations in adult manga in the 1990s was *20QA antique*. Editors type out the contents of the speech bubbles into clusters of vertical and horizontal sentences shaped to fit into the appropriate speech bubbles, on a word processor. This printed sheet of manga script accompanied with an order stipulating the required lettering size and font (*shashoku shitei*) is then faxed to a typesetting company. Magazine editorials tend to have long-term contractual relationships with specific typesetting companies which are familiar with the editorial's production cycle and expect to receive orders for lettering from editors at a certain time each week. Editors who are late for deadlines sometimes fax the pencil manuscripts directly to the typesetting company, forcing the latter to undertake the extra tasks of reading the pencil manuscript, making spelling corrections, and making judgements about which type of lettering is required, where this has not been properly

Figure 2.4 Part-time employees check the spelling of manga manuscripts at desks situated in the corner of a manga editorial office. (1994)

measured or indicated on the manuscript by the editor. This is a point of muted conflict between publishers and typesetting companies. Typesetting companies are determined that this aspect of manga editing will not become an unpaid part of their work.

Lettering companies, or departments, often operate for 24 hours a day, and orders take between 12 and 24 hours to carry out. Lettering ordered on a Wednesday arrives back in the editorial office, via courier, some time during the next day. Thursday is frequently a day of relative rest for manga editors. Completed ink manuscripts (*genkō*) are collected from the artist by an editor on Friday.

Editors or editorial staff cut out the separate pieces of manga script from whole sheets of typeset lettering delivered back to the editorial by the typesetting company. The lettering is then glued carefully into the speech bubbles of the completed ink manuscripts. Figure 2.5 shows speech parts being glued into a manuscript by an editor in an office. At this stage of production the editor and then the chief editor or vice-chief editor of the department both check the ink manuscripts for spelling mistakes, and sentence and picture quality.

Editors may have to re-order new sentences, or badly measured sentences which do not fit properly into speech bubbles from the

Figure 2.5 A manga editor carefully glues typeset lettering into speechbubbles. (1994)

typesetting company. Artists may also be requested to make minor alterations to the ink manuscript. When this checking procedure is complete, typically at some time on Saturday, the entire ink manuscript complete with lettering attached to each speech bubble is sent back to an art-work (*seihan*) department or company. Sunday tends to be the manga artists' day off, though most claim to sleep straight through it.

Art-work (*seihan*) companies or, more typically, art-work departments within large typesetting companies, arrange each manuscript within an industrially standard page-layout and make photographic proofs of the manga manuscript, referred to either as *aoyaki* or *sumiyaki*.[5] The proofs (*aoyaki*) are sent directly back to editors who examine them in the editorial office. At this stage editors may request once again that the typesetting company makes further and final changes to the lettering before the manuscripts are prepared for printing.

Industrial Reproduction

Even the largest of publishers are relatively small companies with several thousand employees which manufacture nothing at all themselves, but subcontract almost all of the mechanical work of making books and magazines out to other companies.[6] Manga publishing in particular involves a range of subcontracting activity.

The four main stages of the industrial reproduction of manga are typesetting (*shashoku*), art-work and proofing (*seihan*), printing (*insatsu*), and cutting and binding (*seihon*). During the pre-war period, all of these functions were carried out as one industrial process by single enterprises. Under the Anti-Monopoly Law of 1947 these enterprises were forced to separate the task of printing from that of binding books and relocate them in separate and formally competitive enterprises. Throughout the first half of the post-war period printing and binding plants were owned by separate companies. Nevertheless, permanent contractual relationships were established between typesetting, art-work, printing, and binding companies. Typesetting companies tend to be the favoured subcontractors (*keiretsugaisha* or *kogaisha*) of large printing concerns, while art-work companies are often the favoured subcontractors of specific typesetting companies. Large publishing companies divide their various manga printing orders between the major competing printing companies, such as Tohan, Kyōdō, or Dai Nippon, in an attempt to prevent any one of these printing companies from establishing a monopoly position in the market, which could quickly be used to demand higher fees for printing from publishers. However, printing companies generally do insist that publishers placing an order also use the services of certain typesetting companies with which the printer has an established arrangement. Manga editorials using Dai Nippon printing company, for example, will be likely to also use the Hirayama lettering company beforehand.

Combined Printing Plants

In addition to these separate but contractually interdependent enterprises, an increasing number of medium-sized independent companies have begun to carry out the full process of reproducing manga, incorporating typesetting, art-work, printing, cutting and binding, in one plant. This has occurred since the growth of manga publishing in the 1960s. Medium-sized combined plants are able to offer manga publishers a faster service with greater flexibility in carrying out late work and changed layout and lettering orders for severe deadlines.

One example of this type of combined plant is Chūō Seihan Insatsu, which became a combined plant in 1967, and has been located in an impoverished industrial suburb to the West of Tokyo since 1980. (During the late post-war period the Kita Koto area has become the centre of a variety of printing, binding, distribution and paper wholesale companies, which take orders from manga publishers.) Typical shop floor employees of Chūō and neighbouring printing companies are unskilled high-school graduates living locally in high-rise housing projects. The average age of regular Chūō employees is 47 years. Regular employees work in eight-hour revolving shifts with regular overtime of approximately two hours, at the end of each day or night shift.[7]

Before printing orders can be placed, publishers must select and buy paper and arrange for it to be transported to printing plants. Paper has been relatively expensive and its distribution quite inflexible in twentieth-century Japan. During paper shortages precipitated by the international oil crisis of 1973, for example, manga publishers were forced to make magazines with fewer pages. Despite using low-quality paper produced largely from cheap wood-pulp imported from Scandinavia, Russia, Malaysia and Australasia, paper nevertheless constitutes approximately one third of the total cost of having manga printed. Cheap paper used for high-circulation magazines is generally dyed to pastel colours in order to improve the lustre of its essentially grainy, dull appearance. Specialist manga printing paper (*comic yōshi*) is currently made in 10 different qualities and is brought from paper companies, such as Mitsubishi located in Niigata prefecture, in rolls up to 6 kilometres in length.

Within Chūō Seihan Insatsu typesetting, art-work, printing and binding plant, which caters particularly to manga publishers, the first stage of production consists of producing the typeset lettering for manga scripts (*shashoku*). Manga typesetting and manuscripts are processed in one large room equipped with two kinds of computer. One quarter of employees use large specialist *Saivert-P* word-processors to type-up and process orders for typeset lettering (*layout*). Another three-quarters of employees in this section are engaged in making corrections to manga scripts on *Macintosh* computers (*naoshi*). Figure 2.6 shows a shift at work in a manga typesetting (*shashoku*) room. Employees of this section are in the

Figure 2.6 Mass-culture: rows of computer terminals in a manga typesetting room. (1997)

habit of logging out of their industrial word-processors during the night shift and running Sony *Playstation* games on their computers instead.

The next stage of production is the preparation of manga manuscripts into camera-ready 'art-work' and making proofs. Manga manuscripts are scanned into computers and the layout of pages as they will actually appear in printed form is arranged on specialist design *Macintosh* machines. In fact some manuscripts are 'combined' (*gōsei*) with the lettering for speech bubbles at this stage. During the 1990s, typesetting, art-work and the production of proofs, began to fuse into one computerized process collectively referred to as *seihan* – which can, in this case, be equated with the job of 'origination' carried out in English printing companies. Figure 2.7 shows an employee creating the page-layout for a section of manga manuscript.

The next stage of the manga factory is to make proofs (*aoyaki*) of the manuscript. Each separate page of the manuscript after art-work is printed on to a specialist fine-grain, high-quality paper (*ingashi*). After checking the quality and layout of this print-out, it is photographed on large shop-floor cameras. Figure 2.8 shows an

Figure 2.7 A young male employee carries out 'art-work' and 'page layout' on a manga manuscript on a computer screen. (1997) Photograph: Akita Daisuke

Figure 2.8 Making manga negatives with an industrial camera. (1997) Photograph: Akita Daisuke

employee arranging a sheet of manga manuscript on to the glass plate of an FCS880 Camera. The industrial camera produces actual-size film negatives of the manga manuscript. Female employees examine the negatives over a light bed and remove small imperfections and white spots with dark cover-up fluid (see Figure 2.9). Corrected negatives are exposed to produce the proofs (*aoyaki*), which are sent back to publishing companies to be examined by editors. Proofs which return to the factory, with requests for a large number of changes or even with whole new pages of ink manuscript re-drawn by the artist, have to be processed from the computer layout stage again.

Corrected sets of negatives are exposed and reversed onto large aluminium sheets. When printing is ready to begin a second aluminium sheet, bearing an oil-based reverse impression of the manga manuscript, is mounted on to the roller of a printing machine. Manga magazines are printed on the same machines – very often these are German machines – as those used to print newspapers. Figure 2.10 shows an impression of the entire manuscript of a manga book mounted on the roller of a *Miller Bookomatic* printing machine. After passing through an automated

Figure 2.9 Manga manuscript negatives are touched-up by a middle-aged female employee. (1997) Photograph: Akita Daisuke

Figure 2.10 The manuscripts of one manga book on the roller of a printing machine. (1997) Photograph: Akita Daisuke

assembly line on which printed paper is dried, moisturised, cut, bound, glued, covered and aerated, stacks of manga books or magazines are packed on to crates ready for distribution.

Manga Distribution Network

The publishing distribution business is organized in a pyramidal network of interconnected and cooperative companies. The largest distributors (*toritsugiya*) receive packages of published material from book printers, binders, or their own depots located close by, and transport them to regional areas. At regional depots material is transferred to middle-sized distributors and taken to local depots. In local depots small distributors with local employees distribute manga to retail outlets in the area. In fact, as *all* the large national distributors deliver books and manga to *all* of the main regions of Japan, distribution is carried out through a series of differently shaped pyramidal networks overlaying one another.

Major distributors each have fixed contractual relationships with specific retail outlets to which they have manga regularly delivered. In 1994 seven distributors were delivering 80 per cent of manga magazines and 98 per cent of all manga books. The two largest publishing distributors, Tohansha and Nippansha, took 80 per cent of Kōdansha's manga books and magazines to regional distribution points. Chūōsha, Taihansha, Ōsakaya, Kurita, Kyōwa, and Taiyōsha delivered a further eight per cent of Kōdansha manga.

Distribution represents a major obstacle for small publishing companies which tend to produce books by unknown authors or specialist manga with small readerships. Distributors may refuse to take deliveries on the basis of their own judgement about how many copies a book will sell. Minor companies, such as Seirindō, which published the low-circulation manga magazine *GARO*, have occasionally resorted to delivering their books and magazines by hand, or paying a larger publisher, such as Shūfu no Tomo ('Houseswives' Companion'), to deliver their magazines for them under their more powerful company name.

While publishers pay printing and binding companies for their services directly, distributors receive a fixed percentage of the total revenue of manga sold. Formally publishers sell all their manga stock to distributors, which distributors then sell to retail outlets. The percentages claimed by distributors and retailers are calculated from the total revenue of manga sold which is based on the actual retail price of books and magazines. Publishers prevent retail outlets from lowering the value of their books by printing the price in large characters on the front of magazines and on the back covers of manga books.

In the 1990s retail outlets took a cut of approximately 20 per cent of total manga revenue, distributors took a cut of between 5 and 7 per cent, and manga artists took a cut of 10 per cent in royalties. A further 10 per cent was paid directly to printers and binders, and approximately 5 per cent was used to purchase paper from paper wholesalers. Large manga publishers received between 50 and 60 per cent of total manga revenue. Powerful tensions exist between publishers, distributors, and retailers, each of which struggle to defend, maintain, or increase their share of manga profits, while at the same time remaining interdependent enterprises. During the early 1990s, distributors responding to falling circulation figures amongst manga magazines and rising percentages of returned stock, managed to force manga publishers to increase their share of the total revenue from 5.5 per cent to 6.5 per cent.

The majority of manga is sold in large, combined book, magazine and manga shops. Distributors prioritize delivery to large book shops, such as Kinokuniya or Zaiseidō, which have space to shelve a wide range of titles. In the 1990s an increasing amount of manga, particularly more expensive artistic manga books, were also sold in fashionable book retail outlets with specialist manga sections, located in luxury department stores such as Parco and Seibu. Twenty-four-hour convenience stores, such as the Seven Eleven, Family Mart, or Lawsons chains tended to sell disproportionate amounts of gag manga (humorous comic strips) and erotic manga. Convenience stores accounted for 10 per cent of total manga stock sold.

After an agreed length of time publishing companies are obliged to buy all unsold manga stock back from their retail outlets, via their distributors. This system of 'sale or return' (*itaku hambai*) necessitates a reverse service from distributors. In the mid-1990s increasingly high percentages of unsold stock (*hempin*) returning to haunt manga publishers and afflict the manga industry world, encouraged distributors to begin deducting extra charges from publishers to cover the cost of returning large volumes of unsold stock. The percentage of unsold manga stock returned to publishers peaked in 1995 at 24.4 per cent. By 1996 this figure had dropped slightly to 22.9 per cent under the streamlining influence of a more selective and brutal distribution service.

A small proportion of returned manga books (but not magazines) are re-wrapped in brand new dust jackets and reissued to retail outlets in the hope that the attractive new covers will attract more readers to buy the manga. Publishers encumbered with unsold magazines sell them to paper recycling plants where they are turned into toilet roll. One popular adult manga satire of the manga world published in 1991, suggested that the toilet paper manufactured from pulped manga magazines is used by male manga readers to masturbate neatly while reading subsequent issues of manga (Akihara and Takekuma 1991).

3

ADULT MANGA AND THE REGENERATION OF NATIONAL CULTURE

Selecting manga from train platform kiosks and introducing it to the roll call of official Japanese national culture required the complicity of a large number of unconnected institutions and companies. Cultural assimilation during the 1990s was a broad social process which involved and connected individuals and organizations with no specific relationship to the manga industry. These individuals and institutions had their own reasons for observing and participating in the promotion of manga. Government agents engaged in cultural policy, in particular Ministry of Education and Culture (*Monbushō*) officials, began to work closely with the manga publishing industry to develop new channels of cultural growth. Media other than manga became crucial to communicating the fact of its new direction and social status. The new power of manga was spread in articles and books written by manga critics, reports and reviews in national newspapers, advertisements placed in newspapers and on trains and billboards, and in television documentary programmes and radio broadcasts. The promotion of manga by other media demonstrated how critical the cooperative relationship between the different branches of the media is to allowing the fluid development of each.

In autumn 1986 a financial broadsheet *Nihon Keizai Shinbun* published *Japan Inc. An Introduction to Japanese Economics in Manga* (*Manga Nihon Keizai no Nyūmon*) drawn by veteran artist Ishinomori Shōtarō. It was based on a series of seminars on the economy (*Seminar Nihon Keizai Nyūmon*) published in *Nihon Keizai Shimbun* over the preceding years. During one year of publication 550 000 copies of the book had been sold in Japan. In

1988 it was translated into English and published by the University of California Press (see Figure 3.1) In 1989 the book was translated into French and published in Paris (Ito 1994:82).

Critics credited the commercial success of a manga book about economics to the rending of a complex and professedly boring subject into a more interesting and digestible form. In *Japan Inc.* economics and management theory is combined with a drama about a company employee and office ladies working for a large Japanese trading company. *Japan Inc.* was the first manga book to be published in which the state of the national economy formed the main theme of the drama. *Japan Inc.* carries a sympathetic attitude towards corporate enterprises and discusses the need for 'business practices that are ethical, socially responsible, and forward-looking'(Duus 1988). *Japan Inc.* became the prototype of a new form of adult manga, published, initially, by large publishing companies with no previous relationship to the manga industry, in which large corporations and national institutions took centre stage in the drama. One manga artist who criticized the laudatory attitude towards the market expressed in *Japan Inc.* was Arimura Sen. Arimura produced a series of adult manga books, written in Japanese, Korean, and English, entitled *The Art of Laughing at Japan Inc.*, which took as their theme the lifestyles and interests of impoverished day-labourers in the Kamagasaki district of Osaka.

Adult manga books produced along the model of *Japan Inc.* are loosely referred to as 'information manga' (*jōhō manga*). The themes of information manga have been characterized by a form of implicit political revisionism: readers are encouraged to think again in a newly positive light about key political and economic institutions such as large corporations, Diet, or military forces. High-quality information manga books exerted a powerful influence both on the way in which manga was perceived in society, and on the themes of manga stories published in weekly adult magazines.

Within the general category of information manga (*jōhō manga*) used since 1986 to describe the new wave of adult manga books, are more specific new sub-genres of adult manga including 'introductory manga' (*nyūmon manga*), *business manga*, 'political manga' (*seiji manga*), 'education manga' (*kyōyō* or *gakushu manga*), 'literary manga' (*bunkashi manga*), and *documentary manga*. As a whole, information manga books and series have been described as 'cultured' (*bunkateki*) and 'high-quality' (*jōhin*) and have been

Figure 3.1 *Japan Inc: An Introduction to Japanese Economics in Manga*, 1988. © Ishinomori Shōtarō's/The Regents of the University of California]

linked favourably with art (*geijutsu*) and literature (*bungaku*). In 1993, for example, the *Asahi Shimbun* newspaper debated whether or not 'the next step forward for manga is literary journals' (*Asahi Shimbun* 1993a). In 1994, cultural critics in *Chūō Kōron* periodical discussed 'the potential of manga as a medium' (*Chūō kōron* 1994).

As the first editions of information manga books ushered in positive new perceptions of the medium, publishers of literature, and even academic books and periodicals which had no previous association with manga, began to jostle for the opportunity to produce new series of high-quality adult manga books, and even manga magazines. Multi-media concerns such as Japan Broadcasting Association (NHK) and the Asahi Shinbun newspaper company also attempted to branch into manga production. In 1987, Asahi Shinbun broke into the manga book market with the publication of a *gekiga* version of Morita Akio's *Made in Japan,* an autobiography of the president of Sony electronic company. A section of the *gekiga* version of *Made in Japan* can be seen in Figure 3.2. In 1994, NHK launched *Mu,* a monthly magazine in which NHK television series and programmes, not already derived from manga series, are serialized in manga format. In 1993, Magazine House, otherwise specializing in fashion magazines, published its first monthly manga magazine *Comic Are,* loosely based on the style of *GARO* magazine. In 1996 Bungei Shunjū, another large and rather respectable publisher with no previous public association with manga, launched an adult manga magazine *Comic Bingo,* for young men.

In 1989, Chūō Kōronsha, an academic and literary publisher, commissioned a 48-volume work, *Manga History of Japan* (*Manga Nihon No Rekishi*), published at a rate of a book a month between 1989 and 1993, from artist Ishinomori Shōtarō. In order to incorporate the necessary facts the artist was linked to a team of 50 academic specialists acting as informants and supervisors, the majority of which were based at Tokyo University (*Japan Times* 1989). The *Manga History of Japan,* which can be seen in Figure 3.3, was later recognized by the Ministry of Education and Culture (*Monbushō*) as suitable for educational purposes in state schools.

In 1995, Sekai Bunkasha celebrated 50 years of publishing literature with the launch of a new series of foreign literary classics produced in manga format, by well-known female manga artists. Girls' manga artist Satonaka Machiko produced Stendhal's *Scarlet*

Figure 3.2 Walkman's on the streets in Paris, America and Japan, and board room meetings in Tokyo. Saitō Takao puts the President of Sony, Morita Akio's, autobiography into *gekiga* in 1987. [*Made in Japan: Comic Version*, p. 230–231 © Asahi Shinbunsha/Saitō Takao]

Figure 3.2 *(continued)*

Figure 3.3 The dawn of Japanese history and the dawn of official manga in the 48 volume *Manga History of Japan*. [*Manga Nihon no Rekishi* 1989 Vol. 1 © Chūō Kōron Sha/Ishinomori Shōtarō]

and Black in manga, erotic ladies' comics artist Morizono Milk produced Emily Bronte's *Wuthering Heights*, and girls' manga artist Igarashi Yumiko drew Shakespeare's *Romeo and Juliet*. The new concept of 'high-quality manga' was also retrospective. Large publishers began to rummage through early post-war manga history to find the early works of well-known manga artists which could be published in new editions, packaged as 'classics'. In this vein the complete works of Mizuki Shigeru (see Chapter 1, Figure 1.2) were re-published by Kadokawa Bunten, while the complete works of Tezuka Osamu (see Chapter 1, Figure 1.6) were republished by Chikuma Bunten. New editions of manga 'classics', originally produced in the 1950s and 1960s, have typically been reissued in either *bunko* format, a standard size and style used for fiction and especially literary classics, or large hard-bound books.

The idea that adult manga books could be considered a form of high-quality culture was a partly practical one based on the high prices of many of these information manga books and reissued classics. Unlike standard manga magazines and books, information manga books were printed on expensive paper, sometimes in full or part-colour, and frequently bound in hard-covers with glossy high-quality dust-jackets. In 1997 a standard weekly adult magazine cost around 250 yen, and a standard manga book cost around 530 yen. Hard-back editions of *Manga History of Japan* cost 1000 yen each. Glossy soft-back first editions of Chen Uen's *Tōshūeiyuden* published by Kōdansha cost 1100 yen. High-quality reissues of Shirato Sanpei's *Kamuiden* and Tsuge Yoshiharu's *Screwceremony* (see chapter 1, Figure 1.5) published by Shōgakukan cost 1100 yen each. Hard-back first editions of Shirato Sanpei's *Savannah* cost 5000 yen.

Information Manga and Corporate Communications

Other companies selected information manga as their medium of choice for communications and public relations exercises. Presenting public relations and internal communications in manga format appeared to be a means of attracting target audiences to read what might otherwise be unattractive or irrelevant information. Sony president, Morita Akio, claimed to have got the idea for having his autobiography, *Made In Japan*, produced in manga format after asking his young, female skiing instructor if she had read his book and being told that she had not, but would consider reading it if it was published as manga. *Made In Japan* was duly written in manga format by *gekiga* artist Saito Takao and published by *Asahi Shinbun* in both Japanese and English editions in 1987. Using manga in official communications also helped companies to project a positive, cool image of their business.

Capitalizing on the success of *Made in Japan*, Sekai Bunkasha launched a series of company profiles in manga. Profiles written in the style of fictional dramas were produced on the history of Honda, Ajinomoto, and Nomura Securities companies (*Fortune* 1989). Large corporations have traditionally distributed expensive, bound volumes of a company rule book to new recruits, or condensed volumes of the company history to graduate job-seekers. From the late 1980s increasing numbers of these rule books and corporate histories were produced in manga format. According to the manga drama of Ajinomoto, the company has helped to revolutionize processed-food production, and is the world's largest producer of the food additive MSG (monosodium glutamate). The Honda company manual describes to new company recruits how Honda developed water-cooled engines in a struggle to produce the best cars in the world.

In each of these public relations manga books, company operations are presented not as profit-making enterprises, but as public services. Corporate activities are dramatized as essentially humanitarian projects designed to improve modern living standards. In this regard corporate information manga books are similar to *infomercial* music-videos distributed amongst the American public by large American companies. Some companies have used information manga to combine advertising exercises with public information projects conferring upon the company the moral legitimacy of a voluntary or public institution. Ohtsuka Pharmaceutical Company, for example, produced medical advice books in manga format. Veteran artists Ishinomori Shōtarō, Akatsuka Fujio (the same artists which had contributed to the Trade Union pamphlet *Manga AMPO* in 1970 (see Chapter 1, Figure 1.10) and Nobaru Baba, produced information manga books about various aspects of health and disease entitled the *Ohtsuka Manga Healthy Kenkō Series*. Over 200,000 copies of the *Ohtsuka* series were distributed to elementary schools and libraries across the country, free of charge.

Politics and Economics in Adult Manga Magazines

The themes of information manga books focused on business and corporate management were partly inspired by some of the new themes being tried out in weekly adult manga magazines. As early as 1982 broadsheet newspapers reported that *Morning* adult magazine was running a series, *Manjū Kowai*, (written by professional stock-market analyst Yasuda Jiro, and turned into manga by Sugaya Mitsuru), in which readers were offered tips and general advice about investing in stocks and shares. In 1983 the same adult magazine began to serialize a realistic executive drama *Section Chief Shima Kōsaku* (*Kachō Shima Kōsaku*), (see Figure 3.4). *Section Chief Shima Kōsaku* increased in popularity through the 1980s and became the prototype of adult manga dramas set within corporations. At the same time factual and frequently historical pedagogical themes of *education* manga books, sponsored by government agencies, influenced the themes of adult manga magazines. Manga series with themes linked to politics, business, or other aspects of current events became referred to as *business* manga, *documentary* manga, and *economics* (*keizai manga*) or *politics* (*seiji manga*) manga. Collectively, the new sub-genres emerging within adult manga magazines were linked by the relative 'realism' of their themes which were oriented towards facts and actual events. As the trend advanced, adult manga began to assume some of the characteristics of newspapers. Like newspapers, political and business manga became directly involved in the wider Japanese economy through providing factual market intelligence, and engaging in topical discussions about politics, social issues, and corporate ethics. The new themes emerging within adult manga contributed towards the regeneration of adult manga publishing and the rapid growth in the total circulation figures of adult manga between 1985 and 1992 (see Chapter 1, Figure 1.16). The realism incorporated in the themes of these new adult manga genres reflected the enhanced status of adult manga within society.

The best-selling manga series of the period stretching from the mid-1980s to mid-1990s belonged to the new genres of political and business manga. In 1990 the third most popular series published by Kōdansha was the political adult manga series *Silent Service* (*Chinmoku no Kantai*). *Silent Service* was launched in 1989 and by 1990 it had sold over one million books (see Figure 3.5). In the same

Figure 3.4 Recently promoted Department Chief Shima Kōsaku looking stylish during business negotiations in Vietnam in 1995. [*Buchō Shima Kōsaku* in *Morning*, 25 August 1995 © Kōdansha/Hirokane Kenshi]

Figure 3.5 Politician Kaji Ryūsuke negotiates military movements live from the committee room, with Japanese armed forces facing twenty kalashnikov wielding Korean terrorists. [*Kaji Ryūsuke no Gi*, 1997. Vol. 17: 203 © Hirokane Kenshi/Kōdansha]

period the second most popular manga series published by Shōgakukan was *Feast* (*Oishinbo*) which began as a 'gourmet manga' series about the joys of eating good food, but rapidly increased in popularity and topicality after focusing on the politics of US–Japan trade relations, during the period of the so-called 'Rice war' between Japanese and Californian farmers. By 1990 *Feast* had also sold one million copies. In this period the sales of political and economic adult manga series began to overtake even favourite children's manga series such as *Dragon Ball* and *Dr. Slump*.

Section Chief Shima Kōsaku by Hirokane Kenshi continued serialization from 1983 until 1992. The lead character of the story is the Section Chief of a Department of General Affairs in a fictional electronics company, Hatsushiba Corporation, loosely based on the real-life Matsushita electronics company. Shima Kōsaku is an able young manager who struggles to avoid joining factions within the company and to create instead a more ethical system of corporate management and promotion. One editor connected to this story explained that 'The original idea was a story about an ordinary salaryman, the pathos, the hardness of their life, the ups and downs. But as the story was written Shima Kōsaku gradually got more and more popular and famous, and he was discreetly transformed from a mild anti-hero into a super-hero'. The heroism of Shima Kōsaku's character, and his effortless popularity with the opposite sex – much scorned by female readers – strayed into the realm of fantasy. Other aspects of the series, such as its focus on favouritism and unfair management techniques within large companies, its detailed portrayal of board meetings and office life, or Shima Kōsaku's business trips to inspect, for example, Hatsushiba's overseas production plants and warehouses, reflected the real activities of company executives in the 1990s. Figure 3.4 shows Shima Kōsaku on a business trip to Vietnam in 1995, following his promotion to the status of Department Chief (*Buchō Shima Kōsaku*).

In October 1992 *Morning* magazine used the popularity of Shima Kōsaku to launch a highly innovative general publicity campaign in which members of the public were invited to find 'The Shima Kōsaku in your company!' (*Anata no kaisha no Shima Kōsaku!*). A series of train advertisements invited commuters to nominate individuals in their company for the position of 'the ideal salaryman'. From amongst those nominated to *Morning* editorial, 100 would be chosen to enter an 'election campaign' involving train advertisements designed like political campaign posters for each of the 100 candidates. The ideal salaryman would then be voted for by readers of *Morning* and the winner offered three million yen in prize money. Ironically, the campaign failed – *Morning* editorial received only a handful of nominations for the post. Clearly few adult manga readers were taken with the competition, or could actually relate the heroism of Shima Kōsaku to the particular attitudes of the managers in their companies (*Tokyo Post* 1992a).

Nevertheless the image of executive masculine success, given a new lease of life through the character of Shima Kōsaku, was considered popular enough that in 1996 Kodansha launched a *New Lifestyle Notes Series, From Shima Kōsaku to his Friends* (*Shinseikatsu teiansho series, Shima Kōsaku kara tomo e*). These non-manga life-style advice books were edited and illustrated by the artist Hirokane Kenshi on behalf of the fictional author, Shima Kōsaku. In the first volume of the series, published in 1996, Shima Kosaku provided his readers with a list of *80 Ways to Become an Adult Man* (*Otona no otoko ni naru 80 ka jō*). In the second volume published in 1997, Shima Kōsaku had further advice to give his readers on *80 Ways to Become a Strong Person* (*Tafu na otoko ni naru 80 ka jō*).

Another best-selling business manga serialized in *Morning* magazine was *Osaka Way of Finance* (*Naniwa Kin'yūdō*) by Aoki Yūji, serialized between 1990 and 1995. *Osaka Way of Finance* incorporated detailed financial intelligence and business information into the unlikely context of an adult comedy; about the fiscal misadventures of lumpen business men in downtown Osaka and a corrupt money-lending firm (*machikin*) called Imperial Finance. The series depicts the insecurity of small businesses and the financial underworld in the 1990s, after the burst of the economic bubble, at the same time as providing concrete lessons in survival for small business men. Detailed drawings of actual promissory notes, bills, and other more obscure financial and legal documents were incorporated into the extraordinary graphic style of Aoki's manga. Former Prime Minister Hata Tsutomu claimed to have used *Osaka Way of Finance* as a source of tips and insights while he was Minister of Finance. In 1994, Kodansha capitalized on the popularity of *Osaka Way of Finance* by publishing a popular *Osaka Way of Finance* guide to economics, (*Naniwa Kin'yūdō: Kane to Hijō no Hōritsu Kōjō*) illustrated, and ostensibly edited, by

Aoki Yūji. By 1995 *Osaka Way of Finance* had sold over 7 million manga books.

A different kind of exemplary manager is portrayed in *A Reliable Person!* (*Kono Hito ni Kakeru!*) by manga artist Yumeno Kazuko and script writer Shū Ryōka, serialized in *Morning* from 1993. *A Reliable Person!* is the story of a female executive called Hiromi, who succeeds as a bank manager through her commitment to a fair treatment of all bank employees and customers and heroic degrees of self-effacement. The series has two main themes, both of which are concerned with reforming business management. In *A Reliable Person!* an image of an ideal career woman was created, which suggested that the appropriate attitude for women wanting to pursue careers within companies was one in which they sacrificed their personal lives to work, while at the same time utilizing their feminine sensibilities to create more just and ethical business practices. Another theme of *A Reliable Person!* was the rehabilitation of a positive image of banks and financial institutions. After the financial crisis of 1989 Japanese banks have been criticized repeatedly for poor financial judgement and internal corruption. *A Reliable Person!* aimed specifically at counteracting some of the public distrust of financial institutions.

Kaji Ryūsuke's Principles (*Kaji Ryūsuke no Gi*) by Hirokane Kenshi, serialized in *Mr Magazine* from 1992, became the prototype of a new wave of political adult manga stories. Kaji Ryūsuke is a young politician fighting for political reform in a realistic drama set in the National Diet. (see Figure 3.6) When Kaji's father, who had been a key figure of Liberal Democratic Politics through the 1980s dies in 1991, Kaji abandons his career in business to succeed his father in politics. Kaji's first post in the Liberal Democratic Party is as prime minister's secretary, after which he becomes vice-minister for the Ministry of Foreign Affairs. Kaji quickly rises through the ranks of the government and in a few years he becomes the Minister of Defence (*bōeichō chōkan*), a position which he uses to campaign for constitutional reform and the re-militarization of Japan. Kaji Ryūsuke, the Minister of Defence, can be seen calling in the Self Defence Forces to deal with submarine terrorists of a yet unknown national identity in Figure 3.6.

In real life the Liberal Democratic Party lost its seat in government in August 1993, just one year after the series began, but in other details it is highly realistic. Artist Hirokane Kenshi has

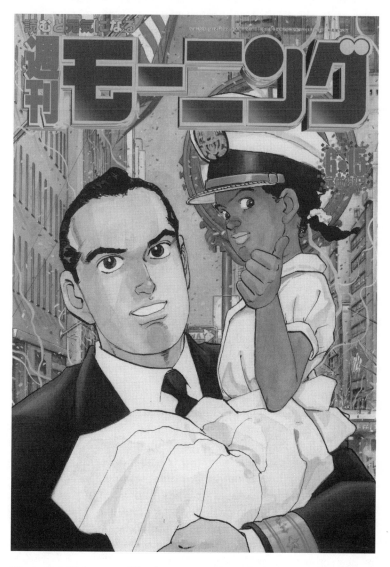

Figure 3.6 Ticker tape fills the streets of New York as American citizens celebrate the arrival of a Japanese international military vigilante who has come to challenge the UN. [*Chinmoku no Kantai, Morning* front cover 15.6.1995 © Kawaguchi Kaiji/Kōdansha]

been provided with insider knowledge of the political world by interviews with real-life political characters including Ozawa Ichiro, the leader of the New Frontier Party (*Shinseitō*), and Ishihara Shintarō, a key member of the Liberal Democratic Party until 1993. The early structure of the story was also loosely based on the real-life story of the conservative Diet member, Nakagawa Shōichi, who entered politics after the death of his father, Nakagawa Ichiro. The drama of the manga series hangs on the fact that Kaji is a new type of politician. Unlike the other members of Diet who are motivated by money, Kaji is intellectual and has political goals, such as the centralization of political power, and eradication of political corruption.

Kinō Yutaka the chief editor of *Mister Magazine* explained its political orientation:

> The media tend to focus on the Liberal Democratic Party powerbroker Kanemaru Shin first, and then on money politics and then corruption. There must be honest people who are working enthusiastically and seriously in politics but we rarely hear about them. Kaji Ryūsuke, a member of a conservative party working to realise his ideals against all manner of temptation, looks fresh to our readers.
>
> (Nikkei 1991)

Kaji Ryūsuke's Principles encourages readers to reconsider conservative politics and to put their trust once again in an institution, the Diet, which has been viewed sceptically by the public throughout the late post-war period. It is not entirely surprising that Ozawa Ichiro, chairman of the New Frontier Party and a highly prominent politician, claimed that a volume of *Kaji Ryūsuke's Principles* was his favourite bed-time reading. In addition to introducing real-life national politics into adult manga fiction, *Mister Magazine* has also published interviews, carried out by artist Hirokane Kenshi, with national politicians, such as Hanada Tsutomu, one time Minister of Finance, slotted between pages of manga series (*Mister Magazine* 1994).

Political themes in adult manga have also been linked to an awareness of the potential for a new role for Japan within the international community. The most popular of all political series set within an international framework is Kawaguchi Kaiji's *Silent Service* (*Chinmoku no Kantai*), serialized in *Morning* magazine from 1989 (see Figure 3.5). *Silent Service* is a military drama with a political plot focusing around the international vigilantism of Commander Kaieda. Kaieda is the captain of the most advanced nuclear submarine in the world, built using Japanese technology and staffed by a Japanese crew to defend Japanese sea-lanes, in accordance with a secret pact made with the United States. During its first test run with a US fleet the submarine suddenly changes course and embarks on a game of global hide-and-seek and a vigilante mission. Captain Kaieda challenges the military actions and moral authority of the United Nations and America on behalf of 'small independent states' and the global citizenry. The submarine is named Yamato, an ancient term for the Japanese archipelago and the name of a famous Japanese battle-ship sunk during the Pacific War, and submarine Yamato declares itself to be an independent state.

Captain Kaieda can be seen marching up to the United Nations building in New York to confront his political opponents while cheered on by crowds of ordinary American citizenry in Figure 3.5. *Silent Service* combined criticism of the US-Japan Security Treaty with questions about the legitimacy of the United Nations, and topical enquiries into globalization and the basis of the nation state. For the duration of the Gulf War, between August 1990 and March 1992, *Silent Service* became linked to the 'PKO discussion' about the possibility of Japanese rearmament, and in 1991 the series was debated in the National Diet. In October of the same year it was turned into a three hour radio drama, broadcast by NHK in a late night slot, listened to by 11 per cent of the population. By 1996 *Silent Service* had sold 22 million books. While accused in 1990 of supporting the ideas of Right-wing military groups, *Silent Service* in fact reflected the experimental fusion of left-wing and right-wing ideas and symbols in a new political era.

The most controversial of all adult manga series in the 1990s was produced not by a manga publisher, however, but by an independent manga artist, Kobayashi Yoshinori, who wrote a political satire for the current affairs magazine *Weekly Spa!* (see Figure 3.7). Noting the topicality of political adult manga in 1991 *Spa!* became one of several non-manga magazines to incorporate a regular manga series into its pages. *Spa!* magazine wanted a controversial adult manga series and Kobayashi Yoshinori produced *The Arrogance Manifesto* (*Gōmanism Sengen*), the title of which is based on a parody of *The Communist Manifesto*, suggesting by implication that the political

Figure 3.7 Kobayashi demands that Japan's post-cold war political parties display their policies, and not their bottoms, to the public. [*Gōmanism Sengen* 1993 Vol. 2: 124 © Kobayashi Yoshinori]

contents of Kobayashi's *Manifesto* are equally radical, while ridiculing the *Communist* original. The title and format of this series celebrate outspokenness and being politically forthright – which were fashionable attitudes during the early 1990s associated with increased confidence about the strength of Japan in the international arena (Ishihara 1991). *The Arrogance Manifesto,* featuring a comic version of Kobayashi himself as the narrator, discussed subjects such as the Buraku caste system, haemophiliacs with AIDS contracted from contaminated blood products, nudity and censorship, and the Emperor's family (which will be discussed in Chapter five), which had previously been governed by a strict code of media censorship. The popularity of *The Arrogance Manifesto's* taboo-breaking political stance made it one of the best-selling adult manga series in the early 1990s.

The Arrogance Manifesto also promoted equally taboo sexist attitudes towards women, belligerent attitudes towards America, and hostile attitudes towards foreigners in general. In 1995 the neo-traditionalist elements of *The Arrogance Manifesto* exploded into an unedited political outburst following, amongst other things (Schodt 1996:226), the full disclosure of the extent of Kobayashi's untimely revisionary stance on Japanese history (Rofuto Books 1997). *The Arrogance Manifesto*, backed by the internet web-site of Kobayashi's fan-club, *Nihon Cha! Cha! Cha!*, argued that there was no objective evidence that Japanese war-crimes, including the Nanking massacre and the use of 'comfort women' (*ianfu*) – Asian and European women and young girls captured by the Japanese army during the Pacific war and made to serve as prostitutes in official military brothels – had taken place.

Episodes dealing with the war-crimes were written with the help of Fujioka Nobukatsu, a professor of history at Tokyo University, who is known both for his orthodox nationalism and the central role he has played in the 'Democratic History Association' network of like-minded intellectuals (*Le Monde* 1998). Kobayashi came into conflict with Taku Hachiro, currently a columnist of *SPA!* magazine, known for his intellectual defence of manga and animation subculture and limited sympathies for drop-out collectives such as *Aum Shinri Kyō* religious cult. After a bitter political exchange between these new-style political adversaries, Kobayashi and Taku, *The Arrogance Manifesto* was moved from *Spa!* to a rival current affairs magazine, *Sapio*.[1] In 1994 Kobayashi Yoshinori felt that the series gave a voice to new political ideas in society: 'The entire structure of the Left versus Right conflict has collapsed and we are searching for new values. I portray these changing circumstances'.

In *Silent Service, Kaji Ryūsuke's Principles, Section Chief Shima Kōsaku, Feast* and *A Reliable Person!* the drama is centred on social and economic élites. This focus on the ideas and experiences of élite sections of society in new genres of adult manga stood in direct contrast to the focus of attention in previous genres of both commercial adult manga and *gekiga*, which had almost invariably been concerned with the lives and aspirations of people from the lower-classes and even the Buraku caste. The implication of this shift in focus was that ordinary people were no longer interesting enough to form the basis of manga dramas. The chief editor of *Morning* emphasized the importance of publishing adult manga about people at the top of society who do things, 'We want to do the top of society – always the most exciting part. We should do manga about Hata and Hosokawa [the Prime Minister]. *That* would be exciting! Or what about doing something on what Zhirinovsky's doing in Russia? *That* would be interesting!'.

As the focus of popular adult manga series shifted to the economic and political discourses and aspirations of individuals in positions of power, so the discursive contents of adult manga began to overlap with those of current affairs journals and periodicals. Indeed the licence of manga to apply a daring, idealistic, and imaginative approach to dealing with current affairs was accused of stealing attention away from serious journals, where similar issues were being debated with rather less innovatory zeal. Large manga publishers sought to attract the attention of readers of serious newspapers and journals to their adult manga magazines.

In 1990 Kōdansha placed large advertisements in the *Asahi Shimbun* and *Nihon Keizai Shimbun* broadsheet which suggested that with the help of series like *Silent Service*: '*Heisei* [post-1989] Japan is finally awakened from its slumber by manga'. Following the prompts of manga publishers, adult manga series were described as being more realistic than reality and more political than the politics being debated in real life. A headline posted in the *Yomiuri Shimbun* newspaper in 1992 made the wry observation that, 'As politics becomes more like a manga scenario, manga stories are becoming more political' (Yomiuri Shimbun 1992).

Another journal of current affairs suggested that adult manga could help to regenerate an active interest in national politics amongst a public which had become disillusioned and 'sick' of the old politicians:

> After seeing the dirty, hidden side of politics [the Kanemaru scandal] the nation is suffering from indigestion. There is a special remedy for this however. I am talking about the current boom in popularity of *gekiga* stories about the political and financial worlds. Realistic struggles between benefactors and heirs, how to gather capital for political campaigns, accounts of terrorist organisations, are being drawn as I speak. The new political manga series have real power: everyone from Diet members to secretaries are reading them.
>
> (*Shūkan Shinchō* 1992)

This journalist observed the potential of adult manga to generate interest in national politics, and especially the struggling Liberal Democratic Party, amongst a public which had become increasingly indifferent to voting in elections.

Adult Manga and Making a New National Identity

Publishers and leading manga artists displayed an acute awareness of the potential new role for adult manga, not only as an alternative arena for domestic politics but as an official representation of Japan abroad. The internationalization of manga appeared to be concomitant with the promotion of its status within Japan. The chief editor of *Morning* anticipated the discursive and diplomatic potential of political adult manga in the mid-1980s:

> Between 1987 and 1988 I changed the content of *Morning*. I wanted to express new Japanese thinking more consciously in manga. I went abroad and travelled around Europe, Asia, and the United States and then I reconsidered Japanese culture. The biggest change which resulted from this exploration was the story *Silent Service* which was launched in 1988. Japan's relationship to other countries is re-evaluated in *Silent Service*.

The History of Japan in Manga by Ishinomori Shōtarō provided ample scope for the expression of revised views of Japanese history which incorporated a more conciliatory attitude towards Japan's neighbours. During the 1990s the question of war-crimes perpetrated by Japan, including the treatment of Allied POWs in Japanese camps in Burma and East Asia, the Nanking massacre (Smalley 1997), and the use of Korean and Chinese women as enforced prostitutes, known as 'comfort women' (Hicks 1995; Howard 1995) during the Pacific war, has formed the focus of an intense criticism of Japan by both neighbouring states such as South Korea, and by the United States and Europe. Japanese politicians have been forced to comply repeatedly with demands that they apologize for Japanese war crimes and acknowledge their guilty status. The presentation of the twentieth century in *The History of Japan in Manga* has responded to this climate of international criticism by introducing a more contemporary and frank account of Japanese activities during the Pacific war. This understated goal is clearly implied in Ishinomori Shōtarō's explanation: 'My aim is to make people born before the war change their views and to enable young people to grasp correct information. Looking back connects us to the future. If the past is recorded inaccurately, how can we look the world in the face?'

The expression of political and economic aspirations in adult manga books and series became intimately bound up with the process modifying the image of Japan abroad. Information manga books were translated into English, French and other languages to ensure that their messages were internationally received. During the first half of the 1990s, articles about adult manga series were published in foreign newspapers such as *The Washington Post, The Observer* and *Le Monde*. Copies of the English language edition of the *gekiga* version of *Made in Japan* found their way on to the shelves of specialist Japanese studies libraries and collections, while other information manga books and magazines became the diplomatic gifts of choice for Japanese government agencies abroad.

If information and corporate manga books, written with a foreign as well as a domestic readership in mind, contributed towards changing the image of Japan abroad, the opposite was also the case. The recognition of manga as a form of contemporary Japanese culture in foreign publications helped it to gain acceptance as culture within Japan. Iwasaki Yoshikazu, the chief curator of the *Tokyo Museum of Modern Art* spoke out against the tendency for Japanese intellectuals and institutions to base their own evaluation of manga on the judgements of foreign cultural experts: 'The Japanese have a tendency to praise anything blindly once it is acknowledged abroad. The same could apply for cartoons [manga]. In any case, Japan should make an effort to introduce a unique part of its culture to the world'. (*Japan Times* 1990)

One of the most comprehensive museum exhibitions of manga was held not in Japan but in San Francisco Cartoon Art Museum in Summer 1992. The exhibition, *Visions of the Floating World: The Cartoon Art of Japan*, displayed 120 framed samples of well-known manga, and was funded by Kōdansha and Shōgakukan publishers, the *Japan Foundation*, and the US Consulate General in Japan.

The title of this exhibition suggested that contemporary manga was part of the canon of eighteenth and nineteenth century woodblock prints, otherwise known as *ukiyoe* or 'pictures of the floating world'. The curator of the San Francisco exhibition, Mark Van Cotta, spelled out this interpretation: 'Given their influences, I think Japanese comics can be considered fine art in the making, just the way woodcut prints were and are.' (*Mainichi Daily* 1992c)

In the 1950s a common arguement made by critics of Japanese film was that they were special because they had been influenced by the choreography of Medieval Nō theatre. The arguement that manga has an aesthetic relationship with Japanese woodblock prints is similar. For its critics, linking manga to *ukiyoe* has been a simple way of conferring artistic status upon it. Nevertheless, as with the shadey relationship between Japanese film and Nō, 'one must look hard, almost invent influences' (Richie 1982:327) to make a case for the association of manga with wood block prints.

Interestingly, it was the discovery of *ukiyoe* wood block prints by French impressionists in the late nineteenth century, notably Dégas, Pissarro and Gauguin (Ives 1974), which persuaded the Japanese authorities of that time to consider that *ukiyoe*, then thought of as a vulgar form of entertainment, might become the key to national art (Noguchi 1933). In a similar vein it was the praise of foreign critics who described manga as 'fine art', which helped to establish manga as serious culture. It was quite logical that the political adult manga artist Hirokane Kenshi (see Figures 3.4 and 3.6) should take the opportunity of an interview with a foreign reporter to define himself not as a manga artist but as a 'novelist who uses pictures and text', producing work that ought to be referred in English, not as manga but as 'graphic novels'.

During the 1990s manga appeared to be the perfect representa-tion of Japanese culture abroad: a more vital and contemporary culture than early modern woodblock prints, and yet clearly distinguishable from any other national culture. Discussing manga on the pages of the glossy fine art magazine *Geijitsu Shinchō*, manga critic Kure Tomofusa suggested that manga was a better representative of Japan than all previous cultural symbols:

> If we were to discuss the aspects of Japanese culture we should be proud to show off to the world I would pick two things. Firstly, manga, and secondly, the mixed writing system of Chinese characters and Japanese *kana* syllabary. There are other examples – the Emperor system, Nō plays, bonsai, *netsuke* [carved toggles], and *kamon* [family crests] – of what is called Japanese civilisation. Some of which I also like. But I do not think they emphasise Japanese characteristics so supremely as manga and our *kana* writing system.
>
> (Kure 1991:86).

Manga and Educational and Cultural Institutions

The only comprehensive archive of post-war manga books and magazines is the Modern Manga Library (*Gendai Manga Toshokan*) created from the comprehensive private collection of one individual, Uchiki Toshio, in 1978. The Modern Manga Library is a tiny private library located above a manga *kashihon* rental shop in Waseda, Tokyo. By 1994 the library contained 120,000 volumes of manga which visitors could read and photocopy on the premises for a small fee. Uchiki Toshio suggested that he had collected manga since the 1960s because of its cultural value and that 'The library's function is to keep manga as objects of cultural research, not as consumer items' (*Mainichi Daily News* 1989). However, for much of the late post-war period, Uchiki's opinion that manga was culture was unorthodox and no funded public institution collected contemporary manga books or magazines until 1988.

In 1988 Kawasaki City Museum began to make a select collection of manga books. At the same time it opened a large permanent display in which the history of post-war manga is illustrated in 90 framed panels – more suited to the display of etchings, prints, and paintings than manga. Since 1988, Kawasaki City Museum has also held exhibitions of cartoons from *Marumaru Chinbun*, and the manga of Tezuka Osamu and Fujio-Fujiko.

The concept of manga as culture which should be displayed in museums spread with extraordinary speed and was linked in particular to home-town regeneration projects. Between 1990 and 1998 no less than 12 new museums displaying the work of a variety individual artists, including Mizuki Shigeru, Yoyoyama Ryūichi, and Ishinomori Shōtarō, were opened in towns across the country.[2] Between July and September 1990 the *Tokyo Museum of Modern Art*, a highly prestigious institution, held a retrospective exhibition of the work of Tezuka Osamu which became its largest exhibition ever. In 1994, Takarazuka municipal council in Hyōgo prefecture opened a modern theme-park-style museum based around the characters and stories of manga produced by Tezuka Osamu. Takarazuka council won the rights to establish a Tezuka Osamu museum in Takarazuka on the grounds that it was Tezuka's home town and a source of inspiration for some of his manga stories.

Manga not only became the resident and guest of local and national museums but also entered the national school curriculum at various levels. In 1984 questions about manga were incorporated into the exam paper of an entrance exam to a public university. In 1985 works by Tezuka Osamu and Satō Sanpei were incorporated into sections of elementary school textbooks on Japanese culture approved by the Ministry of Education and Culture (Ito 1994:81). In 1989, the Agency for Cultural Affairs (*Bunkachō*) announced that manga could, for the first time, be considered for educational awards. Manga critic Kure Tomofusa incorporates manga history into lectures on contemporary culture at Tokyo Rika University. During the 1990s he was joined by other academics, several of them also the authors of books on manga criticism, who began to incorporate teaching on manga history and criticism into degree courses on Art History, Literature, Sociology, Media and Communications, Design, and Human Sciences. By 1997 14 universities and colleges offered some form of teaching in manga studies, two of which, Shirayuri Women's College and Kyoto Seika University, had assembled full courses on Manga Studies I.II (*Manga Kenkyū I.II*) and *Manga Senkō*, respectively.[3] Together with a new wave of books and magazines on manga criticism, these courses combined to create an emergent school of manga studies.

In 1994 the national government made the unprecedented step of producing the *Environment White Paper in Manga Form*. The white paper was published by the Printing Bureau of the Ministry of

Finance under the guidance of the Environment Agency. Figure 3.8 shows Environmental Agency officials discussing the layout of the manga white paper. The points discussed in the government white paper were incorporated into a manga story *Secrets of the Earth*, written by an elementary school student Tsubota Aika, who had died in 1991. *Secrets of the Earth* had already been published in Japanese, English and several East Asian languages and distributed free amongst elementary school students in Japan and foreign countries by *The Foundation for Global Peace and Environment* (*Japan Pictorial* 1995). This action carried out by a national government agency carried the extraordinary message that in Japan writing official documents in manga is normal. The publication of a white paper in manga suggested that manga could be considered a special and official aspect of Japanese culture.[4] Manga had been chosen as a cultural envoy capable of negotiating an improvement in Japan's image abroad.

Accepting manga as a part of national culture appeared to become important to Japanese government agencies and institutions as well. Institutions and individuals concerned with reforming

Figure 3.8 Ministry officials make a photo-opportunity of planning an *Environment White Paper in Manga* in 1993. [Used with kind permission of *Japan Pictorial*, 1995. Vol. 18. No. 1]

national culture and politics, and others concerned with altering the image of Japan abroad, perceived in manga a suitable symbol of change. Within domestic culture the promotion of manga to high-quality culture appeared to portend a more liberal and multicultural social environment, now ready to accept previously excluded social and cultural formations. For companies too, using manga helped to overcome social barriers and counteract passive but profound employee and consumer cynicism about corporate activities. Entering Europe and America manga became a cultural messenger distributed to deliver the subtle message that Japanese culture is still alive, kicking and different.

Manga Studies

At the same time as courses on manga began to appear in colleges and universities across the country the volume of writing on manga increased. Manga criticism conferred intellectual respect and cultural value on manga, and provided an appropriate interpretation of its significance in society. Manga critics who rose to prominence during the 1990s, notably Ishiko Junzo, Kure Tomofusa [Go Chiei], Natsume Funosuke, Takeuchi Osamu, and Yomota Inuhiko, represented the full-time personnel of the project of assimilating manga into national culture. Manga criticism appeared in broad-sheets and literary journals. Regular columns for manga criticism included *Mangakyō* in *Asahi* newspaper, *Manga Geppan* in the *Tokyo Post* newspaper, *Manga Geppyō* in the *Yomiuri* newspaper, and *Manga!* in the *Mainichi Daily News*. From 1989 onwards, a shelf full of books on manga, some of them compilations of articles already published in newspapers, appeared in book shops. Not only did the quantity of manga criticism increase but also the treatment of manga criticism itself changed. It gained respect and new relevance to newspaper readers.

Prior to the publication of Kure Tomofusa's *Modern Manga: The Complete Picture* (*Gendai Manga no Zentaizō*) in 1986, professional manga criticism had been the particular concern of socialist intellectuals active mainly during the 1950s and 1960s. Tsurumi Shunsuke produced his first writings on manga as early as 1949, and helped to found the Scientific Thought Group (*Shisō no Kagaku Group*), concerned with creating a body of critical theory about popular culture (*taishū bunka*).[5]

During the late 1960s Tsurumi developed the theory of 'border art' (*genkai geijitsu*): a new category of democratic culture 'made by and for amateurs', or ordinary people, of which manga was the best example (Tsurumi 1967). Another member of Scientific Thought, Satō Takao, perceived the left-wing political manga of the 1950s and 1960s, such as the work of Shirato Sanpei, as a new force for social change in the post-war period: 'Young people who have been brought up during the manga age are now beginning to make political statements, and political manga has the potential to develop rapidly'. (Satō 1970:344).

In 1986 the earlier emphasis on the importance of manga as a forum for the expression of working class expression and radical politics by Satō, Tsurumi, and manga critic Ishiko Junzo was criticized for its 'over-emphasis' on cultural resistance:

Even today the theory that manga is the weapon of the people is extremely strong. Though of course manga does have a history, there is no basis whatsoever to this argument. During the intense political formations around the period of the Pacific war, some manga, it is true, became critical, but some manga also became complicit with the political order.

(Kure 1990:126)

Previously a contributor to the minor manga criticism magazine *Mangashūgi* (Mangaism), Kure Tomofusa suggested that a new school of manga studies should be created in order to establish manga as a cultural form in its own right, with its own 'rules of manga grammar' (*manga bunpō no tame no riron*) and 'manga structure' (*manga kōzō no tame no riron*), quite distinct from those of either literature or film. Kure's desire to establish a new style of manga criticism without a left-wing bias proved to be prescient. Over the next decade a new generation of books on manga filtered into bookshops, forming the texts of a new academic field of Manga Studies (*manga kenkyū*).

The new school of manga studies is divided into three main subjects: manga history, the life and work of Tezuka Osamu, and manga theory. The majority of new books on manga have been straightforward accounts of mainly early post-war manga history. The overt contextualisation of manga history within a broader social and political framework favoured by Satō, Tsurumi and Ishiko, is replaced in these books by an emphasis on detailed content analysis of specific series and authors. Osamu Takeuchi, author of *Fifty years of post-war manga* (*Sengo manga 50 nenshi*), voices the current view that manga critics should eschew all forms of 'subjectivity' in their relationship to the medium and avoid the 'routine association of manga with the politics of each generation of manga readers' practised by previous generations of critics. Books on manga history (Ishiko Jun 1988; Yonezawa 1996, 1991; Shimizu 1989, 1991; Takeuchi 1995; Murakami 1991) have tended to focus on well-known *gekiga* and avant garde manga works, reinterpreting them not as radical culture reflecting an essentially negative view of Japanese society, but as cultural classics, which showcase the manga medium and the talent of manga artists.

Another group of books on manga history have focused specifically on the life and works of the artist Tezuka Osamu (Nakano 1993; Ishigami 1989; Takeuchi 1992; Natsume 1996, 1995; Imagawa 1996). The death of Tezuka Osamu in 1989 was accompanied by a media wake of sympathetic coverage for the late artist. Through newspaper articles and television documentaries (for example: about the Tezuka Osamu retrospective exhibition held at the Tokyo Museum of Modern Art in 1990, or the construction of a Tezuka Osamu Museum in Takarazuka), Tezuka's existing reputation as one of the most prolific and talented post-war manga artists was inflated to mythological proportions. Tezuka's name became interchangeable with the honorific *prenom* 'God of manga' (*manga no kamisama*), and books and reportage describing Tezuka's work took on an uncritical and eulogizing tone.

The intensity of the focus on Tezuka Osamu's manga, particularly *New Treasure Island* (*Shintakarajima*), *Black Jack, Atom Boy* (*Tetsuwan Atom*), and *Phoenix* (*Hi no Tori*), overshadowed the public presence of other manga artists and helped to create the inaccurate impression that Tezuka Osamu was the sole pioneer of early post-war manga. The exaggerated attention paid to Tezuka's involvement with the development of story manga during the 1950s, was accompanied by a distinctive absence of any reference to the equally important work of the more political *gekiga* artists. The new generation of manga critics found in Tezuka a highly-educated and apolitical manga artist who could be resurrected to create a new and acceptable image for the manga medium as a whole during the 1990s. Tezuka is described as a national hero, as a key figure representing the entire post-war era, in fact, not so much a manga artist as 'a philosopher who passed his ideas on to posterity through the medium of manga.'(*Mainichi Daily News* 1992c)

In terms of the development of a serious academic school of manga studies the most significant titles of the new books on manga are those concerned with manga theory (*mangaron*). Manga theorists, notably Yomota Inuhiko, Ohtsuka Eiji, and Natsume Funosuke, focused their attentions on developing for manga an equivalent of literary theory, referred to as 'manga expression theory' (*manga hyōgenron*), which focuses entirely on the structure and spatial arrangement of manga pictures within the discreet manga product. Manga expression theory takes the lines used to draw manga pictures (*byōsen*), the spatial organization of the boxes (*koma*), and speech bubbles (*fukidashi*), as the starting point of a theoretical deconstruction of the medium.

One manga critic with an academic background, who rose to prominence in the 1990s was Yomota Inuhiko, who published his highly accessible work *Manga Base Theory* (*Manga Genron*) in 1994. Yomota emphasized the unconscious element of expression within the micro-structure of manga pictures:

> Manga poses as an individual experiencing a story, but the manga itself has an ideological existence. If the world-view which is temporarily embodied within the contents of a manga story are put to one side, then manga itself is physically composed of lines, colour, and shapes, which also have to be taken into consideration.
>
> (Yomota 1994:10)

Yomota points out the unique 'flow of time in manga', set up by the multiple cross-readings of each page carried out by typical engrossed readers, and which distinguish manga as a medium from either film or literature, which are based on a chronological time-flow (ibid.:30). *Manga Base Theory* 'lets manga speak on its own terms' and rejects 'base and superstructure and formal sociology' (ibid.:295) in favour of an analysis of the graphic structure of manga stories. In the second section of *Manga Base Theory*, Yomota demonstrates the application of some elements of 'basic manga theory'. In a selection of specialist essays he traces the representation of such random and post-modern subjects as 'playgrounds' or 'monkeys', as represented in manga. Manga theory and the subjects to which Yomota chose to apply it, eliminated conscious intentions and history from the analysis of manga stories.

The introduction of elements of 'manga expression theory' to both highly-educated and general audiences was taken further by Natsume Funosuke in *How to Read Manga* (*Manga no Yomikata*) published in 1995, and a television mini-series accompanying the publication entitled *What Makes Manga Interesting?* (*Manga wa Naze Omoishiroi ka*), broadcast as a part of NHK's People's University (*Ningen Daigaku*) 1996 educational programme.

In contrast to the sociological priorities of the Scientific Thought Group, manga theorist Natsume Funosuke argues that the reason why manga should be taken seriously was that in order to become 'Japan's number one popular culture' the mode of expression within manga had been systematically refined to a point where it embodied a 'highly sophisticated mode of expression' (*kōdo no hyōgen*). In the context of the general trend towards the promotion of manga to the status of high-quality culture, the main significance of the development of manga expression theory was the creation of an apparently objective theoretical reason, based on nothing more than the internal structure of manga itself, as to why manga should be considered an important culture.

The overall orientation of books on manga history and manga theory was uncritical and celebratory, an attitude which veered towards a nationalistic interpretation of the unique aesthetic qualities of the manga medium in the work of some critics. The new approaches developed for analysing the graphic structure of manga stories may have merit in their own right. But the analysis of the graphic devices within printed manga, in isolation from any analysis of the social and economic relations surrounding the production of the same stories, has had the effect of separating manga from concrete developments within Japanese society and politics. The point cannot be made clearly enough: manga expression theory has tended to separate manga from the subjective intentions and ideas of the very producers of the manga stories themselves.

4

AMATEUR MANGA SUBCULTURE AND THE *OTAKU* PANIC

The rapid ascendancy of the weekly manga magazine industry during the 1960s encouraged the development of a sphere of non-commercial and amateur manga production. Artists who were excluded from recruitment or who did not want to work for the new manga magazines developed other ways of distributing their manga. It was the launch of the manga magazine industry which provided the initial impetus for the gradual bifurcation of 'mainstream' manga and 'underground' (*uragawa, angura*) manga, into professional manga and amateur manga. Non-commercial manga produced in the 1960s to mid-1970s was ignored by the publishing industry and the government until the late 1980s, when it began to receive belated critical attention and the interest of large publishers. While 'underground' manga of this earlier period was promoted and partially re-integrated into 'mainstream' manga, during the 1990s the contemporary amateur manga medium was simultaneously ostracized and repressed.

During the 1960s rental manga (*kashihon gekiga*) and the Osaka-based *akabon* manga publishing industries were usurped by weekly manga magazines produced by large publishers based in Tokyo. For the manga artists who managed to make the transition from periodic or monthly production cycles to weekly production cycles this switch-over had two principal effects. Manga artists had to work much faster, and the style and content of their work became more closely monitored and commissioned by publishing companies.

Rental manga publishing companies paid notoriously low wages, but manga artists experienced a great deal of leniency over the details of the series they produced. Large publishers such as

Kōdansha offered rates per page which were up to ten times as high as those offered by the rental manga companies, in order to attract artists to produce weekly series for their magazines. Some experienced manga artists felt that the new mode of production was nipping the internal development of the new story manga in the bud, and that editorial production (*henshū seisan*) was infringing upon the liberty of manga artists to draw properly. Artists argued that the personal space in which artists could express their ideas within their work had shrunk.

Several manga magazines were launched by small publishing companies during the 1960s. These had the goal of providing an alternative space for the publication of manga drawn and developed entirely by artists. In 1967 Tezuka Osamu established *COM*, a monthly manga magazine devoted to supporting the free expression of its contributing artists. In a founding statement published in the first issue of *COM*, Tezuka Osamu explained why this had become necessary:

> It is said that now is the golden age of manga. So shouldn't works of outstanding quality be published? Or isn't the real situation one in which many manga artists are being worked to death, while they are forced into submission, servitude and cooperation with the cruel requirements of commercialism? With this magazine I thought I would show you what real *story manga* is. *COM* is a magazine for comrades who love manga.
>
> (Tezuka 1967:1)

COM was established as an adult manga magazine in which any form of artistic expression, including sexual imagery, could be published. Tezuka Osamu and the core group of *manga* artists, including Nagashima Shinji, Ishinomori Shōtarō, and Fujio-Fujiko, who contributed to *COM*, many of whom were ex-assistants and 'disciples' (*deshi*) of Tezuka, and were mostly childrens' manga artists. It is probable that one additional reason for launching *COM* magazine in 1967 was this group's need to respond to the popularity of adult-oriented *gekiga* stories during the mid-1960s.

Alongside *COM* another alternative magazine, which continued to exist under the same management until 1997, was established by Seirindō publisher in 1964. *GARO* was devoted to serializing in magazine format *gekiga* stories, and in particular the work of Shirato Sanpei. One of the original intentions of the founder of

GARO, Nagai Katsuichi, was to create a space for artists, in particular Tsuge Yoshiharu and Shirato Sanpei, who had been unable or unwilling to work for large publishing companies. In return for retaining freedom over the contents of their series, artists working for *GARO* received no fees. Some of the more individualistic artists of the post-war period, including Yoshikazu Ebisu, Uchida Shungiku, Kazuichi Hanawa, and Maruo Suehiro, as well as Shirato Sanpei, Shinohara Katsuichi, Tsuge Yoshiharu, and Matsui Yukiko, have worked for *GARO* magazine. *COM* and *GARO* existed on the boundary between professional and amateur manga. Both magazines were official publications, but neither developed properly as commercial enterprises. *COM* quickly went bankrupt and folded in 1972, while *GARO* survived on a low turnover until 1997, when the magazine was sold to a new owner. However, prior to the development of cheap offset printing machines in the early 1970s *COM* and *GARO* were the only major non-commercial alternatives to weekly manga magazines and the unpublished hand-written manga (*nikushitsu kaitenshi*), which was distributed by hand. Several 'veteran' artists, including Ishinomori Shōtarō and Akatsuka Fujio, produced hand-written manga until the end of the 1960s (Takarajima 1989:77).

The existence of several unpublished magazines devoted to manga criticism from 1967, suggest that the circulation of amateur manga increased from the mid-1960s onwards. Between 1967 and 1974 an amateur magazine titled *Mangaism* (*Mangashugi*) in a cheeky and competitive reference to Marxism (*Marxshugi*) and other ideological *isms*, was produced on an intermittent basis, and carried the opinion pieces of new, underground manga critics such as Gotō Shin, Ishiko Junzo, Kikuchi Asajiro, Kure Tomofusa, and Kajii Jun. Another amateur magazine for manga criticism, *Nightlife* (*Yagyō*), began circulation in the mid-1970s, following the demise of *Mangashugi* (Kure 1990:26). In common with other virtually unknown material of the 1960s, such as Tokunami Seiichiro's *Human Clock* (*Ningen Dokei*, 1962), issues of *Mangaism* and *Nightlife*, are now highly valued collectors items.

Mini Communications

At the beginning of the 1970s cheap and portable offset printing and photocopying facilities rapidly became available to the public.

Amateur manga and literature could be reproduced and distributed cheaply and easily, creating the possibility of mass participation in unregistered and unpublished forms of cultural production. During the early 1970s the new possibilities opened up by this technology also meant that it was relatively easy for individuals to set up small publishing and printing companies. Many ex-radical students who had ruined their chances of joining a good company through their political activities, or who were turning their energies to youth culture for more specific individual reasons, set up one-man publishing companies producing small, erotic or specialist culture magazines, many of which also contained sections of more unusual manga. Others established small offset printing companies which gradually began to specialize in printing short-runs of amateur manga to professional standards for individual customers.

Using the services of the new mini printing companies, individuals from all walks of life could now print and reproduce their own work without approaching publishing companies. This twilight sphere of cultural production, spreading beneath the superstructure of mass communications, (*mass commi*) became known as the mini communications (*mini commi*). The relationship of Japanese *mini commi* to the mass communications industry corresponds in many of its aspects to the relationship between Anglo–American fanzine networks and television producers (Penley 1991). Sociologist John Fiske's characterization of these Anglo–American fanzine networks as 'shadow cultural economies' (Fiske 1992:30) existing beneath official cultural economies, is also equatable with the structure of Japanese *mini commi*. With regard to its amateur, decentralized and open structure, printed *mini commi* might be compared to the emergence of the computer internet during the 1990s. One of the most extensive forms of mini communications in Japan was to become printed amateur manga.

Contemporary printed amateur manga are known as *dōjinshi* – a term previously used to refer to pamphlets or magazines distributed within specific associations or societies. Alongside the growth of the commercial manga industry, and following the development of cheap offset printing and photocopying facilities, the number of manga artists and fans printing and distributing editions of their own amateur manga *dōjinshi* began to increase, first slowly in the 1970s, and then rapidly during the 1980s.

Manga Conventions

In 1975 a group of young manga critics, Aniwa Jun, Harada Teruo and Yonezawa Yoshihiro, founded a new institution to encourage the development of unpublished amateur manga. The institution was Comic Market (also known by the abbreviations *Comiket* and *Comike*), a free space in the form of a convention held several times a year where amateur manga could be bought and sold. Yonezawa Yoshihiro, the current president of *Comiket* explained how it was established in response to the changing political orientation official manga industry: 'All the independent comics and meeting places of the 1960s were disappearing by 1973 to 1974, and then *COM* magazine folded. It *was* a regression, from being able to publish all kinds of stuff in mainstream magazines to being able to publish only unusual stuff in *dōjinshi* underground magazines. But what else can you do, but start again from the underground?'

Large publishing companies ceased to systematically produce radical and stylistically innovatory manga series around 1972, because they no longer matched sufficiently closely the changed interests of their mass audiences. Younger manga artists and fans interested in developing the manga medium in directions other than those dictated by manga publishers, were forced to turn to amateur production as an alternative outlet for unpublishable material. The amateur manga medium rapidly developed an internal momentum, partially independent of developments in commercial manga publishing.

Between 1975 and 1984, Comic Market was held on three days a year, after which point attendance grew so large that it was rescheduled to two weekend conventions held in the Tokyo Harumi Trade Centre, in August and December. In 1995 these bi-annual weekend conventions were extended to three-day events. The first Comic Market held in December 1975 attracted 32 amateur manga circles, and 600 individuals (*Comic Market 46*:15). Attendance grew slowly between 1975 and 1986, and rapidly between 1986 and 1992.

Comic Market became the central organization of the amateur manga medium, the existence of which encouraged the formation of new amateur manga circles, in high schools, in colleges and amongst amateur manga artists with similar interests across the country. Attendance figures of Comic Market provide a useful illustration of the proportions and growth of the amateur manga medium, which is otherwise a remarkably invisible subculture in Japanese society. Figure 4.1 below illustrates the annual growth of individual attendance to each December Comic Market.

Since 1993, 16,000 separate manga circles, distributing one or more amateur works produced by their members, have participated in each Comic Market convention. In fact there have been approximately 30,000 applications from manga circles wishing to attend each convention throughout the 1990s but no more than 16,000 stalls can be accommodated in the Harumi Trade Centre. Figure 4.2 below illustrates the increase in the number of circles renting stalls to distribute amateur manga works at Comic Market since 1975.

A proportion of the excess demand to attend conventions is absorbed by the staggering of conventions over two and three days and also by a recently established rival convention, known as Super Comic City, which is held in the Harumi Trade Centre each April. Convention attendance gives a loose indication of the number of amateur manga circles across the country, which was estimated at anywhere between 30,000 and 50,000 during the early 1990s (Imidasu 1992: 1094). Figure 4.1 suggests that the amount of amateur manga being produced and distributed has increased greatly since around 1988, and may have totalled anything from 35,000 separate works a year upwards during the 1990s.[1]

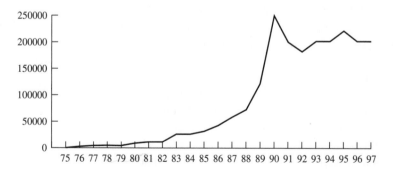

Figure 4.1 Increase in the number of individuals attending *Comic Market* each December 1975–1997. [Source of Data: 1975–1993 *Comic Market 46*, pp. 14–15; 1993–1997 Comic Market President, Yonezawa Yoshihiro]

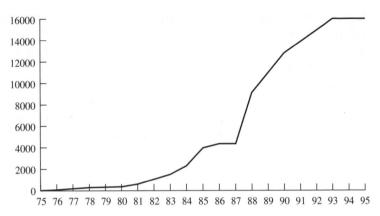

Figure 4.2 Increase in the number of manga circles participating in *Comic Market* each December 1975–1995. [Source of Data: 1975–1993 *Comic Market 46*, pp. 14–15; 1993–1995 Comic Market President, Yonezawa Yoshihiro]

Subculture Industries

Comic Market is ostensibly a voluntary, non-profit making organization, but a range of other commercial enterprises have begun to grow on the margins of the amateur manga pool. In 1986 specialist amateur manga printer Akabubu Tsūshin launched Wings amateur manga conventions, and in 1991 Tokyo Ryūkō [Trend] Centre (TRC) set up *Super Comic City* conventions. Both of these companies hold small to medium-sized conventions in towns across the country every few weeks. It is possible for amateur manga artists and fans to visit a convention to find contacts and friends or to search out new amateur manga every other weekend, though in fact many smaller conventions are limited to specific genres of amateur manga of interest to just one particular group of amateur manga artists.

Timetables of convention dates and locations are advertised in several monthly magazines devoted to the amateur manga world. In the mid-1970s low-circulation magazines such as *June* (San Shuppan), *Peke* (Minori Shobō), *Again, Tanbi* and *Manga Kissatengai* were established. The first of these magazines, entitled *Manga Wave* (*Manpa*) was launched in 1976 and its scions continue to occupy the organizational centre of the amateur manga medium. In 1982 *Manga Wave* magazine split into *Puff* – which specializes in amateur girls' manga – and *Comic Box* – which covers all amateur manga from a distinctive leftist political position. These magazines also carry adverts for small *dōjinshi* publishers, *dōjinshi* books and anthologies, meeting places for amateur artists, and specialist manga book shops which may also sell some *dōjinshi*. *Comic Box* magazine also publishes manga criticism, interviews with manga artists, and otherwise unrecorded indexes of all published manga matter. An increasing number of small companies have also begun to publish amateur manga. Fusion Productions, which makes *Comic Box* magazine, also publishes *Comic Box Jr.*, a 300-page monthly magazine in which collections of already printed and distributed amateur manga organized by specific genre or sub-genre are published, and collected anthologies of *dōjinshi*, which so far include a now infamous, erotic series, *Lolita Syndrome* (*Bishōjo Shōkogun*) published in 1985. In addition to small publishers, the growth of the amateur manga medium has provided custom for a large number of small printing shops such as P-Mate Insatsu and Hikari Insatsu, many of which specialize solely in the production of *dōjinshi*.

Other commercial enterprises directly linked to the amateur manga medium are large manga shops which cater to the specialist requirements of amateur manga artists and fans. In 1984 a chain of manga shops entitled Manga no Mori (Manga Forest), sprang up in the Shinjuku, Takadanobaba, Kichijōji, and Higashi Ikebukuro, sub-centres of Tokyo (Takarajima 1989:246). In 1992, Mandarake, a multi-storey manga superstore, in which staff wear costumes fashioned after those of the better-known manga characters, opened in Shibuya, another sub-centre of Tokyo.

Dōjinshi Artists

In the second half of the 1970s when Comic Market was still a relatively small cultural gathering, a high proportion of *dōjinshi* artists graduated from amateur to professional status. Ishii Hisaichi, Saimon Fumi, Sabe Anoma, Kono Moji, Takahashi Hakkai, and Takahashi Rumiko, all produced *dōjinshi* and distributed them at Comic Market, subsequent to becoming famous, professional female artists (Takarajima 1989:78). As the size of the amateur medium grew in the 1980s this flow of artists into commercial production decreased sharply.

It is evident from Figure 4.1 that the amateur manga movement reached its peak size in 1990 to 1992, when a staggering quarter of a million amateur artists and fans attended Comic Market. Amateur manga conventions are the largest mass public gatherings in contemporary Japan. The tendency towards mass gatherings evidenced at amateur manga conventions has a parallel in rave and festival culture (Glastonbury Festival to Tribal Gathering) which peaked in the United Kingdom during approximately the same time frame.

Most amateur artists and fans are aged between their mid-teens and mid-twenties – the mean age is nineteen. Although no statistics have been recorded, Yonezawa Yoshihiro has also observed that young Japanese from low-income backgrounds, typically raised in large suburban housing projects (*danchi*), and attending lower ranking colleges, or without higher education, are the majority participants of Comic Market. The significance of this observation is not straightforward. Despite the academic and media attention given to higher education and the emergence of a universal middle-class in contemporary Japan, the majority of young Japanese do not go on to higher education, and of those that do, a large proportion attend low-ranking colleges. At the same time the majority of Japanese people now live in suburban housing complexes and apartment blocks. While this could be taken to suggest that the sociological composition of Comic Market is therefore standard and representative, the significance of this observation is, perhaps, that this is one of the very few cultural and social forums in Japan, (or any other industrialized country), which is not managed by privileged and highly-educated sections of society.

This observation is particularly interesting in light of the emphasis on the accumulation of cultural information which can be observed within the amateur manga world. Although largely excluded from professional employment and graduate social circles, many amateur manga artists appear to seek pleasure in being specialized and well-informed. By applying Pierre Bourdieus' theory of the 'cultural economy' to Anglo-American fanzine subcultures, John Fiske has developed the theory that these subcultures operate as 'shadow cultural economies' which provide individuals typically lacking in official cultural capital, namely education and the social status with which education is rewarded, with an alternative social world in which they can get access to a different kind of 'cultural capital' and social prestige (Fiske 1992:30). It is possible that the intense emphasis placed, firstly, on educational achievement and secondly, on acquiring a sophisticated cultural taste, in Japan since the 1960s, has in fact stimulated the involvement of young people excluded from these officially recognized modes of achievement, with amateur manga subculture.

Nevertheless a fraction of the rapid growth of the amateur manga medium at the end of the 1980s is accounted for by the arrival of teenage artists from privileged backgrounds at amateur manga conventions. These new participants, some of them the students of élite universities, are attributed to parents who were active in the counter-culture and political movements of the late 1960s, and who have passed on both their class and some of their positive attitude towards manga to their children.

The huge proliferation of *dōjinshi* production in the wake of the mini communications boom which enabled many ordinary Japanese youth to start producing amateur manga, meant that by the 1980s virtually all amateur manga was being made, not by highly-skilled professional artists seeking alternative outlets for their personal work, but by young artists who had never had a relationship with the manga publishing industry at all. Of the tens of thousands of *dōjinshi* writers active in the medium during the 1980s, only a handful went on to become professional artists. The originally close relationship between amateur and professional manga production had become looser. In an attempt to direct some of these amateur artists towards commercial production, the Comic Market Preparation Committee began publishing an annual journal designed to promote amateur manga artists. In this journal, *Comiket Origin*, published every summer, 15 to 20 amateur artists of the best-selling *dōjinshi* of the previous year are reviewed and introduced to the public.

Early in the development of Comic Market it became evident that printed amateur manga was providing an unexpected new gateway into the manga medium for Japanese women. Though Disney animation and the cute children's manga characters, such as *Princess Knight* (*Ribbon no Kishi*) created by Tezuka Osamu had long been popular with young women, very few of them became manga artists before 1970. Commercial manga was dominated by boys' and adults' magazines, and these publishing categories continue to represent the mainstream of the medium and the

111

publishing industry into the nineties. In 1993, adult manga for men represented 38.5 per cent; boys' manga represented 39 per cent; while girls' manga represented only 8.8 per cent, of all published manga (*Shuppan Nenpō* 1994:188).

The number of women making *dōjinshi* increased quickly after the establishment of Comic Market, so that the first result of the sudden increase in the general accessibility of the manga medium was a new amateur manga movement engendered by women. In the mid-1970s a group of female artists producing 'small quantities of extremely high-quality manga' emerged, and became known as the 1949 Group (*nijūyon-nen gumi*), after the year in which a number of them were born (Matsui 1993). These artists, including Hagio Moto, Oshima Yumiko, Yamagisha Ryoko and Takemiya Keiko, joined other earlier *dōjinshi* artists who had become professional manga artists, when they filtered into commercial girls' manga magazines such as *Margaret, Ribbon*, and *Flowers and Dreams* (*Hana to Yume*).

Until 1988, approximately 80 per cent of *dōjinshi* artists attending Comic Market were female, and only 20 per cent male. During the 1990s however, male participation in Comic Market increased to 35 per cent. The girls' manga genre continues to dominate amateur production but it has now been adopted by the majority of male *dōjinshi* artists. The increase in male attendance of Comic Market at the end of the 1980s was another factor contributing to the rapid proliferation of the amateur medium at this time. New genres of girl's manga written by and for boys sprouted from the fertile bed of the amateur manga medium. Some colleges and universities began to boast not only manga clubs (*manga kenkyūkai*), but also, girls' manga clubs for men. This manga and those men became the focus of the *otaku* [nerd] panic.

Subculture Genres

The realistic, adult-oriented *gekiga* style, which arose out of anti-establishment manga subculture in the late 1950s, and had a strong influence on the genres utilized within commercial boys' and adult manga, has not been a big influence on contemporary amateur manga. Amateur manga production has been far more influenced by girls' manga, which in turn has far greater stylistic continuity with the less politically controversial tradition of child-oriented, cute *manga* pioneered by Tezuka Osamu and his ex-assistants, including

Ishinomori Shōtarō, and Fujio-Fujiko. A typical published sample of girls' manga by Miuchi Sakue can be seen in Figure 4.3. Not only do amateur and commercial manga diverge in their stylistic origins but the social networks of amateur and professional artists have become so distant that they have increasingly come to represent two virtually separate streams of the same cultural media. From amateur manga subculture have emerged new genres which are distinctly recognizable as amateur in origin.

In the early 1980s, *dōjinshi* artists began to produce not only new, original works, but a new genre of *parody* manga. *Parody* is based on revised versions of published commercial manga stories and characters. While often radically altering the content of original stories and implicitly criticizing the morality of the original themes, *parody* does not always imply a specifically humorous re-rendering of texts. The first commercial manga series to attract a whole wave of amateur parodies in the first half of the 1980s was *Spaceship Yamato* (*Uchūsenkan Yamato*). As the amateur manga medium expanded, the proportion of *dōjinshi* artists producing *parody* instead of original works increased too. By 1989, 45.9 per cent of material sold at *Comic Market* was *parody*, whilst only 12.1 per cent was what is aptly referred to as *original* (*Comic Box* 1989).

Most *parody* manga have been based on leading boys' manga stories serialized in commercial magazines. Stories in the best-selling boys' manga magazine, *Jump*, including *Dragon Ball, Yūyūhakusho, Slam Dunk,* and *Captain Tsubasa*, have been particularly frequent sources of *parody*. During the 1990s some political adult manga series also became the focus of interest for *parody* artists. Figure 4.4 shows pages from an amateur *parody* of Kawaguchi Kaiji's *Silent Service* (see Chapter 3, Figure 3.5), printed in 1991. *Parody* based on animation rather than manga series, and referred to as *aniparo* (an abbreviation of 'animation-parody'), became more popular from the mid-1980s onwards. In the same period *cosplay* (an abbreviation of 'costume-play'), where manga fans dress up in the costumes of well-known manga characters and perform 'live *parody*' at amateur manga conventions, also became widespread.

Dōjinshi artists categorized their style of manga, which is dominant in both *parody* and original work, as *yaoi*. This word is a three syllable anagram, *ya-o-i*, composed of the first syllable of each of the following three phrases; '**ya**ma nashi', '**o**chi nashi', '**i**mi nashi', which mean 'no build-up, no foreclosure, and no meaning',

Figure 4.3 *The Glass Mask* of a girl's identity is explored in the most popular girls' manga series of the 1990s. [*Glass no Kamen* 1994 Vol. 1 © Miuchi Sakue/Hakusensha]

Figure 4.3 *(continued)*

Figure 4.4 Noble Captain Kaieda gets silly kow-towing and a silly nickname ('devil') in an amateur *parody* manga of *Chinmoku no Kantai*. (See Fig. 3.5) [*Nani ga Fuman da?: Sea Bat 2* by Creme Creap, 1991]

which are frequently cited to describe the almost total absence of narrative structure, typical of amateur manga from the mid-1980s onwards (Imidasu 1993: 1094). The narrative or story-line, which in many ways is the only remaining link between manga and works generally understood as 'pure literature' (*jun bungaku*), has been very much abandoned to commercial manga publishers, for whom it continues to be of varied but generally substantial importance. The non-linear form of storytelling in *yaoi* work invites categorization as 'post-modern manga', but with little further explanatory effect.

Yaoi is also characterized by its main subject matter, that is homoerotica and homosexual romance between lead male characters of the work. Typical homosexual characters are pubescent European public school-boys, or lean, muscular young men with attenuated limbs and features, long hair and feminine looks (see Figure 4.5). Girls' manga featuring gay love is sometimes identified as *june mono* (after the girls' manga magazine *June*), while love stories about beautiful young men are also known as *bishōnen-ai*. Although the characters of these stories are biologically male, in essence they are genderless ideal types, combining favoured masculine qualities with favoured feminine qualities. Readers are likely to directly identify with 'gay male' lead characters, – and female readers often with the slightly more effeminate male of a pair of characters. Young female fans feel more able to imagine and depict idealized strong and free characters, if they are male.[2]

In 1991 *Comic Box Jr.* published an anthology of *original* amateur manga entitled '*Original* not beaten by *parody* yet!', confirming that amateur manga production has become dominated by *parody*. As parody manga production began to outweigh original manga production in the mid-1980s, original amateur artists have begun to form their own smaller specialist *original* amateur manga circles and conventions. Amateur manga artists producing work more influenced by 1970s *gekiga* than by girls' manga were less likely to be involved in the amateur manga world and more likely to try to get their work published. One such *original* amateur manga artist with connections to *GARO* and to the veteran artist Nagashima Shinji criticized the artistic standards of contemporary amateur manga:

> Manga culture is pathetic at the moment because it is all *parody*. It all looks the same. Me and my friends don't go to Comic Market. The only reason why everyone produces *parody* is because they aren't talented enough write *original*. The only characters they can understand are those that they have been reading for years.

However Comic Market president Yonezawa Yoshihiro sees the expansion of *parody* in manga as an attempt to struggle with and subvert dominant culture, on the part of a generation of youth for whom mass culture, which has surrounded them from early childhood, has become their dominant reality. In this context

Figure 4.5 Transcendental lovers play power games with each other in *original* but amateur *yaoi* manga. [*Nile wo Sakanobotte* front cover, 1989. Used with the kind permission of the artist, Yahagi Takako]

Yonezawa interprets *parody* as a highly critical genre which attempts to remodel and take control of 'cultural reality'. Manga critic Kure Tomofusa, on the other hand, believes that the highly 'personal' (*jiheiteki*) themes of *parody* manga represent, not a critical sensibility, so much as a return to the previous narrow themes of Japanese literature:

> In the 1980s people once again began to forget about dramatic social themes and manga began to move towards petty, repetitive, personal affairs, rather like the I-novels (*shishōsetsu*) of the pre-1960 period. In the 1980s new kinds of *love-comedy*, often set within *parody* works, began in and dominated the amateur manga world.

Yonezawa, representing the more open-minded approach of many independent media-based intellectuals, perceives a progressive political spirit, equivalent with that born by his own generation of the late 1960s, in the cultural activities of amateur manga subculture. Kure, however, insists in a critical appraisal of the themes of amateur manga, and finds them seriously wanting in tangible social and political content. This view is one shared by many editors and artists involved with the commercial manga medium. The implication of this criticism of *parody* manga is that the definition of 'originality' applied to manga, is something linked to the degree to which it embraces current social and political events. 'News', it appears, has a more than merely linguistic association with 'originality'. Amateur manga, whether *parody* or *original*, is widely judged to be low-quality culture, because it lacks direct references to social and political life.

In a survey that I distributed at random to 40 amateur manga artists at Comic Market in August 1994, the respondents were divided in their opinions about *parody*. A total of 29 respondents returned the survey, and of these, 19 respondents said they preferred *parody* to *original* amateur manga. Of these people, 10 respondents cited that it was 'more interesting', as their reason for either producing or buying *parody* manga. Another 9 of the 19 respondents who claimed to prefer *parody* to *original* amateur manga, cited that it was either 'easier to understand' or that they were 'not capable of making *original*'. The remaining 10 respondents claimed not to like *parody* manga at all, because it was 'not interesting'. Thus, approximately one third of respondents, who were all Comic Market participants, did not like *parody* manga at all, another third said they liked *parody* manga because it was easier to write and to understand than *original*, and a final third said they liked *parody* manga because it was more interesting. These judgements, made by convention participants, confirm that producing and appreciating *parody* manga is, amongst other things, easier for many amateur artists to carry out than producing original characters and stories.

Creating new manga scenarios and characters that work, is a more challenging intellectual task than making new versions of already developed manga stories borrowed from popular boys' manga magazines. The presence of the amateur manga medium, which has allowed a great number of ordinary, and proportionately less-talented individuals access to producing manga, may have had the effect of lowering the internal standards of amateur manga and encouraging the expansion of the *parody* genre. Despite the dependency of amateur manga on commercial manga for its scenes and characters, it is clear that *parody* manga has nevertheless developed as a qualitatively separate form of manga in its own right, within which the traditional and commercial understanding of 'originality' has come to have less meaning.

Parody manga often makes light fun of the seriousness of the masculine heroes in commercial boys and adult manga series. While on the one hand favourite manga characters are positively celebrated, on the other hand, their authority and aloofness is punctured, by inserting scatological humour or embarrassing jokes about their physical desires and distresses. The overall effect of this type of naughtiness in *parody* manga is to make popular manga characters in serialized manga magazines more fallible, allowing readers to feel more intimate towards them. This aspect of the amateur manga sense of parody is similar to the Anglo–American sensibility of 'camp'. Both of these cultural modes are based on the subversion of meanings carried in original, and frequently iconic, cultural items. Moreover in the case of both *parody* and camp, this playful subversion is focused particularly on cultural items which contain strongly identified gender stereotypes.

In relation to American films Susan Sontag has suggested that

> Allied to the Camp taste for the androgynous is something that seems quite different but isn't: a relish for the exaggeration of sexual characteristics and personality mannerisms. For

obvious reasons, the best examples that can be cited are movie stars. The corny flamboyant femaleness of Jayne Mansfield, Gina Lollobrigida, Jane Russell, Virginia Mayo; the exaggerated he-manness of Steve Reeves, Victor mature.

(Sontag 1964:108–9)

Contrary to the simplistic notion that there is no sense of 'irony' and therefore no sense of 'camp' in modern Japan (Buruma 1985:117), Jennifer Robertson has pointed out that the style of exaggerated *male* impersonation, referred to as *kizatte iru* or 'camping', forms the principal pleasure of, amongst other things, the all-female theatre, Takarazuka Revue (Robertson 1998:14). There is a also modest parallel between the American camp appropriation of movie sex-symbols and the Japanese *parody* appropriation of well-known male characters from boys' and adults' manga series. Through *parody* manga young women have expressed an ambiguous preoccupation with, and a deep uncertainty about, masculine gender stereotypes, such as those typical of the characters in weekly boys' and adults' manga magazines.

Many of the men involved in the amateur manga medium perceive girls' manga, and the female milieu surrounding it, to be a progressive cultural scene within contemporary society. In 1993, an article appeared in the *Nihon Keizai* financial broadsheet about a company employee who wrote girls' manga, which had been strategically titled 'Active Citizenship through Girls' Manga'. In the article the man explained how, in his opinion, writing amateur Girls' manga was not an escapist activity, but something that actively engaged him with society in a way in which working for a publishing company (producing commercial boys and adult manga) could not (*Nihon Keizai Shimbun* 1993). Further comments about the need to conceal this hobby from work colleagues because 'they would not understand' implied a criticism of the masculine culture and work ethos within large companies. This negative attitude towards traditional models of masculinity was shared by other male fans of girls' manga, including the editorial staff of the magazine *Comic Box*.

Lolita Complex

Towards the end of the 1980s, however, the number of men attending amateur manga conventions increased and new genres of boys' amateur manga began to rise in prominence at Comic Market. The genre into which the majority of this male girls' manga falls is aptly referred to as *Lolicom*, an abbreviation of Lolita complex, a Japanese phrase derived from a reference to Vladimir Nabakov's novel *Lolita*. Lolita complex is widely used to refer to the theme of sexual obsession with young pre-pubescent girls which became particularly strong in Japanese culture during the 1980s and 1990s. *Lolicom* manga usually features a young girlish heroine with large eyes and a childish but voluptuous figure, neatly clad in a revealing outfit or set of armour (see Figure 4.6). The attitude towards gender expressed in most amateur *Lolicom* manga is quite different to that expressed by the male fans of girls' manga, including gay love stores and parody.

The themes of *Lolicom* manga written by and for men express a complex fixation with young women, or perhaps the idea of young women (*shōjo*). The little girl heroines of *Lolicom* manga simultaneously reflect an awareness of the increasing power and centrality of young women in society, as well as a reactive desire to see these young women infantilized, undressed and subordinate. Despite the inappropriateness of their old-fashioned attitudes, many young men have not accepted the possibility of a new role, encompasing greater autonomy for women, in Japanese society. These men who are confounded by their inability to relate to assertive and insubordinate contemporary young women, fantasize about these unattainable girls in their own boys' girls' *Lolicom* manga.

For other young men, however, the infantilized female object of desire held so close has crossed over to become an aspect of their own self-image and sense of sexuality. One sub-genre of *Lolicom* manga tells the story of what might be described as the Lolita-ization of young men. This *Lolicom* manga features entirely feminine, cute Lolita figures which sprout penises to reveal their hidden masculinity (Robertson 1998:201–204). In series published by *Afternoon* magazine for young men the desire to actually become a small pretty girl, or Lolita, is expressed through more subtle and publicly-acceptable means. In *Aaah! My Goddess* the lead male character takes on some of the cute and infantile affectations of a female Lolita character and in so doing, retains the indulgence and friendship of three Lolita-esque goddesses. In *Discommunication*, another infantilized male character indulges in dressing-up in girl's clothes (Kinsella 1998:316). This type of *Lolicom* manga discloses

Figure 4.6 *Lolicom* manga: a half-Indian lady police officer gets handy. [*Gun Smith Cats* in *Afternoon*, 1994 © Kōdansha/Sonoda Kenichi]

an infinitely more ambivalent attitude towards the ideal of infantile femininity.

Despite the differences between these particular male attitudes, the themes by which amateur manga genres are defined have in common a similar preoccupation with gender and sexuality.

Amateur manga genres express a range of problematic feelings young people are harbouring towards established gender roles and, by association, established forms of sexuality. While young people engaged with amateur manga do not fit the social definition of homosexuality, they do share some of the uncertainties and modes of cultural expression, more commonly associated with homosexual men in America and Britain. The sexual themes of *parody*, *Lolicom*, and *yaoi* manga, hint strongly at the possibility that 'camp' is a *cultural* sensibility which is not, or is no longer, the exclusive adjunct of male homosexuality, though it may fail to receive recognition when it ocurrs in other circumstances.[3]

Yaoi, jūne mono, parody and *Lolicom* express the frustration experienced by young people who have found themselves unable to relate to the opposite sex, as they are constituted within the contemporary cultural and political environment. There is, in short, a profound disjuncture between the expectations of men and the expectations of women in contemporary Japan. Young women have become increasingly dissatisfied with the prospect of marriage to men who can not treat them as anything other than women, mothers, and subordinates. Men who persist in macho sexist behaviour – like that often depicted in boys and adults manga magazines, – are gently ridiculed and rejected by the teenage girls involved in writing *parody* manga, or reading gay love stories. Young men who also find masculine behaviour and networking (Allison 1994) restricting and uncomfortable, have also been attracted to amateur girls' manga.

Both the obsession with girls relieved through the different types of *Lolicom* manga, and the increasing interest amongst young men in (girls' own) girls' manga, reflect the growing tendency amongst young Japanese men to be fixated with the figure of the young girl and to orientate themselves around girls' culture. The increasingly intense gaze with which young men examine girls and girls' manga is, to use the words of Anne Allison, 'both passive and aggressive' (Allison 1996:33). It is a gaze of both fear and desire, stimulated not least by the perception of lost privileges over women, which accumulated during the 1980s.

Anglo–American Connection

Points of striking and unexpected similarity between cultural trends in contemporary Japan and those of other late industrial societies often provide social insights which are at least as profound as those discovered at points of cultural difference. Points of similarity in the cultural developments of different societies illustrate the pervasiveness of international social and cultural processes in modern history. Amateur manga is a good example of this point. Genres which have arisen out of Japanese amateur manga subculture in the 1980s bear striking, coincidental similarities to a genre which has been present in the cultural output of television and comic fans in the United States and the United Kingdom since the mid-1970s (Penley 1991:135).

Fine art drawings and paintings and literary parodies of popular television series, such as *Starsky and Hutch, M*A*S*H, Star Trek*, and most recently, *Alien Nation*, from the USA, and *Red Dwarf* in the UK, are central constituents of Anglo–American fanzine subculture. The addition of homoerotica and homosexual romance to these fanzines is also prevalent. Anglo–American homoerotic amateur fanzines are referred to as 'K/S', or more simply still 'slash' (/), in reference to the frequently portrayed relationship between Kirk and Spock, in fanzine versions of the television programme, *Star Trek*.[4] The *yaoi* style emerging from *dōjinshi* is clearly the Japanese equivalent of Anglo–American slash. Like *yaoi*, slash is often characterized by the absence of a strong narrative structure (Bacon-Smith 1992) and the particular fascination with space exploration adventures: for Anglo–American fanzines about *Star Trek* and *Dr. Who* respectively, substitute Japanese manga *parody* based on *Spaceship Yamato* and *Captain Tsubasa*.

In fact there are actual links between amateur manga and fanzine production in these different countries. The most rapidly growing sector of British fan culture in the 1990s was concerned with Japanese manga or animation, while 'Japanimation' has been a popular category of American fan culture since the mid-1970s. Japanese animation companies have attempted to stimulate the interest of foreign fan audiences since the late 1970s as a market-opening devise to introduce their cultural products to wider American audiences (Clements 1994).

A sudden spurt in the popularity of Japanese animation in Britain occurred from the end of the 1980s, at the same time as the explosion in growth of the amateur manga medium in Japan. Fan interest was stabilized by the release of Otomo Katsuhiro's animated film *AKIRA* and the establishment of the magazine *Anime UK*, in 1990. Other

British magazines for new fans of Japanese animation are *Manga Mania*, launched in 1993, and *Anime FX*, launched in 1996. The genres of animation which have become popular within the new fan cultures in Britain and America, and which dominate animation video imports, are derived from *Lolicom* manga which arose out of the amateur manga medium during the 1980s. Girls' manga written by and for men, and featuring little girls, typically armed and fighting for survival in science fiction worlds, has been a major influence on Japanese animation favoured in Britain in the 1990s.

The preoccupation with converting serialized commercial drama into homoerotic parody which emerged spontaneously amongst women in Britain, USA, and Japan, suggests that these women have undergone similar social and sexual experiences. It is not the frequently discussed differences between the role of women in USA and Japan, so much as the apparent similarity of their feelings, which is the source of fascination here. Applying the same logic, the popularity of Japanese animation and manga influenced by the *Lolicom* style, in Britain and America during the 1990s, suggests that many young men in Britain, America, and Japan are also experiencing relatively similar circumstances, leading to closely allied tastes and interests. This type of international manga and fanzine subculture, emerging spontaneously from within amateur media, outside the official organization of the media and culture industries, suggests that the degree to which the commercial media and culture industries in any of these countries have been active in creating specifically national forms of culture, is extensive.

A Serial Infant Girl Murderer

In 1989 amateur manga artists and amateur manga subculture became the subject of what might be loosely categorized as a 'moral panic' of the sort first defined at the end of the 1950s by British sociologist, Stanley Cohen (1972: 9). A sudden genesis of interest in amateur manga artists and Comic Market, amongst the media, began with the arrest of a serial infant-girl killer. Between August 1988 and July 1989, 26-year old printers' assistant, Miyazaki Tsutomu, abducted, murdered and mutilated four small girls, before being caught, arrested, tried and imprisoned (Treat 1993:353–356). Camera crews and reporters arriving at Miyazaki's home discovered that his bedroom was crammed with a large collection of girls' manga, *Lolicom* manga, animation videos, a variety of soft pornographic manga, and a smaller collection of academic analyses of contemporary youth and girls culture including the work of cultural anthropologist, Ohtsuka Eiji.[5] Miyazaki was a fan of girls' manga and in particular *Lolicom* manga and animation, and it was revealed that he had written some animation reviews in *dōjinshi* and had been to Comic Market (Ohtsuka 1989:438).

A heavily symbolic debate ensued Miyazaki's arrest, in which his alienation and lack of substantial social relationships featured as the ultimate cause of his anti-social behaviour. The apparent lack of close parenting given to him by his mother and father, his subsequent immersion into a fantasy world of manga, and the recent death of Miyazaki's grandfather – with whom he had apparently had his only deep human relationship – were posited as the serial causes of his serial murders. Emphasis on the death of Miyazaki's grandfather implied that the decline of Japanese-style social relations represented by older generations of Japanese fulfilling traditional social roles had contributed to Miyazaki's dysfunctional behaviour. Emphasis on Miyazaki's apparently careless upbringing suggested, at the same time, that freer contemporary relationships were no substitute for fixed traditional social relationships, and that there was no real communication between modern, liberal parents of the 1960s generation and their children. Several journals described how Miyazaki's mother had neglected her son so that, 'By the time he was two years old he would sit alone on a cushion and read manga books' (*Shūkan Bunshun* 1989a:36).

Where his family had failed to properly socialize Miyazaki the media, it was suggested, had filled this gap, providing a source of virtual company and grossly inappropriate role models. While one headline exclaimed that in the case of Miyazaki 'The little girls he killed were no more than characters from his comic book life' (Whipple 1993:37) psychoanalyst Okonogi Keigo worried that, 'The danger of a whole generation of youth who do not even experience the most primary two or three way relationship between themselves and their mother and father, and who cannot make the transition from a fantasy world of videos and manga to reality, is now extreme' (*Shūkan Post*, 1989a:33).

In some reports it was deduced that two horror films in particular, *Devilish Woman Doctor* (*Akuma no Joi-san*) and *Flower of Flesh and Blood* (*Ketsuniku no Hana*), had inspired Miyazaki to murder children (Treat 1993:354). Miyazaki, it was argued, after years of reading manga, had become unable to distinguish real life from media images. This aspect of the Miyazaki debate was reminiscent of discussion about the potential role of the 'video nasty', *Child's Play*, in encouraging the two school boys to kill infant Jamie Bulger in Britain in 1993. Within this discussion about the role of culture in influencing anti-social behaviour it was implied that the more fantastical a cultural genre, the more likely it is to directly encourage flights of fantasy (or horror) in its readers. By the logic of this arguement, the greater the stylistic approximation to reality a manga genre formally exhibited the less likely it was to send its readers astray in the real world. Two decades earlier the opposite arguement had been made – as we shall see in Chapter five, it was the stylistic approximation to *reality* of violent *gekiga* dramas which worried critics of the medium.

Following the Miyazaki case, reporters and television documentary crews visited amateur manga conventions, and specialist manga shops. Amateur manga culture was repeatedly linked to Miyazaki, creating what became a new public perception, that young people involved with amateur manga are dangerous, psychologically-disturbed perverts.

Birth of the *Otaku* generation

Otaku, which translates to the English term 'nerd', was a slang term used by amateur manga artists and fans themselves in the 1980s to describe 'weirdoes' (*henjin*). The original meaning of *otaku* is 'your home' and by association, 'you', 'yours' and 'home'. The slang term *otaku* is a witty reference both to someone who is not accustomed to close friendships and therefore tries to communicate with this peers using this distant and over-formal form of address, and to someone who spends most of their time on their own at home. The term was ostensibly invented by critic and *dōjinshi* artist, Nakamori Akio, in 1983. He used the word *otaku* in a series entitled *Otaku no Kenkyu* ('Your home investigations') which was published in a low-circulation *Lolicom* manga magazine, *Manga Burikko* (Takarajima 1989:252).

After the Miyazaki murder case, the concept of an *otaku* changed its meaning at the hands of the media. *Otaku* came to mean, in the first instance Miyazaki, in the second instance, all amateur manga artists and fans, and in the third instance all Japanese youth in their entirety. Youth were referred to as *otaku* youth (*otaku seishōnen*), *otaku*-tribes (*otaku-zoku*), and the *otaku*-generation (*otaku-sedai*). The sense that this unsociable otaku generation was multiplying and threatening to take over the whole of society was strong. While the *Shūkan Post* put about the fear that: 'Today's Elementary and Middle Schools Students: The *Otaku* Tribe Are Eclipsing Society' (1989a:32–33), Otsuka Eiji confirmed that 'It might sound terrible, but there are over 100,000 people with the same pastimes as Mr. M. – we have a whole standing army of murderers' (Ohtsuka 1989:440).

The debate about the Miyazaki serial child-murders evolved into a nationwide panic about amateur manga subculture and *Lolicom* manga which helped to 'reshape the normative, attitudinal, and value landscape of society' (Goode and Yahuda 1994:229) with regard to youth and manga. Urgent discussion amongst journalists, intellectuals and local and national government officers, about the dysfunctional social behaviour and insufficiently developed social consciousness and morality of amateur manga artists and animation fans was 'captured, routinized, [and] institutionalized' (Goode and Yahuda 1994:225) into new laws, and a stricter system of regulating the contents of amateur and published manga (Ohtsuka 1989:438).

Cool *Otaku*

The concept of the *otaku* became so resonant within society that during the 1990s competing positive interpretations of the *otaku* generation were produced in different sections of media, by self-appointed representatives of animation and computer subcultures. Figure 4.7 shows a humorous caricature of a media-friendly *otaku*, which also illustrates an element of conceptual overlap between *otaku* and hippies of the 1970s. Ohtsuka Eiji identified *otaku* as 'the keyword of post-modern society' (Ohtsuka 1989:241) in which cultural experience dominates over social experience. Critic, Asaba Michiaki suggested as a result of being isolated from their friends and made to study relentlessly for exams in their bedrooms, children have grown-up in an environment where their principal source of socialisation and experience has been the mass media. Youth who had spent their childhoods studying hard to pass school entrance

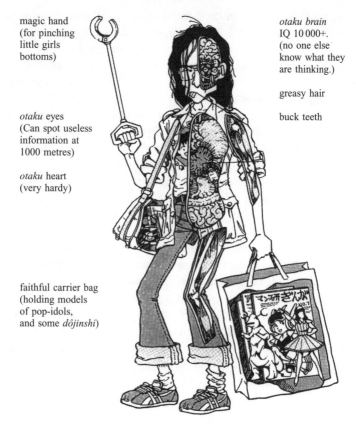

magic hand
(for pinching
little girls
bottoms)

otaku eyes
(Can spot useless
information at
1000 metres)

otaku heart
(very hardy)

faithful carrier bag
(holding models
of pop-idols,
and some *dôjinshi*)

otaku brain
IQ 10 000+.
(no one else
know what they
are thinking.)

greasy hair

buck teeth

Figure 4.7 Caricature of a *manga otaku*. [Taku 1992: 190. Used with the kind permission of Ohta Shuppan]

examinations, apparently formed the core of *otaku* manga and animation subculture (Takarajima 1989:251).

In 1990 a friendly television talent *otaku* called Taku Hachiro (Taku as in *otaku*) appeared on family television. In a 'Nerd Manifesto' for young people identifying with his image, included in *Viva! Nerd Heaven* (*Ikasu! Otaku no Tengoku*), Taku suggested that,

Amidst the rapid flow of events following the serial-infant-girl-murder incident the term *otaku* became a negative keyword. In the 1990s however the meaning has changed. Now *otaku* refers to a high-information handling élite. It is clear, on closer examination, that *otaku* are deeply rooted in the current times.

(Taku 1992:6)

During the 1990s intellectuals sympathetic to young people involved in amateur manga and other *otaku* pastimes continued to discuss the meaning of *otaku* lifestyle (Watanabe 1990; Kiridoshi 1995; Okada 1996 Okada *et al.* 1997), and in 1995 Okada Toshio, author of *Otakuology* began teaching a course on Otaku Studies at Tokyo University.

Police Action

The resurrection of *otaku* as a fashionable concept linked to animation, computer systems and information technology employees and subcultures did not negate the impact of the earlier 1989 to 1992 panic about amateur manga artists and fans. The moral panic about *manga otaku* criminalized and marginalized the amateur manga world. Many *dōjinshi* artists attempted to reject what was seen as an attack on amateur manga subculture by the news-media: 'If I get called *otaku* it is an insult, the word *otaku* is derogatory. At the time of the Miyazaki murder incident we got picked on by the media'. Yahagi Takako, an ex-*dōjinshi* artist who became well-known within the amateur manga world during the 1980s for her *original*, homoerotic stories asserted that the concept of *otaku* had no basis in reality: 'I don't know if I am an *otaku* or not really. What is an *otaku*? Isn't everyone *otaku* really? I am not living in a fantasy world of my own, I live in the real world. How about you?'

Manga critic and Comic Market president Yonezawa Yoshihiro suggested that the news-media debate about Miyazaki Tsutomu and *manga otaku* encouraged a suspicious attitude towards unauthorized intellectual activity in general:

The term *otaku* is being used to single out certain kinds of people for regulation and removal from the public eye. On the other hand the broadening of the concept of *otaku* has provided certain philistine individuals with a term to describe a condition common, apparently, to academic book-worms, film buffs, rock music fans, manga artists and animation fans.

(Yonezawa 1989:84)

The practical results of the new and hostile attention directed at amateur manga were the partial attempts of Tokyo metropolitan police to censor sexual images in unpublished amateur manga and prevent their wider distribution at conventions and in specialist book shops. During April 1991 police arrested the managers of five specialist manga book shops where unpublished, amateur manga was available for sale. This activity began when six officers broke into Manga no Mori manga book shop in Shinjuku, central Tokyo, and confiscated copies of unpublished manga. Police officers collected the addresses of amateur manga circles and took their members into police stations for questioning about the legal status of the printing shops where their manga booklets had been printed. Amateur manga artists and amateur manga printers were subjected to repeated investigations and harassment throughout 1990. Police took in 74 young people for questioning over their activities in making amateur manga, arrested 40 of these individuals, and removed 1880 volumes of manga by 207 authors from Koyama Manga no Mori book shop, and 2160 volumes of manga by 303 different authors from Shinjuku Manga no Mori manga book shop (Tsukuru 1991:18–21).

This scale of direct police activity represents a significant curtailment of the distribution of unpublished manga. Other than in specialist manga book shops in large cities, amateur manga is rarely on sale and is not usually available outside the social circles of young manga fans and artists. The arrest of amateur manga artists by local police forces implies that it was not only the problem of the harmful effects of manga on young minds which concerned the police, but also the independent and unregulated movements of amateur manga artists and amateur manga. A small number of unpublished political pamphlets and manga suggesting Revolution as well as Lolita, were visible on stalls in Comic Market during the mid-1990s. One of the reasons given by the police for their confiscation of amateur manga was their suspicion that the amateur manga world was harbouring terrorist political groups. Some of the small printing companies servicing the amateur manga world had been traced to minor revolutionary groups.

In 1993 guidance about the appropriate contents of *dōjinshi* were distributed at Comic Market for the first time. The Comic Market Preparation Committee determined to attempt the enforcement of local ordinances prohibiting the sale of sexually explicit published materials to minors under 18 years of age, despite the fact that a significant proportion of amateur manga was in any case produced and distributed by minors. In 1994 the Comic Market brochure warned amateur artists that, 'Comic Market is not an alternative society, it is a vehicle orchestrated by you which thinks about its useful role in society. It has become necessary for us to seek social acceptance'. (*Comic Market 46* 1993:12)

The Response of Manga Publishers

The negative stereotype of the *otaku* did not affect all manga artists equally. While *dōjinshi* artists were perceived as dangerous and anti-social, professional manga artists were excluded from this stigma. The general image of a professional manga artist throughout the post-war era, had been that of a reclusive (*naimenteki*), dark (*kurai*) character. During the 1990s this negative image of the manga artist, which had accompanied the general perception of manga and *gekiga* as a violent, pornographic and crude from of culture, was redirected against *dōjinshi* artists. One senior adult manga editor suggested that 'the idea that manga artists were *different* (*kawatta*) peaked in the early 1980s', at which point manga artists were still routinely thought of as 'weirdoes' (*henjin*). By the early 1990s, however, a clear distinction had been established between professional manga artists and *otaku* in media reportage and public consciousness.

Amongst adult and boys' manga editors working for large publishing companies *dōjinshi* were generally described with distaste and derision. Manga scripts submitted to manga competitions run in *Morning* adult manga magazine editorial in 1994, which bore some of the distinctive aesthetic traits of the amateur manga, were described by editors judging the potential of the manuscripts as 'over-personal' (*jiheiteki*), 'childish' (*kodomoppoi*), 'boring' (*tsumaranai*), 'horrible' (*osoroshii*), 'poisonous' (*doku ga tsuyoi*), and 'sickening' (*kimochiwarui*). Editors of ladies' comics, and boys' and adult magazines, described *dōjinshi* artists as 'people lacking talent' who 'could do nothing but talk about themselves', or 'copy other peoples' work'. These editors also suggested that they had no interest in talent-spotting at Comic Market because they had learnt that there were no talented new artists to be found in that environment.

Successful professional artists also expressed negative sentiments about *dōjinshi* and the amateur manga artists. Female celebrity manga artist Morizono Milk was frightened by Comic Market: 'You are brave if you go there. I just went there once to look round. It's a scary place, full of *really* weird people, thousands of them surrounding you'. Leading adult manga artist, Kawaguchi Kaiji described how amateur manga artists had changed since the late 1960s when he had been involved in writing amateur manga at Meiji University manga club:

> I went to university and I was in a manga club for six years until I was 24 years old. Nowadays talented people all go to animation clubs or other things. Manga clubs have changed, they are full of *otaku* and people without talent now. When I was in a manga club we *were* considered a bit 'different' (*kawatta*), because we did not want to join a company. But amateur manga artists now are not just 'different', they are weird and obsessive.

Professional manga artists with a recent history of involvement in the amateur manga world were careful to distance themselves from their previous activities. Fujishima Kōsuke has been contracted to produce the extremely successful series *Aah! My Goddess* (*Aaa! Megami Sama*) for *Afternoon* magazine since 1989. At high school Fujishima had been a member of a manga circle, producing five *dōjinshi* manga books before graduating from high school and becoming an editor of *Puff*, the *dōjinshi* information magazine for amateur manga fans and artists. Discussing the influences on his work in 1994, however, Fujishima appeared to evade any suggestion of his previously intimate involvement:

> There might be some kind of aesthetic influence in my work from *dōjinshi*. I have read a few and I went to Comic Market a few times in the early eighties, but I have not been again since I went professional. People say my work is *otaku*-ish (*otakuppoi*), but I don't deliberately write in an *otaku* style. I don't really see what they mean really. I don't mind if my fans are *otaku* but I don't like the kind of letters and parcels I get from fans. They are creepy. I think those people might get into amateur manga and animation because it's not the real world. They are not really bad, they just seem kind of lonely.

Until the late 1980s *Lolicom* manga was only published in low circulation specialist magazines such as *Penguin Club* published by

Tsutsumi Shuppan, *Boys' Fairground* (*Otoko no Yūenchi*) published by Reed Shuppan, *CANDY* published by Fujimi Shuppan, and *Sukora* published by Sukora Shuppan. In 1989 however *Afternoon* monthly magazine published by Kōdansha began to serialize *Lolicom*-style manga series. Between 1994 and 1997, approximately half of *Afternoon* magazine's 1000 pages were devoted to six *Lolicom* series – *Discommunication, Aah! My goddess* (*Aaa! Megami Sama*), *Gun Smith Cats* (see Figure 4.6), *Assembler OX, Seraphic Feather*, and *Aqua*. Editors estimated that up to a third of *Afternoon* magazines readers 'could be categorized as *otaku*'. The commercial exploitation of these readers' tastes was difficult to resist for a large, experienced manga publisher.

Sonoda Kenichi who has been attending Comic Market since his mid-teens, and continues to produce original and parody *dōjinshi* and amateur manga criticism, has helped to create and establish a more acceptable form of *Lolicom* manga which has gained a limited degree of acceptability with the editors of large publishing companies. Sonoda founded his own manga circle, with several hundred members, while still at high school in Osaka by placing an advertisement in *Animeji* specialist *dōjinshi* information magazine. From 1991, Sonoda, already the artist of three hit stories: *Gall Force, Bubble Gum Crisis*, and *Riding Bean*, drew the series *Gun Smith Cats* for *Afternoon* magazine, utilizing a combination of science fiction and *Lolicom* style. The addition of stronger narrative structures and erasure of all sex scenes from the *Lolicom* series published in *Afternoon* magazine helped to make them more publicly acceptable. One senior editor explained that:

> The *form* of the manga is the same, but the *themes* have been changed to make them easier to read and understand for lots of people. *Aah! My Goddess* is a good example. It looks like *otaku* manga, but the content is different, the story has been changed so it can be read by a wider audience.

Regaining Control of Manga Subculture

During the 1960s large publishing companies were able to capitalize on the incorporation of popular subcultural styles and themes into weekly mass-distribution manga magazines. Publishing companies actively recruited the most innovative and often radical manga artists to work for their magazines. By the mid-1970s attempts to engage with the manga medium by young people had expanded. The development of cheap offset printing, and the establishment of an alternative distribution mechanism in the shape of Comic Market, allowed manga fans to access the manga medium directly by producing their own manga books. The manga medium, which now offered no barriers to participation, became entirely open. The unregulated access to the manga medium meant that publishing companies were no longer able to channel the creative direction of the movement. The expansion of the medium created a huge mass of uncontrolled production. The publishing industry, linked to government and cultural agencies, no longer had complete control over the thematic influences and stylistic development of manga.

In the amateur manga world no alternative system of valuation, artistic discipline, or quality control, replaced that carried out by publishing companies. Artists who could not get their work published in manga magazines took advantage of this unregulated sphere to produce and distribute their work in amateur form. New genres of manga, driven by the strength of their popular appeal alone, emerged from the amateur medium. The same intensity of popular engagement with the manga medium which had helped to fuel the commercial expansion of weekly magazines during the 1960s, encouraged the medium to divide into two separate streams by the late-1980s.

The widespread access young people have had to the manga medium has stimulated concern amongst government agencies. Anxieties which were raised about the commercial propagation of manga and *gekiga* social dramas between 1965 and 1975, resurfaced between 1990 and 1994, when they became redirected towards amateur manga, at that point the most uncontrolled area of the medium. A sense of insecurity about unregulated new spheres of cultural activity found expression in the stereotype of the *otaku*. Yonezawa Yoshihiro suggested that, 'If anything frightful *has* come into being, it is no doubt the existence of this space itself' (Yonezawa 1989:88).

The underlying argument explicit in the *otaku* panic was the view that amateur manga can have only a negative influence on young people, and in particular, on their sexuality. While similar opinions, held by representatives of citizens' organizations, the PTA, or government agencies, about the manga medium in general, were no longer perceived as reasonable or acceptable, more specific criticisms targeted at amateur manga were more novel and engaging. The majority of young people were persuaded by the news media that amateur manga subculture was in fact a serious social problem and not a potentially interesting activity they might like to try out.

Subculture and Social Disorder

The *otaku* panic also reflects many of the contemporary concerns of social scientists about Japanese society. These are powerful concerns about social fragmentation and the contribution of the mass media and communications infrastructures to this change. Since the 1970s, intellectuals have linked their concerns about the decay of a close-knit civil society to the growth of individualism amongst younger generations of Japanese. Individualistic youth culture has been accurately associated with either the failure or the stubborn refusal of contemporary Japanese to adequately contribute to society, by carrying out their full obligations and duties to family, company and nation. The independence of amateur manga subculture from the rest of society, and its growth on the back of new media technologies available to the public, made it an appropriate focus for this sense of chaos and declining control over the organization and communication of younger generations.

The absorption of youth in amateur manga subculture in the late 1980s and 1990s was perceived by many intellectuals as a new extreme in the alienation of Japanese youth from the collective goals of society. The dysfunctionality of *otaku* appeared to prove the unhealthy nature of 'individualistic' lifestyles. For the critics of amateur manga and animation subcultures, *otaku* came to represent people who lacked any remaining vestiges of social consciousness and were instead entirely preoccupied by their particularistic and specialist personal pastimes.

Like generations of youth before them amateur manga artists and fans were also diagnosed as suffering from 'Peter-pan syndrome' – the refusal to grow-up and take on adult social relations. Feminist intellectual, Ueno Chizuko, pressed this theory, asking 'Do the *yaoi* girls and *Lolicom* boys really have a future?' (Ueno 1989). Without social roles, artists and fans who dedicated their time to amateur manga had no fixed identities, no fixed gender roles, and no fixed sexuality. Ultimately they symbolized a group of young people who had become so literally anti-social they were unable to communicate or have social relationships with other people at all. The fact that amateur manga conventions were probably the largest organized public events in the world during the 1990s did not dissuade its critics from criticizing the anti-social tendencies of its participants. At the same time, it seems that it was the domination of amateur manga subculture by young women rather than young men which provoked particular unease. In the mid-1970s early girls' manga was perceived by some left-wing critics as a reactionary cultural retreat from politics and social issues to petty personal themes. Girls manga and soft (*yasashii*) culture were associated with the decline of political and cultural resistance in the early 1970s, sometimes referred to in Japanese as the 'doldrums' (*shirake*). But by the 1990s, individualistic personal themes in girls' manga were being perceived as stubbornly self-interested, decadent and anti-social. The attitude expressed towards amateur manga genres influenced by girls' manga is reminiscent of a general distaste for other aspects of contemporary culture dominated by the activities of young women. In the words of Skov and Moeran there is: '... an almost apocalyptic anxiety that the supposed 'pure' and 'masculine' culture of Japan has been vulgarised, feminised, and infanticised to the point where it has become 'baby talk' beyond the comprehension of well-educated critics' (Skov 1995:70). Drawing attention to the intellectual tendency to perceive girl's culture as an unwelcome *alien* influence within Japan, manga critic, Kure Tomofusa, described how: 'When academics looked at girls' manga they were amazed. They felt like English missionaries discovering that there were different societies in Africa'.

It is striking that although the majority of amateur manga artists and fans are young women, the *otaku* panic has focused almost entirely on the young men who have adopted and adapted to this culture. It has not been girls' manga subculture per se, but the crossover of young men into girls' culture that has provoked particular unease. The universal popularity of manga genres pioneered by women implies that rather than being a discreet feminine section of manga culture, girls' manga is in fact central to the contemporary medium, as indeed young women are to contemporary Japanese culture in general. It also implies that the individualistic and self-interested themes of girls' manga are themes with universal appeal.

5

THE MOVEMENT
AGAINST MANGA

Anxiety about the influence of manga genres arising from the amateur manga world stimulated increased vigilance amongst manga censors. From 1990 the censorship of published series escalated. Censors attempted to stem the flow of influence of amateur manga in published magazines, and to remove sex from manga.

Though manga has not been officially censored at a national level since 1946 it has been affected throughout the post-war period by recurrent bouts of institutional interference in the moral, educational and political content of manga. Concern about the role of manga in society has been expressed through anti-manga activity resulting in stricter manga regulation. In 1963 the content of manga books and magazines came under the surveillance of national quasi-governmental agencies and local government. Anti-manga activism has been carried out by combinations of local citizens' organizations, the PTA, local government, voluntary organizations and national quasi-governmental agencies. Activism peaked once during the period of the initial expansion of the manga industry between 1965 and 1975, and for a second time during the 1990s. In both of these periods the status of manga and its readerships was undergoing a rapid transformation. Anti-manga activity can be understood as a political response to more generalized pro-manga activity in society in the form of the expansion of the manga business.

'Indecent'

A system of surveillance and regulation established in response to anti-manga activities has been established within a complicated web of local and national agencies. Clause 21 of the 1946 constitution upholds the right to freedom of speech and freedom to publish. This internal constitutional wall proved impossible to knock down within the post-war period. Cultural regulation which does limit freedom of speech and the freedom to publish, has been carried out instead through local agencies coordinated by national quasi-governmental organizations.

Since 1964 manga has been regulated by means of Article 175 of the National Penal Code, otherwise known as the Indecency Act. The Indecency Act states that 'indecent' (*waisetsu*) materials may not be sold to minors under 18 years of age. Since minors have free access to most ordinary book stores and manga retail outlets, most manga categorized as 'indecent' is in theory available to minors and is therefore liable to legal restraint. In order to avoid legal action and fines of up to 300,000 yen, retail outlets have tended to refuse to stock manga categorized as 'indecent'. This in turn has strongly encouraged manga publishers to stop producing manga series categorized as 'indecent'. The constitutional right to freedom of speech has not been challenged formally, but in practice the Indecency Act has prevailed over Clause 21, effectively stopping the production of targeted series.

The precise legal interpretation accredited to the term has shifted throughout the post-war period however, and by the early 1990s the definition of 'indecent' had become more lenient. Previously culture containing images of sexual parts or pubic hair was categorized as 'indecent'. This had made Japan the butt of jokes, sending up what appeared to European's as the absurdity of pornography in which hard core sex scenes were allowed, provided that pubic hair and sexual parts themselves were obscured from view by various technical devices.

During the 1990s this systematic approach to defining which materials would be considered 'indecent' gave way to a more flexible quantitative means of interpretation. For the first time the overall degree of raunchiness and extent of sexual imagery in a cultural item was used to determine its status. Increasingly the presence of a few scattered images of pubic hair and sexual parts were being tolerated. The new leniency became public in 1991 following the unhindered publication of a book of nude photographs of the teen starlet, Miyazawa Rie, posing for *Santa Fe* in South America (Shinoyama 1991).

However, the technical evasion of the criterion for 'indecency' extrapolated from the Indecency Act had become an integral aspect in the development of most contemporary commercial manga genres. Stylistic devises such as drawing objects, such as snakes or fruit, which symbolize or vaguely resemble sexual parts, drawing sexual parts as shadows or silhouettes, or simply portraying sex scenes through contorted facial expressions, perspiration, nose bleeds, and suggestive bulges and creases in character's clothing, had rendered the previous definition of 'indecency' relatively ineffectual.

Despite the coy celebration amongst professional photographers and manga artists, of the new freedom to portray pubic hair, the shift in the interpretation of 'indecency' may in fact signify the emergence of a more severe code of decency measured in less clearly defined moral terms, which can bypass entirely the technical devices used by manga artists to evade censorship. In general the new approach to defining sexual 'indecency' has tended to give new leniency to explicit sex scenes which are relatively serious in tone, in which the characters are portrayed in a 'stylish', classical or 'realistic' graphic style; or are portrayed as married partners or long-term couples. On the other hand, frivolous, adulterous and 'tasteless' sexual imagery, in which sex is portrayed as a form of entertainment or physical gratification, taking place between any (unlikely) combination of characters and drawn in the unrealistic, distorted style of caricature, has been severely censored. For example: extraordinarily realistic and vivid scenes depicting sexual intercourse between Miyamoto and his long-term girlfriend (and soon to be wife), the lead characters of Arai Hideki's popular series *From Miyamoto to You* (*Miyamoto kara Kimi e*) were printed in *Morning* adult manga magazine in 1993 and 1994. Four years earlier, in 1990, Hatanaka Jun's also popular series *108 Temptations* (*Hyakuhachi no Koi*), in which lightweight sexual play – such as saucy, adulterous misdemeanours in the public baths – between older characters, living in an older, more rural Japan, was dropped from the same magazine, following complaints from the PTA.

'Harmful'

Local laws (*todōfuken jōrei*) came to be applied instead of the national Indecency Act. *Local Ordinance 756 for the Protection of*

Youth (Seishōnen Hogo Ikisei Jōrei 756), widely referred to as the 'Youth Ordinance' *(Seishōnen jōrei)* states that materials defined as 'harmful' may not be sold to minors under 18 years of age. The Youth Ordinance can be activated by combination with another local law, Ordinance 94, which states that local councils may pass local bylaws so long as they conform to the general direction of national law. In the case of cultural regulation, the Indecency Act has provided the 'general direction of national law' which allows local councils to create new local ordinances preventing the sale of specific manga series to minors.

The Youth Ordinance was adopted first by Tokyo Metropolitan Government in 1964, and by all other city and prefecture councils, bar Nagano, within a few years. Tokyo Metropolitan Youth Ordinance was amended in 1993 and again in 1997 in order to tighten the regulation of erotica and pornographic imagery in manga and elsewhere. Local councils have been able to define which manga is 'harmful' to children, and have it removed from retail outlets. In so far as it embraces a broader range of meanings, 'harmful' has proved a more useful concept to the anti-manga movement than 'indecent'. 'Harmful' has been applied not only to erotic and pornographic imagery, but also to scenes containing 'violence', 'excessive excitation' or simply 'tasteless' images.

Although manga has been regulated according to local law, the organization of local manga regulation has actually been national. The content of manga has been monitored by an internal audit of the publishing industry since 1963, and by a government agency since 1967. Primarily in response to fears about the effect of manga on radical students, the Youth Policy Unit *(Seishōnen taisaku honbu)* of the Ministry of General Affairs *(Sōmuchō)* was established in 1967. The Youth Policy Unit began compiling a regular report on the moral content of manga, including a blacklist of series defined as 'harmful', in each local prefecture. The 'Harmful Designation List' *(Yūgai Shitei Zusho List)*, appears in a quarterly report *(Todōfuken jōrei ni yoru yūgai shitei ranhyō)*, printed by the Youth Policy Unit and distributed to publishers, libraries, the news media and large culture industries.

The government report lists manga categorized as 'harmful' in each prefecture, but the list itself is organized by central government. The existence of this national watchdog and report encourages local prefectures to contribute to the official blacklists of 'harmful' manga. This relationship, in which a national governmental agency induces local councils to make legal changes not legally possible at a national level, is revealing in what it implies about the general political and legal relationship between local and central government in post-war Japan.

The first anti-manga movement took the form of a campaign against 'sadistic images' (*zankoku byōsha*) in rental *gekiga*, which culminated in volumes of Shirato Sanpei's *kashihon gekiga* series *Secret Arts of the Ninja* being removed from book loan shops in 1959 (Tsukuru 1991:220). The years 1967 to 1973 witnessed an ongoing '*gekiga* debate' (*gekiga ronsō*) about the violence and general coarseness of *gekiga* stories published in weekly manga magazines. In 1968 criticism was targeted at *Dawn Combat* (*Akatsuki Sentōtai*) serialized in *Sunday,* which portrayed war-time experiences in a realistic style. The *gekiga* debate eventually resulted in the legal categorisation of *Tomorrow's Joe* (see Chapter 1, Figure 1.9) as 'indecent'. The series was subsequently wound up by *Magazine* at the height of its popularity in 1973 (Tsukuru 1991:223).

The antics of high-school students in a new style love-comedy series by Nagai Go became the focus of a bitter dispute between the publisher, Shūeisha, and the national government. *Shameless School* (*Harenchi Gakuen*) was eventually regulated and removed from *Jump* on the grounds that it contained sexual innuendo unsuitable for children. In 1978 a new *gekiga* debate became focused specifically on low-circulation specialist erotic *gekiga* magazines. The three leading avant garde erotic *gekiga* magazines of the 1970s – *Manga Erogenika, Manga Dynamite* and *Manga Alice* – were forced to remove many of their episodes and series, in particular the work of the erotic manga artist, Dirty Matsugi.

In 1988 manga publishing found itself facing regulatory challenges of a new political character with the foundation of the *Association to Stop Racism Against Blacks* (ASRAB). ASRAB, founded in Osaka by a local civil servant, Arita Toshijiri, gained the support of a variety of American black civil rights organizations, and campaigned vigorously to have allegedly racist manga stories by Tezuka Osamu (see Chapter 1, Figure 1.6) censored. Between 1988 and 1993 ASRAB received high levels of publicity for its attempts to force either the government or Tezuka Osamu's production company, Mushi Pro, to prohibit the distribution of stories such as *Kimba the White Lion* (*Jungle Taitei*), and *New Treasure Island*, in which black people were portrayed in the derogatory style typical of the 1950s. The fact that the late Tezuka Osamu was simultaneously being promoted as a national cultural icon meant, however, that this internationalist campaign against Tezuka's manga eventually did not receive the support of government authorities (*Mainichi Daily News* 1992b).

The Regulation Movement (*kisei undō*)

Adults who read manga are like children; they should read books. History, politics and classics like *The Tale of Genji* are all released in manga form now and I think that is bad. That is a problem. Readers do not have to imagine the scenario themselves, the manga artist draws the entire scene and nothing is left to the imagination. In manga there is no challenge to the reader to think and imagine. It is bad to have history and politics in manga because the reader just takes in the manga artist's ideas without thinking. So really, what I am saying is that there are two things that are strange about manga. Firstly that it is full of perverse sexual images and violence that are bad for children. Secondly that I think it is very peculiar to see a forty year old salaryman and his wife reading manga.

(Kamimura Bunzō, Personal interview 1994)

While the manga regulation movement of the early 1990s publicly identified its concerns as sexual images in manga, the precise nature of its objections remained relatively obscure. For Kamimura Bunzō, an individual closely involved in leading anti-manga activities, the problem with manga was as much to do with regulating the education of history as it was to do with pornography.

From late 1989 headlines about 'harmful', 'violent' and 'pornographic' manga began to appear in national newspapers. These headlines identified a conflict of interest between manga artists and publishers and the nation's women. News media focused on the problem of sexual imagery in boys manga – 'Pornographic manga books with half drawn nudes are selling out fast at local book shops' (*Asahi Shimbun* 1992) – and gave a great deal of coverage to manga regulation activities – 'No giving in: legal restriction of sex pictures' (ibid.: 1993b).

144

Several feminist and women's groups, and 'citizens' organizations' (*shimmin kyōkai*) became involved in the 1990 to 1992 regulation movement. These groups had a variety of objections to manga, ranging from the feminist view that manga was full of sexist images and in this way spread sexism and violence against women through society, to more limited concerns that manga was pornographic and therefore harmful to children. Local women's groups tended to present their concerns about manga as those of 'mothers' or 'housewives', and the origin of the anti-manga movement as a whole was accredited to complaints made about pornographic manga, by 'housewives in Wakayama prefecture' in 1990.

The majority of citizens' groups ranged against manga bore organizational titles such as the Tokyo Mothers' Society (*Tokyo Haha no Kai*); Parents' Society for the Protection of Children (*Kodomo wo Mamoru Oya no Kai*); Society for the Protection of Children from Pornographic Manga Books (*Porn Comic kara Kodomo wo Mamoru Kai*); and the Society for the Protection of Children from Manga Books (*Comic Hon kara Kodomo wo Mamoru Kai*). These groups protested that reading manga interfered with academic study, was not conducive to developing the mental capacities of children, as well as containing violence and pornography harmful to their psychological development.

From 1990 women's organizations such as the Osaka-based, Letters from Japan (*Nihon kara no Tegami*), and the Society for the Protection of Women (*Josei wo Mamoru Kai*), protested against the negative portrayal of women in manga sex scenes (*seihyōgen*). Some feminists argued that manga was central to Japanese patriarchy: 'Comics provide a sort of haven for Japanese men who want to keep the present male power hierarchy' (Ito 1994: 93). Opposing pornographic manga was the main item on the Japanese feminist agenda during the first half of the 1990s.

Feminist arguments that pornography in manga was demeaning to women were linked to the international discourse of political correctness and sat awkwardly alongside more traditional arguments put forward by other women's groups. Feminist professor of Sociology at Tokyo Gakugei University, Muramatsu Yasuko, clarified the distinction between feminist objections and those of local women's groups:

The problem with these manga books is their sexism. A detailed survey demonstrates that these manga often depict violent sex and, more important, that they imply violent sex satisfies women. The major problem with these manga is that they violate basic human rights – the problem is not just with the number or explicitness of sexual descriptions.

(*Nikkei Weekly* 1992)

Both types of women's organizations campaigned against manga by lobbying local Diet representatives, councillors and city mayors to make formal complaints against manga on their behalf. Between October 1990 and June 1991 the issue of 'harmful' manga was raised twice in the Upper House by Liberal Democratic Party and *Rengō* representatives; and on three occasions in the Lower House by Liberal Democratic representatives (Tsukuru 1991:22–23). While most political representation of anti-manga organizations in Diet was carried out by members of the ruling Liberal Democratic Party, which had well-established relationships with local women's and citizens' organizations, opposition parties also engaged in anti-manga lobbying. The Socialist Party Housewives (*Shakaitō wo Ōenshite iru no Shufu*) were particularly active in calling for action against manga and sending letters of complaint to publishers and individual manga artists.

Many of these organizations also contacted their local police forces to make complaints about specific manga books which they believed could be considered 'harmful' or 'indecent', and should therefore be removed from book shops. In most prefectures police forces were sympathetic to complaints about manga and wrote warning letters to the publishers involved. Police authorities also become vocal themselves, calling for a revision of local law which would enable them to remove 'harmful' manga from book shops immediately, rather than after a lengthy legal process to determine the status of each offending manga series. Police argued that the current system was inadequate because in the time it took for a specific series to be legally defined as 'harmful' it had already sold out and disappeared from the shelves of the book shops.

Youth Ordinances were not revised in most prefectures until 1993. In the meantime, however, the activities of the anti-manga movement stimulated a greatly increased application of existing regulation facilities. Within the manga industry world, manga books which had appeared on one of the Youth Policy Unit's lists of manga designated as 'harmful' became known as 'harmful-ized' manga (*yūgai sareta manga*). Figure 5.1 illustrates the sudden increase in the number of officially 'harmful-ized' manga books and magazines between November 1990 and February 1991.

The increase in manga blacklisting can be measured by consideration of the fact that in the year October 1989 to October 1990 (prior to the period of *monthly* blacklisting illustrated in Figure 5.1) the total number of manga books blacklisted was only 554, or an average of 46 books per month. Prior to October 1990, the committee responsible for compiling lists of 'harmful' manga met once every two months. From the beginning of the anti-manga movement in 1990 this committee doubled its activities, and began to meet on a monthly basis. The graph in Figure 5.1 demonstrates that the (large) increase in the number of manga series being placed on the official blacklist began two months after the committee had increased the regularity of its meetings. This suggests that rather than responding to a surge in the number of 'harmful' manga reported in each prefecture, the national inquiry committee had actually initiated the process of categorizing as 'harmful', manga that was perviously considered safe (or harm*less*).

Self-regulation

Despite the pressure of the anti-manga movement, the Youth Policy Unit was more usefully assisted by the manga publishing industry itself in its efforts to regulate manga. Executives of larger publishing companies responded to the external 'regulation movement' (*kisei*

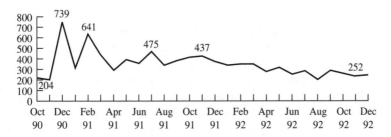

Figure 5.1 Change in the number of number of manga books categorized as 'harmful' 1990–1992. [Source of Data: *Tsukuru* 1993: 159]

undō) with an industry-wide campaign to promote anticipatory 'self-regulation' (*jikō kisei*). In fact the Japan Publishers' Association (*Nihon Shuppan Kyōkai*) established an industry-wide watchdog, the Publishing Ethics Committee (*Shuppan Rinri Kyōgikai*) to monitor the contents of manga as early as 1963. While this committee anticipated organized government regulation by four years, it is probable that it was established to monitor the manga industry at the behest of government officials. Moreover, links between the government committee which produces lists of 'harmful' manga and the industry's own Publishing Ethics Committee were close during the 1990s. In 1994 the Publishing Ethics Committee, which met once a month to discuss the content of published material, consisted of 15 individuals, including a representative from each of the major manga publishing companies and at least one official from the government's Youth Policy Unit.

Throughout 1990 the Ethics Committee became increasingly active in urging its manga publishing members to exercise editorial discretion in reducing sexual imagery. It began to draw up its own list of series which member publishers ought to label as 'adult manga'. Series which had appeared in four or more of the official lists of 'harmful' manga appeared on the Ethics Committee's list of recommended 'adult manga'. It was first suggested that manga books appearing on these 'adult manga' lists should be wrapped in plastic covers and marked with special labels on the dust jackets stating that they were 'adult manga' (*seinen comic*). This project to have 'harmful' manga labelled as 'adult manga', was one way in which the industrial audit could balance the interests of the government, which wanted manga publishers to adhere to the Youth Ordinance, with the interests of their members, who did not want to stop producing manga.

Large publishers followed the recommendation of the Ethics Committee, and began to seal and label some of their manga series, to prevent casual browsing by minors. Despite these precautions, the majority of retail outlets took the opportunity of the clear labelling to refuse to stock any 'adult manga' at all, while a smaller number of book shops created 'adult manga corners'. Rather than easing the problem for publishers, the use of 'adult manga' labels, drew attention to listed manga and greatly strengthened the influence of the government 'harmful' lists. It resulted in the curtailment of erotic and pornographic manga series.

As the number of manga books which the Ethics Committee suggested must be labelled with 'adult manga' stickers increased, the number of manga books listed each month as 'harmful' in government lists decreased. In 1991 the Ethics Committee designated a total of 58 books for labelling, in 1992 this figure rose to 87, and by the end of 1993, 322 manga books had been labelled.

In December 1992 the Ethics Committee stepped up its activities further and requested that all manga books produced by its members which had appeared on any government lists of 'harmful' manga must be recalled and labelled with 'adult manga' stickers. From 1993 most manga produced by large publishers was regulated not by the intervention of police, Youth Ordinances, or women's groups, but through the systematic use of 'adult manga' labels.

Regulation amounting to censorship, effective at an industry level, was a more practical and less controversial means of controlling manga than the arduous process of making local laws against individual manga series. By the end of 1992 the political regulation movement had largely been internalized within the manga publishing industry. A new precedent and agenda for automatic self-regulation by editors and artists at the point of production was established.[1]

Regulated series

Manga series which caused offence most frequently were *Lolicom* series in low-circulation magazines influenced by amateur manga; *love-comedy* in boys' manga containing mildly erotic scenes; and low-circulation pornographic adult manga and ladies' manga. These types of manga generally contained the greatest volume of sexual innuendo and erotica. In other cases, gag manga series, such as *Magazine's Violent Moron* (*Gekiretsu no Baka*), were added to the list of 'harmful' manga on the basis that they were in 'poor taste'.

Manga regulation hit the headlines in October 1990 when the popular series, *Angel: High School Sexual Bad Boys and Girls Story*, by artist U-Jin, was cut from *Young Sunday* manga magazine after complaints that it contained sexual scenes unsuitable for children. In March 1992 another best-selling boys' manga series Yamamoto Naoki's *BLUE*, was 'harmful-ized', provoking an outburst of letters from readers.[2]

In terms of the effect of the regulation movement, manga series which were discontinued, removed from book shelves, or placed in 'adult manga' corners, represented the tip of the iceberg. Within the manga industry the main effect of the regulation movement was a wave of anticipatory self-censorship exercised directly by manga editors and individual manga artists. The dynamics of this process of self-regulation involved both explicit and implicit pressure from manga editors, as well as conscious and unconscious measures taken by artists to evade having their work perceived as 'harmful'. Self-censorship recommended to artists by their editors also tended to become fused with another trend in the manga production process, towards creative editing (this will be discussed in Chapter six).

Manga artists faced compelling reasons for accepting self-regulation. Even manga artists such as Morizono Milk, Nagai Go and Kobayashi Yoshinori, who took a militant line in opposing manga regulation and self-regulation, were nevertheless strongly motivated to produce 'acceptable' work in order to survive in the competitive manga industry. Yamamoto Naoki, artist of the series *BLUE* which was regulated and discontinued in 1992, subsequently succumbed to self-censorship: 'Ever since regulations became stricter I've been shocked every time I notice that I am subconsciously controlling my expression' (*Asahi Evening News* 1993) Artists whose work was categorized as 'harmful' faced severe setbacks in their careers and lost large parts of their incomes in royalties on manga books which could not be sold.

Evidence of the extent of self-regulation which took place in the first half of the 1990s lies in the satisfaction of the anti-manga lobby with the state of affairs by 1994. Kamimura Bunzō suggested that 'The publishing companies have promised not to publish bad manga again, and I think that in general the content of manga has improved from what it was. Yes, it has changed a great deal really'.

The case of manga artist Morizono Milk provides a good example of the process by which the production of certain manga series was effectively censored through the regulation movement. Morizono Milk is a glamorous and media-friendly female artist and the key theme of her manga is wealthy, jet-set young women, enjoying a variety of sexual rendezvous. In 1991 and 1992 Morizono produced an erotic series entitled *Peacemaker* for *Midori* teenage girls' manga magazine published by Kōdansha. During

1990 the Kōdansha public relations department began to receive letters complaining about Morizono's series from police departments, local PTA groups, housewive's groups and local politicians. The management of Kōdansha began to place pressure on the chief editor of *Midori* magazine to stop certain manga series which had appeared on the list of 'harmful' manga. On the top of this list was Morizono Milk's series. Kōdansha subsequently refused to publish collected volumes of Morizono Milk's series unless the entire series was revised. Morizono refused to revise her erotic images with the result that neither she nor Kōdansha received any book royalties from the series. At the end of 1991, Morizono's series in *Midori* was not renewed despite its popularity and Morizono took the series to a smaller company, Shōdensha, who agreed to publish a collected edition of the series in its original 'harmful-ized' form.

Small publishers such as Shōdensha have more limited access to distribution, their books are sold in fewer retail outlets and generate lower royalties for manga artists. Moving from a top publisher such as Kōdansha to a small publisher such as Shōdensha represented a regression in Morizono's career as an artist. In 1994 Morizono continued to work predominantly for Shōdensha, at the same time as being compelled to exercise self-censorship: 'I used to have to be very self-conscious at *Feel Young* because I do "dark" (*kurai*) erotic pictures and their magazine keeps the pages "light" (*akarui*). I kept having to lighten up my pages all the time.' (Pers. Interview, 1994)

'Harmful' manga discontinued by large publishing companies was often published at a later date by small publishing companies. Small publishers were able to avoid the regulation of 'harmful' manga on three accounts. Firstly, in order for re-editions of manga books by different publishers to be categorized as 'harmful' the arduous procedure of legally defining manga as 'harmful' had to be repeated. Secondly, as these re-editions were often available only at larger specialist outlets they were less likely to be widely viewed and cause equivalent offence amongst local government bodies. Thirdly, few of the many small publishers in Tokyo were members of the Japan Publisher's Association, which meant they were outside the internal jurisdiction of the industrial ethics watchdog. After 1990 in particular the regulation movement was indirectly responsible for the flourishing re-emergence of smaller publishers, which had been declining in number since the campaign against erotic manga and minor pornographic magazines in the late 1970s.

Not all manga censorship concerned sex. The case of a manga episode about the 1993 royal wedding illustrates the responsible political role that large publishers also pursued. Kobayashi Yoshinori, a leading adult manga artist (see Chapter 3, Figure 3.7), was asked to produce a special episode of *The Arrogance Manifesto* (*Gōmanism Sengen*) to be used on the cover of *SPA!* magazine during the week of the Crown Prince Naruhito's wedding to Owada Masako in June 1993. Kobayashi produced an episode with the self-referential title, *Front Cover Day* (*Cover Tsuki no Hi*). In this episode Kobayashi spun a fantastic story which made a joke of the dull and uncritical reportage of the wedding in other sections of the media. On the day of Kobayshi's version of the royal wedding, Owada Masako, the incumbent bride of the future emperor, jumps out of the royal carriage to join an anti-Emperor demonstration. At the same time she reveals to the world that she is a member of the Central Core Faction of the Revolutionary Communist League (*Chūkaku-ha*). Two days before this story was due to be published the management of the parent organization of Fusōsha publishers, the Fuji-Sankei Communications Group, ordered the episode to be cut from *SPA!*. *Front Cover Day* was later published in the October 1993 issue of the *GARO* magazine (*Shōkun!* 1994:272–273).

During the 1990–1992 regulation movement, series influenced by the graphic style of girls' manga were far more frequently categorized as 'harmful' than manga stylistically related to *gekiga,* which dominates adult and boys' manga series. In particular, a significant proportion of 'harmful-ized' series bore the influence of amateur *Lolicom* manga. Manga regulation helped to stem the flow of amateur manga styles into low-circulation manga magazines, and fortified the separation of amateur and published manga.

Domestic non-governmental organizations

When asked about regulation, the great majority of artists and editors cited 'interfering housewives' ('*osewazuki na obāsan*') as the chief activists, followed by the PTA and local police authorities. Hara Takao, an ex-assistant of Tezuka Osamu and founder of the manga artists' organization, Manga Japan, represented the opinion of most manga artists:

> There is no complex thought behind censoring manga. Middle-aged women simply see manga and phone up the police or their local Diet member to complain, and then manga gets criticized. The Japanese government just censors manga when people complain about it. As always it is entirely passive in its actions. (Interview, 1994)

Few artists or editors were able to specify the names or contact details of individual women or citizens' organizations opposed to manga. On closer inspection the two most prominent groups opposed to manga revealed themselves to be ambiguous organizations, more directly connected to local and national government agencies, than to any independent citizens' movement.

The National Assembly for Youth Development (NAYD) is a domestic non-governmental organization (NGO) which was established by the government in 1964, to deal with the problem of juvenile delinquency. National and international youth training and exchange programmes are organized by NAYD. NAYD also co-ordinates the activity of the majority of official youth organizations in Japan including voluntary organizations such as the Young Women's Christian Association (YWCA), National Youth League (*Seinendan*), the Boy Scouts' Association, and the Youth Volunteers. It is linked at the executive level to the Youth Affairs Office (*Seishōnen Sōmu Kyōiku*), another department within the Ministry of General Affairs (*Sōmuchō*), from which it also receives the great majority of its funding. Local branches of NAYD exist in every prefecture, and are connected to a national NAYD headquarters, based in the grounds of the National Olympic Memorial Youth Centre (NYC) in Yoyogi, central Tokyo.

The NYC complex is located in an expanse of former military park land and buildings, used briefly by the Allied Occupation Forces between 1945 and 1951. The land was donated to the NYC by the government in 1964 and it is here that NAYD activities are co-ordinated. NAYD was an organization closely involved in shaping the anti-manga movement of 1990–1992. Kamimura Bunzō, the executive director of NAYD described the objectives of a national speaking tour he gave in 1991 in the following terms:

> We felt that manga full of sex is not good for children's development so we announced a plan to oppose manga. In

1993 we managed to get a local law passed against 'harmful' manga in four cities simultaneously: Tokyo, Kyoto, Hiroshima and Osaka. NAYD representatives gave speeches in every prefecture about the need to regulate manga. (Interview, 1994)

Since 1991 the process of channelling complaints about manga towards local government agencies became a job undertaken by local NAYD branches. On the other hand the task of detecting and collecting 'harmful' manga has been allocated to members of the Youth Volunteers Association (also co-ordinated by NAYD). Each week several Youth Volunteers go to local book shops to search for potentially 'harmful' manga and then take samples of what they find to a designated representative of NAYD. Typically this NAYD representative, who is in fact appointed by local government officials, is also a voluntary group leader, professional citizen, or teacher active in the PTA.

After receiving potentially 'harmful' manga books from Youth Volunteers, local NAYD representatives make immediate contact with the regular members of a quasi-governmental committee, in order to call an emergency meeting to evaluate the contents of the manga in question. If this committee decides that a manga book is 'harmful' an official proposal is made to local government to create a local injunction immediately, to stop the sale of the series in question in book shops throughout the prefecture.

Cultural regulation is a relatively systematic part of the functions of local government. Rather than reaching the attention of local councils through the efforts of independent protests, 'harmful' manga is systematically sought out by youth volunteers and judged by a team of individuals selected principally on the basis of their opposition to manga.

A large number of similarly titled organizations campaigning against manga, such as the Parents' Society for the Protection of Children (*Kodomo wo Mamoru Oya no Kai*), the Society for the Protection of Children from Pornographic Manga (*Porn Comic kara Kodomo wo Mamoru Kai*), or the Society for the Protection of Children from Manga (*Comic Kara Kodomo wo Mamoru Kai*), had been launched by the same network of community, youth and voluntary leaders as were engaged in the bureaucratic process of regulating manga. Available evidence suggests that the anti-manga activities of the early 1990s did not stem, as implied in the news media, from a popular, independent movement against manga, so much as from committees organized by local government. The overlapping of local citizens' organizations into the bureaucratic process of cultural regulation provided a semblance of political legitimacy to what might otherwise be seen as an undemocratic and censorious aspect of government policy.

The Tokyo Mothers' Society is another example of an citizen's group with suspect independence, which campaigned against manga. The Tokyo Mothers' Society is organized from a room in a Tokyo police station. Members of the group apparently visited the room on occasions but were otherwise not directly available. Enquiries to the Tokyo Mothers' Society had to be fielded through contacts in other similar organizations, or through the police. The Tokyo Mothers' Society also attended committee meetings to determine the status of manga books, which were convened in the exclusive office space of the new Tokyo Metropolitan Government building in Shinjuku, central Tokyo. The Tokyo Mothers' Society are unwilling to enter into discussion about their work with members of the general public. This fact, combined with the fact that their activities are balanced between a police station and the Tokyo Metropolitan Government offices suggests that they are not an open and autonomous citizens' group, so much as a group of individuals working as volunteers, on a semi-professional basis, for the Tokyo Metropolitan Government.

NAYD accredits the initiation of the anti-manga lobby to a housewives' organization in Tanabe city, Wakeyama prefecture, which protested against manga in late 1990. The protest of the Wakeyama housewives had apparently become a nation-wide movement through the actions of the Young Women's Christian Association (YWCA) and the Womens' League (*Fujin Domei*). These organizations publicized the protest in Wakeyama prefecture and turned it into a national movement against manga. The exact details of how this small, local protest against manga, led by a group of housewives, was transformed into one of the most important single-issue movements of the early 1990s, remain open to investigation.

The involvement of women in local government agencies, local citizens' campaigns and NGOs linked to government offices, has an established history in the organization of Japanese local politics. In late post-war Japan, women who have been discouraged from pursuing professional careers, chiefly through the effects of discrimination in the labour market, have sought involvement in other spheres of public life. Many women have attached status and importance to the education of their children and attending local PTA meetings. Women who were students during the 1960s and who, through student protests, experienced an active involvement with society during their youth, have tended to complement their lives as housewives with educational activities and involvement in local citizens' campaigns. These women are sometimes referred to as 'professional activist housewives' (*katsudō sengyō shufu*). During the 1980s and 1990s approximately 10 per cent of married Japanese women were actively involved in some form of citizens' organization. Feminist scholar Iwao Sumiko points out that 'Leaders of all kinds of local campaigns tend to be drawn from this pool of activist housewives' (Iwao 1993).

The nature of the relationship between local branches of organizations such as NAYD or the YWCA, and the government, is one which resembles the style of citizens' organizations which have been described by Gregory Kazsa as 'administered mass organizations' (AMOs). According to Kasza AMOs typically originate as pressure groups or NGOs, and draw ordinary members of the public into an active involvement with government policy making, through the course of populist political campaigns. In Japan, Kasza categorizes the pre-war Housewive's League and the National Youth League (*Seinendan*) as AMOs (Kasza 1995). NAYD, and local women's groups such as the Tokyo Mother's Association, which have been involved in the anti-manga movement, fall into a similar pattern of political campaigns which are membered by citizens but administered by government.

Several individuals have perceived broader coincidences between the timing of the anti-manga movement and changes in the structure of Japanese politics. In the opinion of a senior editor of *Magazine*, manga regulation has been a vote-raising issue amongst Liberal Democratic Party politicians since the late 1960s:

> The PTA are largely composed of LDP members and they get financial support from the LDP. So when it comes to election time the LDP candidates become vociferous complaining about manga. They know that it makes them look good and attracts the votes of conservative housewives and local citizens. (Interview, 1994)

Chief editor of the Aoba Shoten company dated the cooling off of the manga regulation movement with the decline of the ruling LDP government in 1992: 'The government is not as difficult as it used to be about managing manga. Since Hosokawa came into government they haven't bothered us so much at all. I think it is basically because it is no longer an LDP government.' (Interview, 1994) The gradual climb-down of anti-manga activities and discourse in the media may have been related to the decline of the LDP's power after August 1993.

Campaign for the Freedom of Expression

During the manga regulation movement of 1990–1992 Japanese state authorities gained more control over what manga people could produce and what manga people could read. The initial freedom of the publishing industry made manga more vulnerable to this heavy-handed bureaucratic treatment. However the move to restrict manga did not go unopposed. From 1990, publishing companies and the Publishers' Union (*Shuppan Rōren*) resisted the move to utilize local laws to effectively censor manga.

Manga artists themselves were not involved in this low-key counter-movement until March 1992. In the post-war period manga artists have been badly organized, and when they finally got their own voice in this dispute it was through an organization created for them, rather than by them. The Society to Protect the Freedom of Expression in Manga (*Manga Hyōgen wo Jiyū ni Mamoru Kai*) was founded by Shinoda Hironori, the publisher and chief contributor of *Tsukuru*, a periodical devoted to a critical analysis of the media and communications industries. Shinoda Hironori had been following the manga regulation issue for several months in *Tsukuru* and felt that manga artists ought to be more organized in order to defend their work.

By 1994 the Society for the Protection of Freedom of Expression in Manga had successfully recruited over 1000 members. Members were composed of household-name manga artists such as Satonaka Machiko, Saitō Takao, Chiba Tetsuya, and Saimon Fumi, while Ishinomori Shōtarō became the formal president of the Society. In addition to manga artists, individual manga editors, publishing company executives (such as Kōdansha's chief publisher), the Publishers' Union, independent lawyers and manga fans also joined the Society. Each member payed a minimum fee of 1000 yen a month, through which the Society supported its activities.

Between March and May 1992 the Society arranged for a special appeal to be placed inside the pages of all major manga magazines published by major publishers. This single page advertisement entitled the Appeal to Protect the Freedom of Expression in Manga Books (*Comic Hyōgen wo Jiyū ni Mamoru Appeal*) aimed to inform manga readers about the problem facing artists and the manga industry. Readers were encouraged to send letters of support and membership fees to the society. The manga publishing industry was able to counteract the accumulation of negative media publicity by using manga itself to deliver its message. The Appeal alerted manga readers to the extent of manga censorship, and made the case that this censorship was generally arbitrary, resulting in needless restrictions placed on manga series. Shinoda Hironori, who also distributed a Bulletin of the Readers' Civil War (*Shigaisen Kaihō*), believed that the gradual decline in the figures of manga books blacklisted after 1992, was due to the success of the Society for the Protection of Freedom of Expression in Manga.

Manga artists also took the opportunity provided by this campaign, to challenge the general image of manga as a crude form of culture. Many manga artists wanted the same status as practitioners of the fine arts or craftsmen, i.e. to be independent creators in control of the content of their own manga books. Older, veteran, artists such as Ishinomori Shōtarō, Satonaka Machiko and Nagai Go, acted as the public representatives of concerns of manga artists.

Veteran female artist, Satonaka Machiko argued that:

> It is possible to view the control of manga as a way of concretely enforcing the idea that manga is a low form of culture. But, just as literary figures do not expect to be challenged over their responsibility towards their work, individual manga artists can assume responsibility for judging the value of their own work – work that might later be made into films or television dramas.
>
> (*Asahi Shimbun* 1993c)

Here, Satonaka makes an appeal to more conservative lines of thought by making creative use of a keyword of the conservative political lexicon, 'responsibility'. Satonaka uses the concept of 'responsibility' to argue not for institutional censorship, but to describe and defend a competing notion of autonomous individual responsibility in a mature political state. Satonaka suggests that artists should be trusted to censor their work themselves without the interference of official agencies.

Publishing companies also wished to challenge prejudice against manga because it affected their ability to recruit larger readerships composed of broad sections of the adult population. Uchida Masaru, the ex-chief editor of *Magazine,* suggested that in order for the medium to develop it must be perceived at least as positively as literature:

> There is still a strong prejudice against manga in society, and so long as this continues to exist manga won't develop any further. If adults don't read manga then there won't be an audience worth writing for and manga will not develop any further artistically. (Interview, 1994)

Manga artists fought for a new privilege: to be seen as a reliable and respectable group in society with the right to pursue their interests beyond the arbitrary control of government. The strength of this assertion and the degree to which it was entertained within the media suggests that manga artists had already become sensitive to signs that there was a real potential for them to move beyond the previously limited role and status they generally worked within. The majority of members of the Society for the Protection of Freedom of Expression in Manga opposed censorship, while simultaneously claiming that artists could censor their own creations. By arguing for self-censorship manga artists emphasized that aspect of their demands which involved being perceived as serious and respectable individuals. Only two famous artists, Morizono Milk and Kobayashi Yoshinori, were vocal in opposing both institutional regulation and self-censorship, though both artists admitted that in practice they did censor their own work. Thus the artists' struggle against manga censorship was a twofold movement. It constituted not just an attempt to resist new areas of government control, but also a self-interested project to raise the commercial value of their work.

In 1993 an organization was formed for the exclusive member-ship of manga artists and explicit exclusion of manga editors and publishers. Manga Japan was launched by Hara Takao, a multi-media entrepreneur and former assistant of Tezuka Osamu. Manga

Japan entertained a loose alliance with the Society for the Protection of the Freedom of Expression in Manga, and supported artists of erotic manga, such as Nagai Go and Morizono Milk, against editorially imposed self-censorship.

At the same time, Manga Japan was also explicitly concerned with improving the status of manga and manga artists in society. For Manga Japan the order of concern was, firstly, promoting high-quality respectable manga and, secondly, opposing censorship. Hara Takao explained:

> We want to prevent the government from censoring manga. Because the environment is so restrictive artists give up trying to draw well, but Manga Japan thinks that artists can be responsible for themselves and decide for themselves what they ought to draw. Basically we want to heighten artists' awareness of these problems and to make them take more responsibility for their own work. So you could say that Manga Japan is a group designed specifically to help *story manga* artists produce good work and to maintain the quality of that work. (Interview, 1994)

Manga Japan represented manga artists who actively anticipated the potential new status of manga as culture, and of an enhanced social role for themselves in Japanese society. As the English title, Manga Japan, suggests, its concern with the status of manga artists also encompassed a desire to promote manga and manga artists internationally. More specifically, many manga artists wanted to defend their copyrights abroad. From the late 1980s many best-selling manga series were being illegally copied and translated by foreign publishing companies based in East Asia, especially in Hong Kong, Taiwan and Bangkok. Artists were frustrated to find that in these cases their copyrights were not being actively defended by the publishing companies for whom they were contracted to produce work.[3]

Manga Japan may be seen as a new form of collective organization, which is neither a political movement, nor a trade union, nor a guild, and yet borrows elements from each. It is also illustrative of how business and political interests may maintain an influence upon independent organizations not under their direct control. Although Manga Japan made no reference to any sponsor-ship or business interests in its literature, it was in fact backed by the

Dentsu media and advertising corporation. Manga Japan meetings were held in lavish conference rooms inside Dentsu headquarters overlooking the Sumida river. Dentsu was interested in the potential for marketing the work of best-selling artists, internationally, in CD-ROM format.

The ambitions of the group of manga artists active in the Society for the Protection of the Freedom of Expression in Manga and Manga Japan converged. The orientation of individual manga artists who had joined organizations to defend the freedom and reputation of manga were closely, though not explicitly, aligned to the trend towards the promotion of new adult manga to the status of a serious culture by cultural institutions and manga publishing companies. The majority of well-established manga artists were keen to receive their new status and produce a more respectable manga which focused on national political and economic goals.

In many cases, artists most active in Manga Japan and the Society for the Protection of the Freedom of Expression in Manga, were the selfsame individuals as those featured in flattering reports about the manga medium or who had been commissioned to produce information manga books. The ubiquitous Ishinomori Shōtarō, provided the most obvious example of this convergence of promotion and anti-censorship activity. In the first half of the 1990s Ishinomori was titular president of both Manga Japan and the Society for the Freedom of Expression in Manga, as well as being the artist of both *Japan Inc. An Introduction to Japanese Economics in Manga* (see Chapter 3, Figure 3.1) and the officially sponsored book series *Manga History of Japan* (see Chapter 3, Figure 3.3).

CREATIVE EDITORS AND UNUSABLE ARTISTS

Through observation of both manga self-regulation and the creation of a new style of adult manga, it has become evident that editors employed by publishing companies played an important role in introducing changes into the content of manga series. Closer examination of the personnel engaged in making manga provides important clues as to the full character of the changes affected. In the 1990s artists and editors were involved with two major trends changing the face of manga production.

The first of these trends involved the increasing creativity of manga editors. Manga editors became more active in taking on intellectual and creative functions in manga production. They did this not only to ensure the production of manga series which were socially acceptable to their critics, but which were, in addition, ideal expressions of contemporary national culture. Editors helped to create model manga series which fitted the criterion of model manga being defined in other areas of society. As manga editors took on more creative roles in adult manga production, so the manga they produced became characterized by the fact that it was produced not by *artists,* necessarily living on the fringes of organized social and economic life, but by company employees immersed in white-collar corporate society instead.[1]

The second major trend hinged on the negative assessment of the contemporary manga medium and of younger manga artists by adult and boys' manga editors. These editors believed that contemporary manga artists no longer had the special quality of passion and social direction which could be harnessed by a publishing company to make popular, and by the same token commercially viable, manga series. Editors shared the view that manga artists were increasingly 'unusable' (*tsukaenai*), a critique which carried a hint of the more derogatory notion that artists were themselves 'useless'. In response to these misgivings some manga editorials introduced foreign artists and specially contracted manga editors into the manga production process. It was hoped that these new social elements might contribute some of the special quality of passion and social direction which Japanese manga artists apparently lacked.

These two trends worked on two distinct but eventually interacting registers. The creative lead taken by editors making realist manga, accompanied by the devaluation and substitution of the work of manga artists, interacted at the point of determining the contents of manga. This resulted in an overall shift in the source of intellectual leadership and creativity in the medium. The creative balance of power between artists and publishing companies, was re-órdered in favour of company employees and, in broad terms, the social class that these privileged publishing company employees represented. This development also created a new cultural space in which the social and cultural preoccupations of this particular social group found expression.

Making Respectable Manga

The new genre of realist political and economic manga (see Chapter 3) was grounded in a change in the established division of labour in commercial manga production. The work of manga editors became creative. The role of manga artists who could neither agree nor collaborate with the creative vision of the editors became increasingly limited to mechanical and decorative func- tions. As manga editors employed by large publishing companies belonged to a distinctive social elite, the changes wrought in the content of realist manga incorporated the political consciousness and cultural predilections of one privileged section of society. The new genre of realist manga which became popular from the late 1980s is sometimes referred to as 'business manga'. In fact it was *business manga* by virtue not only of its visible focus on corporate life, but also by virtue of being made by and for privileged company employees (commonly referred to as 'business men' in contemporary Japanese argot), and those identifying with that image.

The promotion of manga to the position of an official form of Japanese culture encouraged editors to look at the manga they managed in a new light. The self-regulation or censorship of manga series, carried out in response to the anti-manga movement, forced editors to undertake a closer and more critical examination of the contents of manga series. Larger publishing companies accepted the responsibility for producing morally 'good' manga. Their editors were disciplined to the physical task of removing potentially offensive images and ideas from manga series.

This task was literally performed on manga manuscripts with pieces of tape, ink pens, cover-up fluid, cover-up spray, and other techniques. The threat of blacklisting placed on manga publishing companies by the government's Youth Policy Unit and the quasi-governmental National Assembly for Youth Development, induced editors to actively ensure that the contents of the manga they produced would not aggravate these authorities. In other words, pressure from political and government organizations influenced editors to take a more active role in determining the contents of manga series.

At the other end of the critical spectrum, the praise showered upon realist manga, such as *Japan Inc: An Introduction to Japanese Economics in Manga* (1986), also inspired manga editors to attempt to emulate this style of manga series which would receive critical acclaim and institutional support. It was precisely this type of serious critical attention which publishers had sought (in vain) since the beginnings of the era of manga mass-production (Kure 1990:46).

In common with book publishing and cultural production in general, manga editorial policy was developed through a conscious and considered interaction with national culture. Michael Lane's observation that amongst book publishers 'Editorial decisions are influenced by more than the narrow world of their house, let alone their individual tastes and preferences. Willy-nilly they are both influenced by and help to shape the culture of the society in which they live ...'(Lane and Booth 1980: 86) is as accurate in Japan as it was in Britain. Producing the type of model manga favoured in the news media required that publishers took it upon themselves to shape the contents of manga series in an appropriate fashion.

One senior editor in Shōgakukan spelled out how the new trend of describing manga as 'culture' automatically encouraged editors like himself to take a more active and conscious role:

When people start saying that manga is culture they also have to think about the impression manga gives. At present we just make it and don't care about what it is like or what anyone thinks of it. From now on I think that we should take responsibility for manga and recognize it as our culture. (Interview, 1994)

Another senior editor in Kōdansha spoke of increasing the scope and even scale of manga, of turning manga as a whole into a medium with more 'power', 'energy', and 'impact'. Manga series were no longer to be produced as if they were a trivial form of entertainment for commuters, but as if they were large and important projects 'on a par with Hollywood films'. Rather than being male-oriented magazines randomly peppered with semi-pornographic imagery, manga magazines ought to be sound and 'upstanding' (*rippa*), containing manga which salarymen could 'read openly', 'discuss with their colleagues', and 'take back home for their wives and children to read'. Adult magazines should feature 'outstanding characters' (*rippa na shujinkō*) in their series, who were 'worthy of respect' (*sonkei subeki*) from the readers. If manga was to be 'culture' then it should get 'serious' (*majime*) both in terms of scale and in terms of content.[2]

The zeal with which editors embraced the idea of making serious manga of which they (or their companies) 'could be proud', varied between publishing companies and editorials, depending largely on how much resources (capital and personnel) were available to invest in such a project. The position which the company as a whole occupied in relation to the major political and cultural institutions was also an important factor. One publishing company which had the resources to invest in making 'good' manga, as well as a long history of close relations with national political leadership, was Kōdansha (Noma 1934:260).

Dai Nippon Yūbenkai Kōdansha was founded in 1909 by Noma Seiji. Originally this was a small two-magazine enterprise based on a magazine titled *Yūben* composed from notes taken at lectures delivered at Tokyo University, and a children's story magazine titled *Kōdan Club* (Noma, 1934:130). Kōdansha continued to be a family enterprise, which was headed by Noma Sawako during the 1990s. Kōdansha is one of the oldest and most distinguished publishing houses in Japan, known for its particular brand of conservatism and responsible role in the mediation of intellectual debate and political affairs. Its continued sensitivity towards public debate is reflected in the number of current affairs magazines and periodicals it publishes in addition to manga and books.

Kōdansha's distinguished reputation as a publisher and its general tendency to be political and conservative, meant that it, even more than other large publishers, had been particularly embarrassed by the growth of its manga publishing departments. During the 1990s, manga editorials most conspicuously involved in developing the new style of realist manga were based in Kōdansha. Not only did Kōdansha have an affinity with the idea of producing a more respectable kind of manga, but its editors were at a special advantage in producing political and economic manga, because the coverage of current affairs and politics was already one of the company's specialities.

Several manga editorials run from within Kōdansha, including *Magazine*, *Mister Magazine* and *Morning*, began producing realist manga series from the late 1980s. *Morning* magazine in particular received a great deal of attention, both within the publishing industry and amongst the news media, for pioneering new style realist manga series.

Elite Editors

There have been hints as to which social class editors belonged. If we examine this subject more closely, the wider significance of the intellectual and creative role taken by editors in developing economic and political manga series begins to emerge. Virtually all company editors enter Kōdansha or Shōgakukan immediately on graduating from a prestigious university. Most editors graduate from the handful of universities occupying the top of the academic ranking system, which descends from the awe-inspiring peaks of Tokyo, Waseda, Keiō, Chūō, Meiji, or Kyoto, through to the unmentionable troughs of a myriad unknown and virtually unlisted private colleges. Passing through one of the former prestigious institutions has been shown to be powerfully (Azumi 1969:90–91) – and since around 1970 even more exclusively (Rohlen 1977:37–71) – dependent upon a privileged social background.

Despite changes to the rigid structure of the professional labour market during the 1980s, and the increased popularity of working for small flexible companies (Kimindo 1995:50–55; Miyanaga 1993), employment in a large publisher, such as Kōdansha or Shōgakukan, is still regarded, by university graduates, as highly desirable. These are large, well-established companies which provide a range of welfare programmes and perks for employees, as well as the security of life-time employment, accompanied by wage rises guaranteed with ability, if not seniority (*nenkō seido*). Employees also enjoy the high social status, personal confidence and power bestowed on them by becoming an employee of a prestigious (Bowman 1981:240–244) and all but indestructible company. One young manga editor, who had recently graduated from university, described finding himself an employee of Kōdansha as quite frankly 'paradise'.

A high proportion of Kōdansha employees are recruited from Waseda university, one of the most prestigious universities in the country. In July 1995 Kōdansha had 1171 employees, of which 894 were men and 277 were women. In April 1996, 322 of these Kōdansha employees were graduates of Waseda University, 95 were graduates of Keiō University, 47 were graduates of Chūō University, 46 were graduates of Tokyo University, 37 were graduates of Sophia University, 36 were graduates of Meiji University, 34 were graduates of Rikkyō University, 30 were graduates of Tsukuba University (previously Tokyo Education), 23 were graduates of Tokyo Gaigo University, 21 were graduates of Nihon University, 16 were graduates of Aoyama Gakuin University, and 14 each were graduates of Kyoto and Hōsei Universities, and so on, in order of decreasing numbers.[3] This list illustrates that in general the more prestigious the university, the greater its graduates number amongst Kōdansha employees.

Before they are members of specific manga editorials, the employees of large publishing companies are company employees and salarymen with prestige careers. A number of editors in *Morning* and *Magazine* were able to candidly categorise their social status as 'élite'. Within Kōdansha, company employees were separated into two streams. A minority of employees were posted to specific departments within the company and stayed within those departments, accumulating highly specialized experience, through-out their careers. These employees aspired to get promoted to managerial positions within their departments – though the bottle-neck of employees in their mid-forties and fifties who belonged to the huge post-war baby-boom generation had made this transition more competitive in the 1990s.

The majority of company employees moved between different departments, spending anything from between two and eight years – eight years was considered about the maximum length of stay – in one department, before being moved elsewhere. Thus in any manga department in Kōdansha there was a core group of individuals working their way towards management positions, who through their accumulated departmental specialism, lent continuity, internal cohesion and leadership to the editorial.

A larger group of more mobile editors moved in and out of different editorials according to their changing personnel requirements, and for other reasons not disclosed by company management. Manga editors in Kōdansha had generally worked in a range of other editorials, producing magazines or books, before being transferred to a manga editorial. One company editor in *Morning* had spent most of his career producing the serious intellectual journal *Gunzō*, while another had been involved with foreign children's books in translation.

Virtually all company employees were unfamiliar with manga before being moved into a manga editorial. Few had been in the habit of reading manga as children or even during their days at university. The majority of editors in Kōdansha struggled to properly disguise their basic disdain for the medium, while one senior editor in *Morning* admitted, 'Manga is a load of rubbish. I would not let my children read it'. Editors came from the type of socio-cultural milieu for which manga was a vulgar phenomenon, and for which this was a judgement so uncontested that it did not really require spelling out. Only one Kōdansha employee in *Morning* editorial had had any personal experience of manga prior to entering the company.

While ignorant about manga, company employees did, in many cases, arrive in the manga editorial with sophisticated cultural tastes. The activities pursued by editors during their student years suggested that they had come from social backgrounds that were privileged not only in terms of living standards and higher education, but also rich in cultural capital. A group of manga editors in their forties, who had been students at the time of the explosion of the manga medium, described their interests while young men as 'amateur drama', 'theatre', 'play writing', 'ballet', 'avant garde cinema' and 'surfing'.

Editors tended to display the characteristics attributed especially to members of 'the professions' by sociologist Pierre Bourdieu. They tended to be 'relatively well-endowed' and inclined to 'invest in their children's education but also and especially in cultural practices' (Bourdieu 1986:122). More specifically, the tastes and values of many editors in Kōdansha had a tangible overlap with those typical of that 'extraordinarily narrow' socio-economic group which dominates British publishing. This group of British editors was described in the following terms: '... it's almost as if the Bloomsbury set was still alive, but had managed to keep its identity and expand somewhat'. (Lane 1980:88) Editors in Kōdansha tended to be bookish, opinionated, individualistic and sometimes eccentric.

Manga editors in large companies formed a distinctive and homogenous social group. All had graduated from a high-ranking university and succeeded in entering a prestigious publishing company immediately on graduation. Here they received social prestige and high monthly salaries. Most intended to remain in the company until they retired. These editors were not the 'ordinary salarymen' or white-collar employees engaged in routine office work, with whom they occasionally made an indulgent identification. Editors were financially comfortable and highly-educated: they belonged firmly to a social group whose existence both predates and transcends the large undefined post-war middle classes identified in either 'middle-mass' or later 'micromass' social theory (Ivy 1993:241, Kelly 1993:195–197, Fujioka 1986).

Working-Class Artists

Editors did not share the typical social origins and experience of the great majority of manga artists, even less so did they reflect the medium's unglamorous social origins. That manga artists come from poor families, and that manga is a working-class culture, has became a knowledge so ubiquitous that it has become a mythology. In his memoirs, Nishimura Shigeo, the ex-chief editor of *Jump*, described artists as youths driven to try their hand at manga by poverty and lack of formal education:

> No matter what kind of low social position they come from boxers get to the top using their arms alone ... The same thing could be said about boys' manga. In the manga world lack of

169

education is an additional anxiety too ... It was never possible to know which of the youths with their faces buried in a bowl of food in the Shūeisha company dining hall would become popular manga artists'

(Nishimura 1994: 81).

Consciousness of the working-class origins of manga artists also features in manga series themselves, and is focused on directly in work from Nagashima Shinji's opus, *The Cruel Tale of a Manga Artist* (*Mangaka no Zankoku Monogatari*), to Fujio-Fujiko's *Manga Road* (*Manga Michi*). Both of these works tell the story of how little boys in their early teens, made the journey to Tokyo, from the impoverished villages of early post-war Japan, in a bid to make their fortunes as manga artists. While the stereotype of the poor manga artist undoubtedly is based on a preceding reality, the precise character of these social origins is difficult to ascertain.

Descriptions of the impoverished, itinerant and isolated lifestyles of early picture card show (*kamishibai*) and rental manga (*kashihonya*) artists seem to suggest that perhaps many of the earliest manga and picture card artists may have originated not simply from the lower classes but, more controversially, from the oppressed Buraku caste. Cultural critic Tsurumi Shunsuke has suggested that manga artists in the early post-war period were people who did not benefit from the 'increase in the standard of living and rise in educational standards':

There were segments of society which were left behind and hard hit by this change. To this group belonged the generation of young cartoonists [*sic*] who made their debut in the 1960s, and they greatly appealed to readers who were frustrated by this smug social milieu of the 1960s'

(Tsurumi 1987:32–33).

While artists from the lower end of the social spectrum dominate the medium – something that continued to be in evidence at amateur manga conventions in the 1980s – it seems that the children of small shop keepers and local professionals accounted for most of the rest during the early post-war period at least. In a survey of 31 *successful* veteran manga artists and cartoonists aged over 50, that I handed out in 1994, most said that their father had owned fish, sake, rice and haberdashery stores. Others said that their fathers had been a doctor, a local civil servant, a school teacher, a local trader, and a farmer.

The apparent heterogeneity of the social origins of manga artists suggests that, like art (Bourdieu 1993:43), the manga medium has attracted artists from a variety of social backgrounds. A closer examination reveals that this heterogeneity is found only amongst famous artists working for high-circulation magazines. Famous artists, however, represent only a small fraction of all those making their living in manga. Graduate manga artists from privileged backgrounds are few and far between amongst the approximately 4000 unknown artists working for small publishers for minimal financial rewards.

Most manga continues to be produced by artists from the lower end of the social scale who are prepared to accept a life of poverty and insecurity in the hope of one day becoming rich and famous. Highly-educated artists have been disproportionately successful and disproportionately visible in high-circulation magazines. This bias towards highly-educated artists was particularly marked amongst artists producing realistic adult manga series in the 1990s.

Graduate Artists

Not only were the editors of large publishing companies, especially Kōdansha, members of a social élite, but the artists they most favoured to draw manga series also came from relatively well-educated and privileged social backgrounds. Manga artists who had attended professional manga courses run in higher education institutes such as Yoyogi Animation Gakuin in Tokyo, rather than élite universities, were discussed scornfully by editors of large publishing companies. The great majority of *successful* graduates of such courses, which tend to cater for individuals isolated from contacts in the field of cultural production by their lack of university education, eventually got work in low-circulation manga magazines.

One editor in *Morning* observed that 'Academic qualifications (*gakureki*) are very important for manga writers if they want to write for *Morning*, *Spirits*, or other top manga magazines, but for low-quality (*gehin*) manga magazines there are no restrictions'. Artists of the four most popular realist adult manga series produced during the late 1980s and 1990s, *Silent Service, Section Chief Shima Kōsaku, Kaji Ryūsuke's Principles*, and *The Arrogance Manifesto* were produced by three artists, Kawaguchi Kaiji, Hirokane Kenshi and Kobayashi Yoshinori. Kawaguchi graduated from Meiji University, Hirokane Kenshi graduated from Waseda University and Kobayashi graduated from Tsukuba University. Watase Seizō and Aoki Yūji, both drawing series for *Morning*, had previously run their own companies, while Hirokane Kenshi had previously been employed as a management-track salaryman in the Matsushita electric company. Élite editors and a select group of highly-educated key manga artists were suited to producing manga with an educational bent and pro-business bias.

Factual Manga

The objective of creating respectable manga series required editors to select suitable themes for their stories. In *Morning* editorial great emphasis was placed on the process of thinking up interesting ideas for new manga series. A senior editor of *Morning* outlined the process of editing in a way which made clear the central role of editors in making new stories:

> The editorial process has four main steps, those are – one; think of a plan for a new story, two; get the plan ratified by the chief editor, three; find a manga artist suitable to write the story and start it, four; control the story well and keep feeding it with new components. The speciality of *Morning* is that we have a stage one – thinking of a good new idea for a story. (Interview, 1994)

In this editorial story-building was also loosely divided into two tasks widely referred to as *create* and *keep*. *Create* was the function of thinking-up suitable subjects and stories for manga series, while *keep* was the function of maintaining a story for months or years after it had been launched, by feeding it with interesting new directions.

The awkwardness with which most editors approached this task of creating new manga series is conveyed in exhortations made by one senior editor, encouraging other editors to get used to the idea of being creative animals:

> The editors here have got a salaryman mentality, you're like civil servants on life-time employment! You have got to be

editors, not salarymen! You have got to have enthusiasm, energy and curiosity. This is a lifeless editorial. It is getting more and more conservative and boring! (Editorial meeting, 1994)

The work of creating manga stories, even model ones, did not appear to come naturally to editors, who were not closely engaged with other kinds of independent creative activity.

Competition had emerged within *Morning* editorial over how well editors were able to 'create' new manga series. Those most successful in the creative task were ostensibly the most highly respected individuals in the editorial. Ideas for new stories were discussed in editorial meetings (see Introduction, Figure 1). In one editorial meeting I attended in 1994, editors took turns to describe the new manga stories they were developing. One editor was working on a story about people and iron, set in a period of industrial revolution. This editor had read an article about the iron industry, in a business magazine, and thought it would provide a good setting for a 'strong industrial age male hero'. The next editor was working on a story about the world of illegal money-lending and its links to the Tokyo stock market. It was a series in which he hoped to examine the issue of 'grey areas' which exist at the interstices of legal and criminal business activity. This was a controversial topic visible in the media in 1994 following the BCCI bank practice scandal. This editor had already asked a small American research company, Dynasearch, to collect the factual details necessary to set such a story in the USA.

Another editor explained his plans regarding a story based on the themes of an extremely strong-willed woman who married repeatedly. The editor had found a female artist to put this story into manga, but described the problems caused by the artist's demonstrated inability to actually draw a strong female character. Another editor proposed a documentary manga series about how ex-members of the Red Army (*Sekigun*) now spent their lives. The documentary style series was to be based on real-life interviews with previous Red Army members carried out by the editor. This plan was abandoned when it was pointed out by other editors that former members of the Red Army were still on police wanted-files across the country! Another editor explained that he was investigating the possibility of launching a new series charting the history of colonialism, a theme which appeared to have been inspired by his memories of studying a university course on the subject. Lastly, one female editor described her research into the theme of smell, which she felt might form the basis of an interesting new challenge to effectively describe smells through manga drawings.

What is apparent from the themes chosen to form the basis of stories is that many of them were culled from subjects recently topical in news magazines, television, foreign films, or books. In this respect the themes editors pursued were often 'original' only in the sense that they had not previously been featured in manga. The editor planning a manga series about smells, for example, got the idea after reading the Japanese translation of the international best-seller, *Perfume*, written by Peter Süskind, which received a high profile in the Japanese media in 1994. Where editors took their ideas from real issues in the news media – for example, the editor considering a story on insider trading or the editor considering a series on the iron and steel industry – these themes were often taken from broadsheet newspapers, current affairs and business maga-zines. Quite logically the subjects editors found in these publications tended to be about the state of the economy from the perspective of business and finance.

Another characteristic of themes developed by editors was the presentation of copious volumes of specialist information. Series such as *Osaka Way of Finance* (*Naniwa Kin'yūdō, see Chapter 3*), *Feast, Kaji Ryūsuke's Principles* (see Chapter 3, Figure 3.6) had an educational content and purpose. These political and economic series had been strongly influenced by the form of Ishinomori Shōtarō's *Japan Inc: An Introduction to the Economy in Manga* (1986) and *Manga History of Japan* (1989). Research had become necessary to produce well-informed, specialist series. Research involved carrying out extensive fact-gathering surveys into academic, literary and secondary sources, as well as making direct contact with individual informants and advisers.

The editor of the *Morning* series *Osaka Way of Finance* featuring state-of-the-art financial and business information, spent a large part of his time reading specialist business magazines and books in order to incorporate the latest business information into the plot of the series. In the case of other series based in professional worlds such as the police station, hospital, large companies, or Diet, key individuals professionally engaged in the area of interest were employed to act as occasional or regular advisers. Advisers provided editors with personal anecdotes and descriptions of the relationships, key issues and insider talk of their professional worlds. *Super D K*, serialized in *Magazine*, was a story about the life of a surgeon and included detailed information about the medical profession and human biology. The editor in charge of this series regularly read specialist surgeons' textbooks and medical journals, had interviewed surgeons and even made observations of operating theatres during surgery. Extensive editorial research was carried out in the preparation of the *Morning* series *Silent Service*, about a Japanese-built nuclear submarine crew which mutinies. This included discussions with military specialists and academics acting as informants, and the purchase of expensive original aerial photographs of naval boats and submarines from military photographers.

The number of additional individuals drawn into the process of creating the series *Silent Service* had inspired the chief editor of the story to develop the theory that the best way for adult manga to become a more serious medium was to produce it in teams based in the editorial office. The concept of 'group-art' (*shūdan geijutsu*) was formulated to describe how manga could be made by a large production team of editors, advisers, informers, specialists and artists, in a co-operative group similar to that of a television or film crew.

Editors themselves appeared to be predisposed to take an educational approach to producing manga by partial virtue of the fact that in their own social backgrounds the pursuit of educational goals had dominated over other forms of experience. Series based on factual specialization tended to embody an objectifying approach to their subjects in which facts and specialised data displaced the explicit expression of social experiences and subjective attitudes. Manga series which deployed a large number of educational facts appeared to be more closely related to real life, and to be, by extension, more realistic and objective. At the same time the presentation of new political ideas within stories dense with factual detail tended to give the impression that these ideas were not political aspirations so much as educated descriptions of objective reality.

For example, the graphic style of the series *Silent Service* contained a great deal of photographic realism. However, the storyline – presenting a Japanese military leader as a vigilante fighting for global justice – was a highly subjective political fantasy. Specialism and pedagogy gave a sense of authority to the themes of realist adult manga series. The educational approach to making manga instigated by editors became a driving force behind the trend towards photographic realism which characterized the graphic styles of realist and business manga. Figure 6.1 shows a sample of *Kaji Ryūsuke's Principles* in which Hirokane's illustrations of war-ships are so realistic that the artist has chosen to acknowledge the copyright of the original photograph on which the drawings are based.

In some cases editors took their artists on research field-trips. A young editor in *Morning* took a two-week trip to Tibet with a manga artist in 1994 in order to gain experiences and take enough photographs to form the basis of a new story on religious beliefs and the afterlife. In Tibet the editor and artist stayed in the Lhasa Holiday Inn and the editor interviewed several monks and local experts of Tibetan religion. The editor of the series *Silent Service* travelled to New York with the artist Kawaguchi Kaiji and some of his assistants, in order to gather ideas and experience, and amass photographs, before shifting the location of events of this important series to just outside the United Nations headquarters in New York. Figure 3.5 (Chapter 3) shows a scene from *Silent Service* in New York. Another editor took Watase Seizō, the artist of the series *Sai*, to Kyoto for a weekend visiting temples and expensive tea houses run by geisha.

The role of artists, particularly those who did not share the interests or opinions of their editors, became more manual and less intellectual. *Osaka Way of Finance*, a series similar in the main aspects of its plot action, lead characters and social setting, to the British television sitcom *Only Fools and Horses,* was extremely popular in the first half of the 1990s. The editor of this series applied to it his own experiences of investing in property on the Tokyo stock exchange, as well as painstaking research into small-scale finance, banking and investment. Though the artist of the series, Aoki Yūji, was famous, the editor devised the story and dialogue. Aoki's main role was to convert these speech parts into downtown Osaka argot, popular with the readers, and drawing pictures to match the story line. The editor believed that if a percentage could be made, he was responsible for 80 per cent of the story, while the artist merely

Figure 6.1 Photographs of real war ships help to create adult manga with the appearance of real war coverage. [*Kaji Ryūsuke's no Gi*. 1997. Vol. 17: 196. © Kōdansha/Hirokane Kenshi]

embellished the plot. The absolute control which this editor exercised over the content of this series caused the artist, Aoki Yūji, a highly opinionated middle-aged man, to 'hate him' with a public vengeance.

Another editor in *Morning* commissioned the novelist Shū Ryōka, winner of a Kōdansha book prize in 1990 with his novel *Bankers*, to write the script for a manga series about a heroic female bank manager. The original novel was an intra-company drama based on Shū Ryōkas's experience as an employee of Fuji Bank. In the series this theme was fused to the issue of 'career women', and in particular to the editor's political belief that women demanding careers should carry out the same amount of overtime work as their male colleagues. The editor in question wanted to create a manga series which responded to feminist criticism of current employment practices. From the 1980s sexism in the labour market was a controversial subject, particularly following the passing of the Equal Employment Opportunity Law in 1986 (Buckley 1995:357–359). Feminist criticism that the practice of demanding regular evening overtime from career track employees, effectively prevented women with children from having careers, and prevented men from participating in domestic duties, had become widely accepted.

A popular manga series, *A Reliable Person!*, featuring an idealized, stoic female bank manager was the result of this editor/ script writer collaboration. Female manga artist Yumeno Kazuko, who had previously drawn girls' manga for which she had been accustomed to devising the plot, dialogue and drawing, was contracted to draw the pictures to fit the plot action and script already finalized between the editor and script writer. Yumeno reported that as she had no input into the theme of the story she felt 'cool and disinterested in the plot', and that for her it was nothing more than 'business'.

Rather than the social experiences of artists being transmitted to editors through the medium of manga, it was largely editors' ideas, research and experience which were conveyed to artists before each episode of the series began production. The social experiences of manga artists, on the other hand, were not rejected entirely. While artists' interests and experiences were not generally included in the plot, theme or speech parts of the series, they were present to varying degrees in the graphic styles of manga series. Manga artists were discussed by editors with reference either to their drawing styles and unique visual techniques, *or* to their personalities and general level of tractability towards editorial instruction. As one senior Kōdansha editor remarked 'The *best* artist is both obedient and a genius draughtsman'.

Making Corporate Manga

The sub-genres of business manga, salaryman manga and economic manga which fell within the new canon of realist manga series reflected editors' own experiences as white-collar company employees. Editors lacked the type and range of social experiences collectively represented by manga artists but they had a great deal of experience within the field of white-collar corporate life. Adult manga magazines began to feature stories revolving around scenes in board-rooms, shareholders meetings, offices, taxis, hotels, and impressive buildings. These series, such as *A Reliable Person!* staged largely within a bank, or *Section Chief Shima Kōsaku* set largely within the interior of an electronic company, or *Kaji Ryūsuke's Principles* set within Diet and government offices, were thematically similar to corporate manga books such as Morita Akio's *Made in Japan,* in which shop floor and board-room scenes dominate the pages.

Through the themes of leading series based in and around companies, manga became a vehicle to examine topical issues related to business ethics and employment practices. *A Reliable Person!*, for example, tells the story of a fictional female bank manager who exhibits a heroic commitment to justice and fairness. The series set an example not only of new employment practices favouring the installation of women at a managerial level, but also of the importance of ethical business, as decorously practiced by this lead female character. *Section Chief Shima Kōsaku* meanwhile gained his popularity fighting against factionalism within a large joint stock company, and for his transparent and just management and promotion practices.

Some of the most successful, fluid and imaginative new adult manga series created by editors were stories about the personal and working lives of male company employees. *Ironman* (*Tetsujin Ganma*) was frequently the most popular series in *Morning* magazine during the 1990s. *Ironman* explored the Freudian fantasies and sexual misadventures of a small, fat and exceedingly ugly company employee, suffering from a severe sexual inadequacy complex. The series was popular with male readers who, in reader response surveys, claimed that it reflected their own social and sexual experiences and related to their broader identities as 'salarymen'.

The themes of realist adult manga series shrank away from the kaleidoscopic range of social experiences and fantasies for which the manga medium had been noted, and towards life within corporations and the corridors of power. Inevitably the corporate theme selected by editors was also one which both reflected and appealed to the most immediate experiences and concerns of a more privileged band of society.

In 1991 *Big Comic Spirits* magazine began serializing a realistic story about a manga editor working for a large publishing company which converted the work experiences of editors employed in boys' and adult manga editorials in Shōgakukan directly into manga. *Editor!* (see Chapter 2, Figure 2.3) became a popular series portraying the adventures of an idealized manga editor working in a contemporary manga editorial office and managing manga artists. The focus of this manga story on the process of making manga itself, encapsulates the tendency of editors to turn to themes progressively closer to their own personal interests and social experiences.

Lack of Passion amongst Manga Artists

To view the shift towards editors of the intellectual centre of realist manga production as a straight-forward case of cultural appropriation would, however, be too simplistic. This shift in the division of labour between editors and artists was based on a more complex dynamic than just the increased desire of manga editors to control the contents of manga. In fact there is considerable evidence that manga editors were confronted with a drying up of the very passion and social consciousness that had originally made manga popular in the 1960s. The same evidence suggests that it was manga editors, rather than manga artists, who were increasingly frustrated by the state of the medium and driven to instigate new visions, and to recruit new personnel and foreign artists, to the manga production process. As adult manga artist Kobayashi Yoshinori observed:

> Previously manga editors encouraged whatever was a big hit according to the circulation figures of their magazines. Now manga is so homogenous that they have started trying to let artists be more experimental. The thing is I don't think there

are many artists who actually want to express themselves!' (Interview, 1994)

In the first half of the 1990s a large number of editors, and even artists, involved in the adult manga industry, shared a strong but diffuse sense that adult manga production was facing problems. The accuracy of their fears was proven by 1995 when the circulation figures for manga magazines began to fall across the industry. The drop in these circulation figures is illustrated in Figure 1.1 (Chapter 1). Editors and artists complained of 'boring manga series', 'dull magazines', 'lack of direction', 'lack of heroes', the 'narrowing of story manga themes', the 'lack of originality in artists' work', the 'over-saturation of the market', 'insufficient interest in manga on the part of readers', and many other problems besides.

Amongst the great majority of adult manga editors was held the view that manga artists were simply not as good as they used to be. The greatly increased number of young people accomplished in drawing manga as compared with the relative rarity of graphic skills found in previous generations of the 1960s and 1970s, was widely acknowledged. However, few of these newcomer artists were felt to have what it took to make a hit manga series. The formal goal of manga editors, like music producers, is to produce big hits which will generate maximum profits from minimum initial investment and production expenditure. Few of these artists were the so-called manga 'geniuses' (*tensai*) who could produce best-selling series, which editors hoped to discover. The manga industry had seen increasing numbers of small hits, many of which had been planned meticulously by editors. A senior editor of *Young Sunday* magazine made the expansive suggestion that in fact 'There have been no natural hits since 1985 when *Dr. Slump* became a huge hit all over Japan. *Dr. Slump* was a real hit – it was not arranged by editors'.

Editors linked the loss of manga geniuses capable of making 'natural' best-seller manga hits, to the usurping of the manga readership by computer games and information technology: 'The number of geniuses has become very few compared to before because the manga world has lost its charm. The geniuses have all gone somewhere else, like computer-game software design' (Interview, with an editor 1994). For the most part, however, editors saw the lack of creative genius amongst artists primarily as one aspect of a broader social phenomenon, 'The problem of not having enough geniuses is related to the period we are living in' (editor of an adult magazine, Interview 1994).

Over-Particularism

Editors complained frequently about the inability of newcomer artists to think up stories or subjects around which to create manga series – it was suggested that artists were unable to draw anything because they lacked imagination. As they had no particular thing in mind they wanted to draw, the repertoire of newcomer artists' work was frequently limited to imitations of better known artists' works or single-page illustrations. Newcomer artists' drafts were criticized for being excessively introverted (*naimenteki*), particularistic (*jiheiteki*), and limited to petty (*kudaranai*), personal or individual (*kojinteki*) themes.

One senior editor described how in his experience newcomer artists were increasingly incapable of producing anything more than pictures of cute girls which he characterized derisively as 'masturbation manga'. The same editor went on to describe the scale of the problem,

> It's not Romeo and Juliet you know. We have been reduced to making stories which hinge on whether the lead character does or does not wear glasses. There is a big problem in manga. Nothing seems to have any energy or a powerful impact anymore. We do not make big hits, just lots of little ones. Manga has become so individualistic and inward-looking that it just cannot go any further. Even the artists talk about it. A lot of artists are tired these days, they can't write any more. They ask me over and over again, 'What is interesting?' (Interview, 1994)

Some editors related the limited repertoire of newcomer artists to the breaking up of popular culture into smaller interest groups, a cultural process referred to as subdivision (*saibunka*), which can be loosely equated with post-modernism and the fragmentation of mass-society and mass-markets. Manga drafts submitted to *Morning* editorial by newcomer artists were not infrequently described by editors as 'nerdish' (*otakuppoi*), meaning that the manga was excessively subjective and particularistic. Many of these 'nerdish' artists were influenced by the distinctive genres and graphic styles of the amateur manga medium. While editors liked the energy and typically uncritical nerdish enthusiasm for hard work displayed by these newcomers, they were on the other hand made anxious by what they perceived to be an absence of ability to create new stories. The inability of newcomer artists to produce viable themes and plots for manga series meant that many editors doubted if the majority of young artists were really *manga artists* at all. Rather than being representatives of the 'younger generation' and 'in touch' with society, newcomer artists appeared to be entirely 'out of touch', and this severely limited their ability to bring astute new insights and ideas to the editorial. One deputy chief editor of a boys' magazine linked the excessive subjectivity of young artists and their inability to develop stories to the limited nature of their social experience:

> Lots of young artists only read manga and do not know about anything else so we editors have to feed them information and ideas about what people, *the readers*, are like and what they are interested in. They do not understand anything at all about society, let alone have something to say about it. They just draw. We can only use a tiny fraction of the themes thought up by even the very best artists. (Interview, 1994)

The accounts of young manga artists tended to confirm the opinion of editors. One young artist drawing his second major series in *Young Magazine* gave a particularly candid account of his own lack of ideas, 'I don't believe in anything, so I am faceless. I do not have a clear idea about what I want to draw so it just develops as it goes along. I have no plan and no message, so I am very dependent on my editor for ideas'.

The exhaustion of ideas amongst manga artists meant they were reliant upon editors to help them to create manga stories and less likely to conflict with them over the content of their series. As one older manga artist, Hatanaka Jun, suggested, 'Young artists today are all conformist. I don't think there are many artists left which find it so difficult to co-operate with their editors like I do'. Editors supervising artists whom they felt lacked social perspective and ideas were forced to carry out more of the intellectual work involved in making manga series, in order to produce manga of interest to the readers, and which was by this criterion commercially viable.

The problem presented by artists who appeared to be ill-prepared to create their own stories was connected to a second problem concerning the *arbitrary* quality of their work. Artists who had developed their own ideas that they wanted to turn into a manga story, came to the manga editorial not just with their drawing skills, nor even with just a good imagination, but with a package of attitudes and insights expressing their social experiences. The attitude expressed in a manga story is a primary source of interest for manga readers. An attitude embodied within a manga story is able to transform a phenomenon, fact, or simple drawing into culture: an expression of subjectivity. Editors found that artists who did not appear to have social attitudes and ideas to express were difficult to employ and exploit, because the themes eventually incorporated into their manga series tended to be too arbitrary and accidental. Their work did not communicate ideas which had a subjective drive, immediacy and urgency that could relate back to, attract, inspire and compel manga readers.

Criticisms made by editors of new artists corresponded with the self-defined characteristics of amateur manga genres at the other cutting-edge of the medium. Whereas editors complained of newcomer artists who were utterly incapable of writing their own manga stories, amateur manga artists had created *yaoi:* a genre which self-consciously identifies itself as manga without direction, narrative, or meaning (see Chapter 4, Figure 4.5). Editors who complained of new artists' lack of passion about anything but 'cute girls' and 'masturbation manga', were in effect also summarizing the main themes of Lolita complex manga which had been popular in the amateur manga world. The attempt by manga publishers to prevent *otaku* genres from branching out of the amateur medium and into high-circulation adult manga magazines was connected to the more generalized criticism made by editors, of the lack of passion and social perspective amongst the professional artists linked to their own editorials.

Editorial Nostalgia for the 1960s and 1970s

Throughout the period of its expansion, stories characterized by the themes of 'pride' and 'passion' were the bread and butter of commercial boys' and adult manga. These stories, referred to as *konjō*, inspired boys and adolescents to struggle to realize their ambitions. *Konjō* pride and passion transposed into sports stories gave rise to the huge genre of *sports-konjō*. '*Spokon*' stories include classic series such as *Tomorrow's Joe* (see Chapter 1, Figure 1.9) and *Star of the Giants* (*Kyojin no Hoshi*), baseball manga. Though passion and aspiration were the key sentiments around which commercial boys' manga had expanded, editors found that aspiration and passion were precisely the qualities which artists appeared to be lacking in the 1990s. Editors saw the emotional qualities of manga artists active in the 1960s and 1970s, and the style and themes of manga produced during the 1960s and 1970s, as an ideal against which all other manga decades were measured.

The loss of direction and drive amongst manga artists was linked to the idea that there had been a gradual loss of direction and passion in society in general since the beginning of the 1970s. Okamoto Makoto, the late owner of the Ginnansha contract manga editing company and elder brother of artist Shirato Sanpei (see Chapter 1, Figure 1.3), gave voice to the quasi-Marxist theory that

> The level of energy manga artists invest in manga goes up and down according to the period and according to the degree of dissatisfaction manga artists feel with the current state of innovation and expression in manga culture. During the 1960s, the time of student unrest, the level of activity on the part of manga artists was very high, then it began to drop off. (Interview, 1993)

The pervading view of the 1960s was that youth were materially impoverished, and that this poverty had encouraged them to aspire, thus inspiring manga artists to narrate these aspirations and dreams in manga. The contemporary Japanese usage of the English term 'hungry' refers to both physical poverty epitomized by a shortage of food, and a fighting spirit, 'hungry' for more from life. The first post-war baby-boom generation (*dankai sedai*) are often described as the 'hungry generation' (*hungry sedai*) and the 1960s in general as the 'hungry years' (*hungry jidai*). These loose historical concepts are popular with manga editors too. Uchida Masaru, ex-chief editor of *Magazine* felt quite certain that rising living standards caused artists to produce dull, unimaginative work and that 'poverty is good because it stimulates energy and creativity'.

Social and political movements such as *AMPO,* and organizations such as *Zengakuren*, had generated new ideas about society, which could be funnelled into manga. There were no equivalent movements in the 1990s. The nineties were described as a 'watery period' (*usui jidai*), a period in which it was difficult to make strong manga with powerful heroes, which could attract large readerships. One editor in *Young Sunday* magazine outlined the origins of the editorial predicament: 'In the 1960s success-story manga about struggling and winning were popular. Then sadness, love and nostalgia took over in music *and* manga. Now I cannot see what period this is, nor what kind of new manga there could be either'. Editors suffered uncertainty and loss of confidence about how adult and boys' manga could relate to the current period. Nostalgia for the 1960s and even 1970s permeated editorial consciousness and the breadth of the adult and boys' manga industry. This nostalgia for a period when the manga industry was expanding rapidly, and when social and political movements surrounded manga artists on all sides, was evident in the themes of adult manga series themselves in the 1990s.

In the early 1990s *Morning* magazine ran a series by Ose Akira titled *What Happened in my Town* (*Boku no Mura no Hanashi*). The series dramatized the political conflict between local farmers and radical students, against the national government and riot police, over the construction of Narita airport on agricultural land, which took place between 1965 and 1972. In 1990 *Big Comic* magazine began serialization of *Medusa* by Kawaguchi Kaiji (see Chapter 3, Figure 3.5). Medusa is the story of a love-hate relationship between two students with opposing political perspectives involved in campus occupations, political demonstrations, and clashes with riot police in Tokyo, at the end of the 1960s. The lead female character, Yoko, is modelled on the female leader of the Japanese Red Army (*Sekigun*) Shigenobu Fusako. The lead male character, Tatsuo, is a non-affiliated student from a wealthy family. As they grow older, she makes a career of being a revolutionary while he becomes a conservative politician in the Liberal Democratic Party. The pair become engaged in a bitter political struggle, which reflects both the conflict and the interaction between left and right in late post-war Japanese politics.

In 1994, *Manga Action* adult magazine ran a story titled *Pendako Paradise* which told the story of how a young boy was inspired to write manga in 1970 after watching political demonstrations at the US naval base in Sasebo, on his parents' television. The older artist of this semi-autobiographical series tried to infuse his younger readers with some of the excitement he had felt as a lad caught up in the political whirlwind of students and police at anti-*AMPO* demonstrations (see Figure 6.2). *Manga Action* editors encouraged the production of a series which was openly nostalgic for both opposition politics and manga drawn with conviction in the heat of a moment.

Allusions to the passion with which manga was drawn by artists of the 1960s' generation are also made in *Editor!* (Chapter 2, Figure 2.3) serialized in *Big Comic Spirits* from 1994, which bears the subtitle *Tomorrow's Joe* in reference to the popular boxing story serialised between 1968 and 1973 (see Chapter 1, Figure 1.9). The first pages of the story open with scenes of a gang of little boys reading the original *Tomorrow's Joe* in 1973 and crying over their shared magazine as they reach the final scene in which Joe, the boxer, dies in the ring. One of these little boys is the lead character, Momoi Kampachi, who is so influenced by his childhood reading of the late-1960s/early-1970s manga classic that he decides to follow in the footsteps of his manga idol and become a champion boxer: a

Figure 6.2 Gabon Chan decides to be a manga artist in the second year of middle school: 'I'm gonna throw my "ordinary life" away... I can't do it no matter what'. [*Pendako Paradise* in *Shūkan Manga Action*, 1994 © Futabasha/ Yamanaka Osamu]

man who fights back to the end. When an eye injury terminates his career, Momoi becomes a manga editor. Whereupon editor Momoi literally brings a new fighting spirit into the manga editorial.

In *Editor!* however it is not manga artists who are portrayed as the source of passion, but the editors themselves. Artists are portrayed as cynical and disinterested. *Editor!* reflects the consciousness of real adult manga editors who have decided to act out for themselves the role of passionate artists, in the process taking over some of the tasks of producing manga. Figure 2.3 (in Chapter 2) shows Momoi, the editor, with the middle-aged *manager* of a famous artist. The latter has just been forced to agree with Momoi that his artist's manuscripts are simply not good enough. Under the watchful eye of Momoi the artist's manager is forced to re-draw the manga manuscripts *himself*. Together these characters act out an idealized scene of cultural conflict and engagement which they believe ought to take place between a manga artist and editor.

The unease which editors feel about the habits of the younger generation of artists in the 1990s and their nerdish manga, is expressed in their constant attempt to look back over their shoulders at the 1960s. Adult manga magazines have taken refuge from the 1990s in the social atmosphere, politics, and culture of the 1960s.

Retro Manga in a New Culture

Editors also attempted to compensate for the lack of social consciousness and passion which they found amongst newcomer artists. Compensation was found in three main forms. The first of these was the use of artists who were disconnected from the main trends of the contemporary manga medium. Artists who preferred to employ graphic styles reminiscent of realist *gekiga* typical of *kashihon* manga and boys' manga stories published in the 1960s, or avant garde *gekiga* influenced by the styles promoted by the avant garde manga magazine *GARO*. Graphic styles influenced by 1960s and 1970s *gekiga* (see Chapter 1, Figures 1.2–1.12) were associated with the more subjective and opinionated manga artists and readers of that era. Both of these graphic styles also carried a somewhat retro and nostalgic feel to them published in magazines during the 1990s.

Between 1986 and 1989 *Morning* magazine published a special edition (*zōkanshi*) series titled *The OPEN*. Newcomer artists working in a variety of graphic styles reminiscent of 1960s and 1970s *gekiga* were published in this special series. Several of the artists recruited to produce work for *The OPEN* had previously been working for *GARO*. These artists used unusual and 'artistic' styles not previously published in high-circulation commercial magazines. One senior editor of *Morning* admitted: 'In 1986 and 1987 we published lots of manga, such as the work of Taisho Yaro, which won the *Morning Open* competition top prize in 1987. When you look at it from a distance it is stuff that would not be out of place in *GARO*'.

Of the artists recruited in this period, several, including Iwaaki Hiroshi, later to produce a leading series titled *Parasite!* (*Kiseijū*, see Figure 6.3); Takamochi Gen, Tsuchida Seiji (see Chapter 2, Figure 2.3), and Tanaka Masashi, went on to become leading artists working for *Morning* and other high-circulation adult manga magazines. Manga critic Kure Tomofusa described the effect created by capturing old-fashioned *gekiga* artists and styles into high-circulation adult manga magazines as '*GAROtique*'.

In 1994 Kuroda Iō, a newcomer artist in his early twenties, began to produce a folk-tale-inspired series *Words and Pictures of the Great Japanese Troll* (*Dai Nippon Tengu no E to Kotoba*) for *Afternoon* magazine, while still a university student. Kuroda's manga, which can be seen in Figure 6.4, was produced using a technique which gives the appearance of a traditional art drawn by brush strokes and has a lo-tech atmosphere, similar to that of avant garde *gekiga*. Kuroda cited the famous artist Tsuge Yoshiharu (Chapter 1, Figure 1.5) – active mainly in the 1950s and 1960s – as his main stylistic influence. The editor in charge of Kuroda was at pains to point out how the decision to serialize Kuroda's work had been a conscious choice to introduce different stylistic elements into adult manga magazines:

> He is the type of artist only a narrow range of people can relate to. But the fact that such a talented artist exists at all is very important so I want to publish him anyhow. Someone with skill like he has can have a good influence on the state of the manga industry generally. (Interview, 1994)

Fukumoto Yōji was another artist contracted to produce an artistic and surreal series titled *Gamurakan* for *Morning* from 1994. Fukumoto (Figure 6.5) was one of a minority of professional adult manga artists who preferred not to use assistants, but to produce

Figure 6.3 Parasites discuss the pitfalls of getting drunk in company, over dinner. [*Parasite!* 1992 Vol. 4: 212 © Kōdansha/Iwaaki Hiroshi]

Figure 6.4 Retro style. [*Dai Nippon Tengu no E to Kotoba* in *Afternoon* magazine, January 1994 © Kōdansha/Kuroda Iō]

Figure 6.5 A sucubus emerges from the face of an office lady and bites off her colleagues nose. [*Gamurakan* in *Morning*, 25 August 1994 © Kōdansha/ Fukumoto Yōji]

their manga entirely by their own hand. In this way Fukumoto tried to maintain the strength of his artistic vision and the cohesion of its execution. Fukumoto's slow drawing technique and unusual graphic style were indulged by *Morning* editorial: 'We have no problem with his strange pictures. In no sense would *Morning* attempt to restrain his imagination'.

Foreign Artists

The second and more controversial route by which adult manga editorials attempted to compensate for the lack of passion and informed subjectivity in Japan, was to look for new talent in different societies abroad. In 1989 *Morning* launched an international project through which they were able, amongst other things, to locate and employ foreign comic artists in other countries around the globe. It was reasoned that foreign artists, in particular European artists, might have more ideas, direction and passion than Japanese artists. *Morning* editorial's international project operated between 1989 and 1998, and involved 10 foreign and Japanese editors resident in foreign countries employed to contract, translate, and edit suitable comic artists. *Morning* editors attended the Angouleme comic festival held in France each January, and the International Comic Festival held in San Francisco in 1994.

By 1994 *Morning* was in regular contact with a stable of over 50 foreign artists, including many already major figures such as Herve Balu, Jacques de Loustal and Joly Guth from France, Chen Uen from Taiwan, and Hwang Mina from South Korea. Chen Uen, one of the most popular manga artists throughout East Asia, drew for *Morning* a popular series titled *Heroic Stories of the Eastern Chō Dynasty* (*Tōshūeiyūden*) about a fantastical pan-Asian empire (Figure 6.6). Hwang Mina, a female Korean artist, produced another popular series about life in South Korea titled *Uni*.

The first full-length story by a European artist, Herve Balu, titled *Highway to the Sun* (*Taiyō Kōsoku*) was 400 pages long and serialized in *Morning* in 1994. Sera (Ing Phousera), a French comic artist who visited the *Morning* editorial office for three months during 1994, produced a manga series titled *Retour de Soleil* in the editorial offices under the supervision of a senior *Morning* editor. Spanish comic artist Luis Alberto Maldonaldo decided in 1995 to join forces with *Morning*'s production experiments by accepting a

Figure 6.6 Pan-Asian historical fantasy. [*Tōshūeiyūden* 1993 Vol. 3 © Kōdansha/Chen Uen]

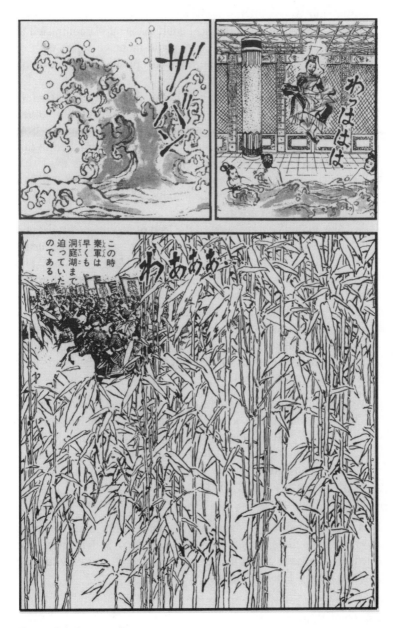

Figure 6.6 *(continued)*

full-time job as an artist's assistant with Kawaguchi Kaiji (see Chapter 3, Figure 3.6), the political adult manga artist contracted to both Shōgakukan and Kōdansha. A photo-montage series entitled *Dominator* by British artist Tony Luke was published in *Afternoon* magazine from 1993.

The majority of European artists began their work for *Morning* by submitting short stories published in a foreign manga cameo series titled *Pierre et Ses Amis*. Artists from Italy, Germany, USA, Belgium, France, Britain, Yugoslavia, and Spain contributed to this series between October 1992 and April 1994. Throughout the 1990s a French comic editor was employed as a permanent member of staff in *Morning* editorial to help Japanese editors to organize contracts with foreign artists.

In 1994 *Young Sunday* followed the lead of *Morning* editorial and began introducing North East Asian artists into its magazine, using the vehicle of an *Asian Manga Festival* (*Asia Manga Matsuri*). The festival began with a series of four short stories by manga artists from Hong Kong, Taiwan, and Korea, edited by a manga editor fluent in Chinese and Korean, specially contracted into the editorial to manage East Asian artists. A senior editor of *Young Sunday* magazine explained that the main attraction of artists from other Asian countries was that, unlike newcomer artists in Japan they 'don't have passive characters':

> We have got three Asian artists working for *Young Sunday* now. They all write manga about the young people in their own countries. We do ask them to write along certain themes, for instance, our artist in Hong Kong is producing a series about violent youth brought up in slums who join the local Mafia. However we also want them to contribute their own style, interests and feelings as much as possible. (Interview, 1994)

In manga produced by young artists coming from other societies *Morning* and *Young Sunday* hoped to capture a dynamism and orientation towards social themes, which they felt was now lacking amongst young Japanese artists.

Contract Editors

The third and less visible approach by which editorials compensated for the lack of passion and idealism amongst manga artists was through the introduction of unusual and varied individuals into the process of creating manga, in the shape of contract editors. During the late 1980s adult manga offices began to introduce new sorts of editors into their editorials who were sub-contracted either from specialist manga editing companies such as Gauche, Comic House, and Ginnansha, or by individual negotiation.

The number of contract manga editors working in adult manga editorials expanded rapidly during the 1990s. By 1995, 18 of the total combined staff of 52 editors in *Morning* editorial offices were contract editors. Other editorials, including *Big Comic Spirits* and *Young Sunday*, also employed extra contract editors during the same period. Contract manga editors had quite different social experiences to those of company editors and remained outside of the employment structure of publishing companies. Adult manga magazines could draw both the specialism and enthusiasm for manga, and the varied social experiences of contract editors, into the production process.

The oldest and largest of the contract manga editing companies is Ginnansha. In 1994 Ginnansha employed 70 individuals who were either contracted out to work within publishing companies or else carried out contract work at Ginnansha's own offices, situated alongside the offices of Shōgakukan and Shūeisha. As the elder brother of *gekiga* artist Shirato Sanpei, the president of Ginnansha, Okamoto Makoto, was in a good position to establish a contract editing company which could link individuals, 'with special potential', to large manga publishing companies. From the mid-1980s Ginnansha began to develop a reputation for the high quality of its ideas, which it had sold in the form of brief reports to manga editorials. Later Ginnansha began to contract individual editors to work inside the manga editorial offices of publishing companies themselves.

The job of manga editing has been extremely popular amongst university graduates who have dropped out of conventional career routes. In addition to having a strong attachment to manga, contract manga editors were frequently individuals who could have gone to high-ranking universities and even entered large publishing companies directly, but who had pursued other academic or cultural interests instead. Contract editors were individuals who had missed a real opportunity to enter life-time graduate employment, by dropping out of university courses or the graduate recruitment process operated by universities.

Each vacancy advertised by Ginnansha in 1992 attracted between 700 and 1000 applicants. From amongst these only two or three individuals were employed as contract editors. Okamoto Makoto described the kind of people he wanted to hire as those who were both creative and 'in touch': 'We do not want childish people who can only imagine the issues of their own generation. All the editors at Ginnansha are outstanding individuals who really understand society in one way or another.' (Interview, 1994)

One young man in his twenties, selected by Ginnansha in 1993 to work in the editorial office of *Young Sunday* magazine, represented well the exceptional social and cultural experiences common amongst contract editors. This contract editor was fluent in Chinese, Korean and Spanish, and had the experience of living abroad for many years. As a child this editor had been encouraged to read manga by his expatriate father who believed that manga was a progressive part of Japanese culture. Both his father and his brother had attempted and failed to debut as manga artists, while he had attended Waseda University to specialize in Asian culture. Prior to becoming a contract editor he had trained as a social researcher during an abandoned academic career. In addition to a personal enthusiasm for manga, this editor had unusual socialist leanings.

Another contract editor was employed by Comic House in 1994, specifically to fill a contract to work as a permanent member of staff in *Morning* editorial office. This contract editor had studied Biology for four years before dropping out of university and forming a rock band. The rock band did not succeed, and prior to starting his placement in *Morning* editorial this editor had alternated between selling jewellery on the streets, and doing part-time shifts as a telephone salesman. Although he had read manga since his teenage years and become something of a connoisseur with a taste for avant garde *gekiga*, he had never been a fan dedicated to manga to the exclusion of other interests in literature and music.

Both of these young contract editors appeared to be better equipped for the broader project of intensifying creative editorial activity than company employees. The majority of employees of large publishing companies shared a distinctive personal history. Almost all had graduated through a series of good schools, attending a high-ranking university, and then entering the company, around the age of twenty-two. Contract editors were generally more experienced individuals, able to apply different social experiences and feelings to making manga. One contract editor described contract editors as 'unusual people' (*kawatta hito*) with more 'individualistic' (*kojinteki*) attitudes. Okamoto Makoto felt that the position of contract editors outside of the homogenized social experience of publishing companies meant that they were more creative than company editors: 'If just the same old companies continue to make manga then it will just cycle round and round and get boring. We are a different sort of people with new ideas'. (Interview, 1994) Contract editors helped editorials like *Morning* to overcome the problem of company editors who were perceived to be apathetic and uninterested in creating new manga, as well as contributing social consciousness, passion and ideals to compensate for these qualities lacking in newcomer artists.

In addition to the cultural advantages, hiring contract editors became increasingly important to adult manga editorials in the 1990s for economic reasons. As editors became more active in the production of manga, the number of editors allocated to manga editorials by parent publishing companies became insufficient to cover the amount of work that these editorials now had to perform. Hiring contract editors became a means by which editorials could attempt to cope with their increasing work loads.

Contract manga editors were paid at a rate far lower than that of the salaries of publishing company employees. The majority of contract editors were also prepared to work harder than company editors, not simply because they wanted to work with manga, but because their job-security depended on it (Miyanaga 1994:68). In the words of Okamoto, 'There are no lazybones and no nerds (*otaku*) in Ginnansha. There is no competition or incentive to work hard in big companies and keeping lazy workers has become expensive. They need cheap "hungry" hard workers from small companies like mine ...'

New Social Relations in Manga Production

During the 1990s the typical roles of manga artists and manga editors producing adult and boys' manga were reorganized. Artists no longer originated and controlled the intellectual ideas and political and social attitudes on which their stories were based, whilst editors began to create and control entire manga series.

199

Additional staff contracted into the manga production process further enabled editors to take on the role of originating and developing new cultural ideas. This shift in the division of labour within the industry was both influenced by and contributed towards the progressive re-definition of the manga medium as a respectable form of national culture.

The producers of manga were influenced both by the censorship *and* promotion experienced in different stages from the mid-1980s onwards. In the hands of company editors adult manga became a more standardized form of contemporary culture, exhibiting characteristics common to television and the national news media. Uncultivated tastes, interests and attitudes, along with uncultivated manga artists, were no longer included in the production of adult manga. In the words of one Kōdansha editor: '*Morning* magazine is more high culture (*jōhin*) than low-culture (*gehin*), it is middle class manga made by élite salarymen in companies for normal salarymen in other companies. It is not for street vendors, if you know what I mean'. (Interview, 1993)

Historically, however, manga has been a predominantly working-class culture. The popularity of manga has been linked to poverty, and long and dull commutes between home and work place. Adult and boys' manga has been a portable television set for men who work long hours. For 40 years, manga provided the cheapest and most easily available form of entertainment in post-war Japanese cities. Manga had been produced by artists from the lower end of the social scale, and read by all those lacking the education to know better.

During the 1920s comic strips became a cultural form closely linked to the political organization and consciousness of the working class. Bohemian and workerist splinters of the middle-class also began to take an interest in manga for the first time during this period. During the 1950s manga became the saviour of a new generation of poor young workers. During the 1960s college students made manga the loadstone of their counter-culture and used it to express radical and left-wing politics (Sato 1996:155–156).

During the 1990s, the working-class origins of the manga medium, which had been filtered through the middle class since the 1960s, were severed entirely. It was no longer possible to say that manga gave 'a voice to a class of people who failed to make the grade in a society where academic credentials determine class'

(Sato 1996:158). The preference for highly-educated middle-class artists in adult manga editorials and the taking-over of the creative and intellectual role of other artists, removed traces of specifically working-class style and attitude from high-circulation adult manga. In a small way the emergence of realist adult manga, managed by editors, reflected the end of an historical era. Its emergence marked the final vanishing point of any remaining vestiges of working-class culture yet haunting late post-war Japan.

7

CONCLUSION: THE SOURCE OF INTELLECTUAL POWER IN A LATE TWENTIETH-CENTURY SOCIETY

From the mid-1980s large corporations, cultural institutions, and government agencies reached out towards the manga medium and attempted to draw it closer to the state. This happened through two superficially antithetical trends – a censorship movement and an active process of cultural assimilation. The general process of assimilation by educational and cultural institutions has been aptly described as granting 'cultural citizenship' to manga, after a long period of 'outsider' or 'immigrant' status (Kure 1990 208–217). Tezuka Osamu's pedagogical manga stories, avant garde *gekiga*, new genres of political and economic adult manga, and information manga were positioned in the centre of this official promotion. The selective assimilation of specific genres of manga continued alongside a powerful trend, between 1990 and 1992, towards closer government regulation of the contents of all categories of manga.

Between these twin campaigns of depreciation and promotion a new official definition of *good manga* was carved out, and an institutional apparatus established for separating *good* from *bad* manga. Manga which did not fit the criterion of national culture was criticized, blacklisted and discontinued. Fortified regulation strongly discouraged the commercial production of such manga, in particular sexually explicit and highly contemporary genres of girls' manga, including *yaoi* and *Lolicom*, which did not conform to the new definition of high quality (*jōhin*) culture (*bunka*). As female manga artist Morizono Milk detected: 'Before 1990 none of the companies censored sexual imagery, there was just a big taboo against things about politics and gossip about the emperor'. Subsequently there was a basic shift in the type of manga which provoked concern or praise amongst government agencies. Renewed manga regulation was accompanied by new political values which favoured greater flexibility over the themes of 'old politics', such as the emperor system, and less flexibility over the themes of 'new politics' (Beck 1992), namely those of gender and sexuality.

Not only did this shift in the focus of manga regulation capture the transition from one political era to another, it also recorded a shift in the organizational location of political activity. In general, manga regulation was carried out by local government and local organisations such as prefectural branches of NAYD (National Assembly for Youth Development), and community and women's groups attached to local government agencies and resources. However, the promotion of manga was orchestrated largely through national government agencies, such as the Ministry of Education and Cultural Affairs, national cultural institutes such as the Tokyo Museum of Modern Art, and through the national news media. As such, the regulation movement was propagated by older political interests based on local government, which had been quite central to the 'grass roots' structure of LDP rule in the post-war period, while the manga promotion movement was fostered by national organizations attempting to strengthen a new, more centralized political leadership.

The movement for stricter censorship and the movement for greater cultural status did, in the case of specific individuals, represent a clash of values. However the two trends ultimately dovetailed into a general process of increasing interference in the manga medium and the imposition of new agendas and values on manga by bureaucratic agencies. The increasing amount of attention paid to manga by government and business was one indication of the extent to which these governing organizations felt that it was imperative to find new means of communicating with society. From the mid-1980s, there appeared to be a desire amongst large corporations and institutions to formulate new social and cultural values which might help to cohere society in a new mould.

Following the publication of *Japan Inc. An Introduction to Japanese Economics in Manga* in 1986, these corporations and institutions began both to use and to promote manga. Manga became the medium through which they attempted to communicate their ideas to employees, young people, children, and society in general. In the absence of political discussion or political movements connecting individuals into national politics, large organizations concerned to understand more about the society around them and to create new lines of communication with masses of unorganized individuals, turned to the cipher of pop culture. Adult manga provided corporations and agencies with a means both of presenting their own ideas to the public, and of gathering insights into contemporary attitudes and experiences which had found limited expression in manga but none in intellectual discussion.

Through the promotion of manga to the status of national culture, Japanese government agencies and institutions demonstrated, and inadvertently tested, the potential for a more inclusive, modern and flexible style of government which employed contemporary cultural symbols as much as political messages. Accepting adult manga as a part of the national cultural heritage carried the message that the government had become willing to recognize and integrate political ideas and social groups linked historically to adult manga, namely those of the post-war left. Individual politicians, such as Ozawa Ichiro, the president of the New Frontier Party, positively identified themselves with political adult manga in an attempt to express the modern and liberal aspects of their ideas.

At the same time that large corporations and government agencies experienced difficulties relating to society in a manner which might enable them to govern it effectively, adult manga editors also experienced what eventually became the same problem, though in a different way. Editors believed that they faced the hurdle of reproducing a medium created in an environment defined by social movement and social expression, in a society in which apathy and individualism had reached a point of apotheosis. The disappearance of even nostalgia for mass movements and accompanying forms of social consciousness was a problem for these producers of mass culture. At the end of the twentieth century, editorial confidence about what high-circulation magazines should look like, and who their readership was, had been eroded. In governing organizations adequate insight into how politics should be conducted, and what the true nature of contemporary society in fact was, had become correspondingly tentative. Essential assumptions about how individuals and their consciousness should be organized, within culture and society, had broken down.

The negative characterization of the amateur manga world, which was constructed during the 1990s, was linked to broader debates about social fragmentation and the decline of a sense of social awareness amongst youth. Both of these discussions influenced the way in which adult manga editors viewed the manga medium, and added to their anxieties about how to produce commercial manga. Publishers noted the absence of large nation-wide manga hits and the increasing frequency of minor, less profitable hits, amongst small, fragmented readerships. Many in the manga industry felt that this problem had its roots in the disunity and particularism of youth engaged with either a diverse consumer culture or a diverse amateur manga subculture. Young artists at the spontaneous cutting-edge of the manga medium appeared to be too individualistic and subjective. They were judged to be incapable of producing stories with universal or social themes, with mass appeal, which could be published and sold in large quantities. Moreover, the majority of amateur manga was in fact *parody*, based on series which had already been published in commercial magazines. The amateur manga medium, which released cohorts of major manga artists during the 1970s, was no longer thought to be a rich source of exploitable ideas and artists, by manga magazine publishers.

Instead of pursuing amateur genres, some adult and boys' manga publishers attempted to turn adult manga into an innovative new cultural medium which could thrive in the new and still undetermined social and political circumstances of the 1990s. The enhanced official status of manga increased the potential for producing manga for precisely the type of people who would not previously have wanted to read, or be known to read, manga magazines. Commitment to shrinking traditional readerships and popular manga dramas was gradually supplanted by conservative, political and social themes, which might appeal to a more political and culturally mature new manga readership.

Manga publishers responded to the rapid promotion of adult manga within society by producing more respectable and 'cultured' manga over which they exercised greater intellectual control. The appropriation of manga by cultural and educational institutions and powerful corporations was paralleled by the appropriation of the key intellectual functions of manga production by publishing company editors. The intellectual contents of adult manga, its public perception, and the social relations of its production, were different aspects of the same process. The transformation of manga permeated through society and connected individual manga artists, publishing companies, cultural and educational institutions, local and national government bureaucracies, quasi-governmental organizations, the national news media, the literati, politicians, academia, local citizen's organizations, feminist organizations, and manga fans. It illustrated 'the indissoluble connections between material production, political and cultural institutions and activity, and consciousness...' (Williams 1977:80) in the formation of cultural phenomena.

In order to overcome the problem of manga artists who appeared to be unable to produce new forms of political and social realist manga, editors took over the role of thinking up and researching new manga series. Creating a more respectable and cultured form of adult manga led to the concentration of new intellectual functions in manga editors. Between the mid-1960s and the mid-1990s the flow of ideas in adult manga reversed. From originating amongst (extraordinary) ordinary individuals in society during the 1960s – many of them self-appointed intellectuals and artists from lower class backgrounds – and moving upwards, ideas for adult manga themes started to originate with editors in highly privileged positions in society, and to filter downwards into amateur manga, where they were turned into *parody* by amateur artists. Corporations, government agencies and publishing editors became relatively more powerful in determining the contents of manga, while manga artists and readers became relatively less able to contribute. The balance of intellectual power within manga shifted significantly. The relocation of the social origins of intellectual expression, traceable in one of contemporary Japan's largest and most diverse and inventive cultural formations, reflected a broader process of intellectual re-alignment taking place across Japanese society in the 1990s. During this decade, the stream of individuals actively involved in politics and culture since the 1960s was dammed up and broad swathes of society ceased to have any active role in intellectual and cultural exchange whatsoever.

Editor-centred manga production influenced the political ideas embodied within manga stories. As a group, editors tended to be relatively politically alert and they were, moreover, sensitive to new trends in social discourse which emerged particularly during the Gulf War, from August 1990 onwards. Editorially-inspired manga tended to combine traditional moralism with more contemporary politically correctness. New political ideas were expressed in series run in *Morning* and *Mister Magazine* magazines, such as *Silent Service*, or *Kaji Ryūsuke's Principles*. Manga serialized in these magazines tended to have deliberately realistic themes and distinctive political plots based on contemporary events. Key concepts – the need to take individual and national 'responsibility', show 'strong leadership', reform political and corporate 'factionalism', and re-establish the Japanese military – which were ubiquitous to political discussion during the 1990s (Ishihara 1991; Ozawa 1994) featured strongly in the themes of adult manga series.

Editorial offices favoured political artists who could match their own interests and values, even where these artists were unrepresentative of the general attitudes of other manga artists. As Hirokane Kenshi, the artist of both *Section Chief Shima Kōsaku* and *Kaji Ryūsuke's Principles* which were published in leading adult manga magazines, himself pointed out, there simply were no other manga artists with conservative political persuasions equivalent to his own in circulation in the manga industry.

Realistic political manga, which appeared in adult manga magazines from the mid-1980s onwards, marked the return of explicitly political themes, accompanied by a version of the realist *gekiga* graphic style, for the first time since the early 1970s. In its second life, however, political adult manga had changed in disposition from being anti-establishment to pro-establishment. For some individuals who were active in the first explosion of adult manga at the beginnings of the commercial manga medium, who have been willing to produce essentially conservative or uncritical corporate manga in the *gekiga* style in the recent period, the reversal of political ideas in adult manga has represented a final abandonment of left-wing objectives. *Comic Box* publisher, Saitani Ryō, and veteran manga artist, Nagashima Shinji, use the term *tenkō* to describe the 'political conversion' of adult manga magazines during the 1990s.

With the end of the Cold War and the end of the left, the basis of popular culture in wealthy industrial societies was undermined. Popular culture has gradually been replaced by a retro corporate culture fashioned by producers and editors employed within culture industries like the manga industry. This corporate culture is fashioned according to cultural producers ideas about the present and according to their recollection of the mode of popular culture of the past.

NOTES

Introduction

1 For a full list of all the interviewees and interviews carried out between 1993 and 1996 refer to the 'Methodological Appendix' attached to my doctoral thesis (Kinsella 1996).

Chapter 1

1 The full titles are: *Magazine* (*Shūkan Shōnen Magazine*); *Sunday* (*Shūkan Sunday*); and *King* (*Shūkan Shōnen King*).

2 Tsuge Tadao is the brother of Tsuge Yoshiharu, who committed suicide while still a young man.

3 Following the Sarin gas attack in October 1994 these recycling bins were removed from all stations in Tokyo. Commuters were strongly discouraged from discarding manga magazines in public places. This official campaign to reduce the visibility of manga was premised on allegations that there was a link between manga and the beliefs of the Aum Shinri Kyō cult which had perpetrated the gas attack.

4 The serialized format of post-war manga production is similar to the serialized form in which popular novels were produced in Victorian Britain (Sutherland 1995).

5 The Publishing Research Centre compiles detailed statistical information on the publishing industry which is published in monthly and annual reports. The reports are used extensively both within the publishing industry and by academics and researchers. The Centre is funded by Tohan Hambai, one of the largest book and magazine distributors in the country. Tohan Hambai was originally established by a group of six large publishers, including Kōdansha, Shūeisha, and Shōgakukan, in order to maintain a large-scale and efficient distribution service which would prioritize the distribution of each of their books and magazines. Tohan Hambai's other services to the large publishers include the provision of a

highly efficient research centre for the benefit of the entire publishing industry.

6 The overall category of adult magazines (*seinen-shi*) bears the same pronunciation, but not the same Chinese characters, as the term for the sub-category of 'youth magazines' (*seinen-shi*). On the other hand, 'mature magazines' (*narunen-shi*) are differentiated from the main category of 'adult magazines' (*seinen-shi*) only through the different pronunciation of the two terms: on paper they share the same Chinese characters.

Chapter 2

1 The concept of 'editorial production' developed within the manga industry correlates with the role of *editors* and producers in the culture industries more generally. As Nicholas Garnham has pointed out: 'We need to recognize the importance, within the cultural industries and within the cultural process in general, of the function which I shall call, for want of a better word, editorial: the function not just of creating a cultural repertoire matched to a given audience or audiences but at the same time of matching the cost of production of that repertoire to the spending powers of that audience. These functions may be filled by somebody or by some institution referred to variously as a publisher, a television channel controller, a film distributor, etc. ... It is a function, moreover, which will exist centrally within the cultural process of any geographically dispersed society with a complex division of labour.' (Garnham 1990: 162).

2 The 'production system' also helps best-selling artists to reduce the amount of tax deducted from their royalties.

3 Readers interested in detailed ethnographic material about manga competitions, recruitment techniques, artists' assistants, artists' training, manga courses and colleges, manga circles, and controlling artists, should consult my doctoral thesis: Kinsella 1996:89–155.

4 Only a small minority of series are produced using a script writer. In Summer 1995 only 3 out of 28 stories in *Morning*, 2 out of 19 series in *Young Sunday*, and 5 out of 21 series in *Manga Sunday*, were written by script-writers.

5 Previously, proofs had been printed in blue ink and referred to as 'blue-prints' (*aoyaki*), but later they were made with black ink, which is easier to examine, and became known as 'ink-prints' (*sumiyaki*).

6 Excluding the giant text-book publisher, Gakken, which although relatively unknown by comparison with Kōdansha or Shōgakukan has approximately ten times as many employees across the country.

7 The average wage of a 40-year-old male employee working in Chūō Seihan Insatsu was described by a sales manager as 3.6 million yen per annum.

Chapter 3

1 Kobayashi Yoshinori's political activities extended beyond *The Arrogance Manifesto*. In November 1997 he successfully prevented 176 photographs of the Nanking Massacre from being shown in Nagasaki on the basis that they were not sound evidence as they were stills from American propaganda films (*Le Monde* 1998; www.jp.comfort women).

2 These were the Sarashina Home Town Manga Hall (1990), Yūzen Manga Museum (1992), Kamiwakibecho Manga Museum (1993), Takarazuka City Tezuka Osamu Museum (1994), Kibikawakami Community Manga Museum (1994), Manga Summit House (1994), Matsudachō Manga Museum (1995), Tsuribaka Hall (1996), Kahokuchō Takashi Yanase Memorial Hall (1996), Mizuki Shigeru Memorial Hall (1998), Yokoyama Ryūichi Memorial Hall (1998), and Ishinomori Manga Hall (1998).

3 The other 12 colleges in which Manga Studies were taught are: Tsukuba University, Osaka Education University, Tohoku Art and Industry University, Tokyo Zōkei University, Tōyō University, Musashino Art School, Senshu University, Ritsumeikan University, Osaka International Women's College, Osaka Art School, Otemai Women's College, and Kurume University.

4 This unprecedented respect for pop culture by a national government also shared some similarities with events taking place in the USA and Britain with, for example, President Bill Clinton's public interest in jazz, and Prime Minister Tony Blair's affection for the pop group *Oasis*.

5 The Scientific Thought Group (*Shisō no Kagaku Group*) can be usefully compared to the CCCS school founded in 1950, which launched a Marxist school of popular culture theory, later to become known as British Cultural Studies, and to become known later still, in Japan, as *karusuta*.

Chapter 4

1 This figure of 35,000 is calculated on the basis that there are currently three conventions held in Harumi Trade Centre each year. Each convention is attended by approximately 16,000 circles, each renting a stall, and ostensibly distributing one work per stall. In 1994, 74.1 per cent, or 11,856 circles attending Comic Market, produced manga (as opposed to music, costumes, software, computerized illustrations or CD ROMs). Thus approximately 11,856 circles distributed a single item of manga three times a year. About 35,568 pieces of amateur manga may have been produced each year.

2 This is not an approach unique to Japanese girls' manga: fanzine subculture in the United States and Britain also features a strong vein of male homosexual romance for women. Fans use material featuring gay homosexual love affairs as devices for staging the type of independent and free characters in which they are most interested. (Jenkins 1992)

3 Aside the campness of Japanese girls' fan and manga culture, there are other incidences of unrecognized camp, in for example the style of dress adopted by Jamaican youth.

4 According to Henry Jenkins: 'The colourful term, "slash," refers to the convention of applying a stroke or "slash" to signify a same-sex relationship between two characters (Kirk/Spock or K/S) and specifies a genre of fan stories positing homoerotic affairs between series protagonists.' (Jenkins 1992:186)

5 A comprehensive photographic survey of the rooms of Japanese youth living in and around Tokyo in the late 1980s and early 1990s confirms that Miyazaki's room, stuffed with a large collection of manga, books and videos, was in fact fairly typical (*Tokyo Style*, Tsuzuki 1993).

Chapter 5

1 Manga series labelled 'adult manga' under the direction of the Ethics Committee, which had already appeared on government lists of 'harmful' manga included volumes of the following series: *Bad Invitation* (*Ikenai Invitation*) and *108 Temptations* (*Hyakuhachi no Koi*) by Kōdansha; *O Genki Clinic* (*Feel Good Clinic*) and *Okusama Lunch* (*Wife Lunch*) by Akita Shoten; *Lets Get Funky* (*Funky De Ikō*) by Issui Sha; *Renai Express* (*Express Affair*), *Just Like You* (*Kimi to Omoikiri*), *Dangerous Woman* (*Abunai Onna*), *Go Ahead Wife* (*Dōzo Okusama*) and *The Loving Time* (*Ai shite Doki*) by Matsubunkan; *BE MY SISTER* by Tokyo Sanyo Sha; *Like An Idol* (*Maru Maru Idol*), *EVOCATION*, *Triangle* and *Sisters Panic* by Fujimi Shuppan publishers.

2 Examples of these types of series which appeared on the government lists of 'harmful' manga in 1990 to 1992 and which were subsequently discontinued include volumes of: *Bad Invitation* (*Ikenai Invitation*), *108 Temptations* (*Hyakuhachi no Koi*), *Feel It BABY* (*Kanji Sasete BABY*), *Bad School Mistress Luna!* (*Ikenai Luna Sensei!*), and *1 + 2 = Paradise* published by Kōdansha; *Feel Good Clinic* (*O Genki Clinic*), *Wife Lunch* (*Okusama Lunch*), *I wanna do it* (*Yaritai Hōdai*), *ANGEL, AMORE*, and *BROTHERS* by Akita Shoten; *Lemon Angel, Cinderella Express* and *Bad BOY* (*Ikenai BOY*) by Shūeisha; *Happy Gorakubu* (*Happy Club*), *Sotchi ga Ii No* (*That's Good*), *Junk Boy, SIGH*, and *100%*, by Futabasha; plus *The Ultra Heaven of Love* (*Ai no Ultra Heaven*) by Kōbunsha.

3 Between the late 1980s and around 1993 many Japanese manga series were pirated illegally by small publishers in other Asian countries. Whilst the readership of these pirated series increased, Japanese publishers did not attempt to press legal charges against the foreign publishers but allowed the illegal pirating to continue instead. This policy paid off in 1993 to 1994 when many pirated Japanese manga series had become so popular and lucrative that their Asian publishers sought to legalize the business arrangements and willingly entered into copyright agreements with Japanese publishers. Japanese publishing companies had accrued large new readerships abroad, had their manga

series regularly translated and re-set, and evaded a costly and potentially touchy legal battle at no cost to themselves. Several top manga artists paid for this tactic, however, through the loss of their own share of royalties on these series.

Chapter 6

1 One manga editor gave a succinct explanation as to why manga artists tended to exist on the edges of social and economic life: 'There is no system whereby the manga artist is a salaryman employed by the company. Manga artists with low ability might want to join the company. But we wouldn't want them would we?'

2 In the general and editorial idiom of this time, 'serious' (*majime*) was a keyword with multiple nuances, including 'commitment', 'conformism', 'hard work', and 'conservativism'. Its equally common antonym 'not serious' (*fumajime*) carried the connotations of 'playful', 'distant', 'uncommitted', or 'lacking respect'.

3 Kōdansha personnel department.

REFERENCES

Abramson, Paul and Hayashi, Haruo 1984 'Pornography in Japan: cross-cultural and theoretical considerations', in Neil Malamuth and Edward Donnerstein *Pornography and Sexual Aggression*, London: Academic Press Inc.

Adams, Kenneth and Hill Jr., Lester 1991 'Protest and Rebellion: Fantasy Themes in Japanese Comics', p. 99–111 in *Journal of Popular Culture* 25 (1), January 25, pp. 99–111.

Adorno, Theodor W. and Horkheimer, Max [1944] 1972 'The Culture Industry', in *Dialectic of Enlightenment,* New York: Herder and Herder.

Adorno, Theodor W. and Horkheimer, Max 1975 'The Culture Industry Reconsidered', *New German Critique*, December 6.

Akihara, Kentaro and Takekuma, Kentaro 1991 *Saru demo Kakeru Manga Kyōshitsu* (Even a Monkey Can Draw Manga Classroom), Tokyo: Shōgakukan.

Allison, Anne 1994 *Nightwork: sexuality, pleasure, and corporate masculinity in a Tokyo hostess club*, Chicago: University of Chicago Press.

—— 1996 *Permitted and Prohibited Desires: mothers, comics and censorship in Japan*, Colorado: Westview Press.

Aramata, H. 1994 *Aramata no Shōnen Magazine Daihakurankai* (Aramata's Grand 'Magazine' Retrospective), Tokyo: Kōdansha.

Asahi Evening News 1993 'Cartoonists say Sex Restrictions Hinder Free Speech', September 16.

Asahi Journal 1965 'Daigakusei wa Manga Suki' (University Students Like Manga), November 20, pp. 107–12.

—— 1969 'Manga Bunka no Jidai' (The Age of Manga), August 24, pp. 94–113.

—— 1971 'Manga ni Tsuite' (About Manga), January 1 pp. 14–16.

—— 1971 'Marx and Manga – Part 2', April 2, pp. 31–35.

—— 1971 'Marx and Manga – Part 3', April 9, pp. 31–35.

Asahi Shimbun 1992 'Sugata kesu porn comic, gai no honyasan kara tsugitsugi to', December 11.

213

—— 1993a 'Manga, aitsugi bungeishi ni' (The next step forward for manga is literary journals!), March 18.

—— 1993b 'Yurusuna, seibyōsha no hōkisei', August 16.

—— 1993c 'Mangaka kara seibyōsha rongi' (Manga Artists Enter the Debate about Sexual Expression), September 9.

Asian Advertising and Marketing 1987 'Japan held fast in the grip of manga', May.

Azumi, Koya 1969 *Higher education and Business recruitment in Japan*, New York: Teacher's College Press.

Bacon-Smith, Camille 1992 *Enterprising Women: television fandom and the creation of popular myth*, Pennsylvania: University of Pennsylvania Press.

Bakhtin, M.M. 1984 'Carnival ambivalence', in *Rabelais and His World*, Bloomingdon, Ind.: Indiana University Press, pp. 194–244.

Banks, Toby 1991 'The Historical Development of the Video Music Industry', unpublished Ph.D. thesis, University of Chicago.

Barker, Martin 1989 *Comics: ideology, power and the critics*, Manchester: Manchester University Press.

Beck, Ulrich 1992 *Risk Society: towards a new modernity*, London: Sage

Becker, Howard 1982 *Art Worlds*, Berkeley and Los Angeles: University of California Press.

Ben-Ami, Shillony 1981 *Politics and Culture in Wartime Japan*, Oxford: Clarendon Press.

Benjamin, Walter [1936] 1992 'The work of Art in the Age of Mechanical Reproduction', in *Illuminations*, London: Fontana.

Benedict, Anderson 1983 *Imagined Communities: reflections on the origin and spread of nationalism*, London: Verso.

Bourdieu, Pierre 1986 [1984] *Distinction: a social critique of the judgement of taste*, London: Routledge and Kegan.

—— 1993 *The Field of Cultural Production: essays on art and literature*, London: Polity Press.

Bowman, Mary Jean 1981 *Educational Choice and Labour Markets in Japan*, London: Chicago University Press.

Buckley, Sandra 1991 'Penguin in Bondage: a graphic tale of Japanese comic books', in C. Penley and A. Ross (eds) *Technoculture*, Minneapolis: University of Minnesota Press.

Buruma, Ian 1985 *A Japanese Mirror: heroes and villains of Japanese culture*, London: Penguin Books.

Chūō Kōron 1994 'Media to shite no manga no Kanōsei' (The Potential of Manga as a Medium), p. 223–46, April.

Clements, Jonathan 1994 'Tales from the Edge of the World: A survey of Japan's manga and anime exports, with special reference to economic, legal and cultural influences upon sales', unpublished MA thesis, Leeds University.

Cohen, Stanley 1972 *Folk Devils and Moral Panic: the creation of mods and rockers*, London: Granada.

Comic Box 1989 'Comic Market 15 Nenshi' (Fifteen Years of Comic Market), November.

REFERENCES

Comic Market 46 Sanka Mōshikomusho Set (Comic Market 46 Participant Application Form Brochure) 1993, Printed by Comiket Junbikai (Comic Market Preparation Committee), October.

Comiket Catalogue 1994 Comic Market 46, August 4–6.

Daily Yomiuri, The 1989 'Japanese Cartoonists Animate the Old Testament', November 5.

—— 1992 'The enigma of Japanese comics', December 1, p. 9.

Duus, Peter 1988 'Introduction', in Shōtarō Ishinomori, *Japan. Inc. an introduction to the Japanese economy in manga*, Berkeley and Los Angeles: University of California Press.

Etō, Jun 1995 'A Nation in Search of Reality', p. 63–71 in *Japan Echo* 22 (Special Issue) pp. 63–71.

Fiske, John 1992 'The Cultural Economy of Fandom', in L. Lewis (ed.), *The Adoring Audience: fan culture and popular media*, London: Routledge, p. 30.

Fortune 1989 'Japanese Comics are all Business', October 9, p. 87–90.

Frith, Simon 1978 (1976) *The Sociology of Rock Music*, London: Constable.

Fujioka, Wakao 1986 'The rise of the micromasses', *Japan Echo* 13 (1), pp. 31–38.

Garnham, Nicholas 1990 *Capitalism and Communication: global culture and the economics of information*, London: Sage.

GARO 1994 '69nen no Kakujō to GARO' (GARO and the 69 Uprisings), May, pp. 14–19.

GARO Mandara 1992 *TBS Britannica* Tokyo: TBS Britannica.

Gekkan MOE 1994, October 1 pp. 84–85.

Gendai Fūzoku Shi Nenpyō 1945–1985 (Modern Popular History 1945–85) 1986, *Kawashutsu Shobo,* Tokyo: Kawashutsu Shobō.

Gluck, Carol 1985 *Japan's Modern Myths: Ideology in the Late Meiji Period*, Princeton, N.J.: Princeton Universtiy Press.

Goode, Erich and Yahuda, Ben 1994 *Moral Panics: the social construction of deviance*, Oxford, U.K and Cambridge, Mass.: Blackwell.

Goodman, Roger and Refsing, Kirsten (eds) 1992 *Ideology and Practice in Modern Japan*, London: Routledge.

Gordon, Andrew (ed.) 1995 *Postwar Japan as History*, Berkeley and Los Angeles: University of California.

Hammond, Phil (ed.) 1997 *Cultural Difference: media memories: Anglo-American images of Japan*, London: Cassell.

Hatano, Kanji 1959 'Children's Comics in Japan', in H. Katō (ed.) *Japanese Popular Culture*, Tokyo: Tuttle, pp. 103–108.

Havens, Thomas 1982 *Artist and Patron in Post-war Japan*, Princeton, N.J.: Princeton University Press.

—— 1986 *Valley of Darkness: Japanese people and world war two*, London: University Press of America.

Hicks, George 1995 *The Comfort Women*, London: Souvenir Press.

Honda, Shiro 1994 'East Asia's Middle Class Tunes into Today's Japan', *Japan Echo* 21 (4), pp. 75–79.

Howard, Keith (ed.) 1995 *True Stories of the Korean Comfort Women*, London: Cassell.

Imagawa, Kiyoshi 1996 *Sora o Koete Tezuka Osamu Den* (Traversing the Skies – Tezuka Osamu's Tale) Tokyo: Sōgensha.

Imidasu 1993, Tokyo: Shūeisha.

International Herald Tribune 1990' O-batalion v Oyaji-gal in the great manga war', July 14–5.

Ishigami, Mitsutoshi 1989 *Tezuka Osamu no Jidai* (The Era of Tezuka Osamu) Tokyo: Tairiku Shobō.

Ishihara, Shōtarō 1991 *The Japan That Can Say No*, London: Simon and Schuster.

Ishikawa, Jun 1995 *Manga no Jikan* (Manga Time) Tokyo: Shōbunsha

Ishiko, Junzo 1980 *Sengo Mangashi Notes* (Post-war Manga Notes) Tokyo: Kinokuniya Shoten.

—— 1994 [reprint] *Sengo Mangashi Notes* (Post-war Manga Notes) Tokyo: Kinokuniya Shoten.

—— 1989 *Comic Ron* (Thoughts on Comics) Tokyo: Hokutō Shobō.

Ishiko, Jun 1988 *Nihon Manga Shi* (Japanese Manga History) Tokyo: Kyō Bunko.

Ito, Kinko 1994 'Images of Women in Weekly Male Comic Magazines in Japan', *Journal of Popular Culture*, 27 (4), pp. 81–95.

Ito, Masami 1978 *Broadcasting in Japan*, London: Routledge and Kegan Paul.

Ito, S. 1979 *The Historical Development of Media Systems*, UNESCO.

Ito, Takatoshi 1992 *The Japanese Economy*, London: The MIT Press.

Ives, C. F. 1974 *The Great Wave: the influence of Japanese woodcuts on French prints*, New York: Metropolitan Museum of Art.

Ivy, Marilyn 1988 'Critical Texts, Mass Artifacts: The Consumption of Knowledge in Postmodern Japan', M. Miyoshi and H.D. Harootunian (eds.) *South Atlantic Quarterly: Postmodernism in Japan*, 87 (3), pp. 417–442.

—— 1993 'Formations of Mass Culture', in A. Gordon (ed.) *Japan as Postwar History*, Berkeley and Los Angeles: University of California Press, pp. 239–258.

Iwao, Sumiko 1993 *The Japanese Woman: traditional image and changing reality*, New York: The Free Press.

Jansen, Marius (ed.) 1989 *The Cambridge History of Japan*, vol. 5, The Nineteenth Century, Cambridge: Cambridge University Press.

Japan Pictorial 1995, Tokyo: NTT Mediascope 18(1) pp. 19–23.

Japan Times 1989 'New textbooks to present Japanese history in pictures', November 5.

—— 1990 'Museum memorialises man of manga', July 11. p. 12.

—— 1992 'Jump manga provides escapist fare for all ages', January 3.

—— 1992 'Koreans Jump for Japanese Comics', October 22.

—— 1993 'Day labourer "manga" a laugh at society', November 9.

Japan Times International Weekly 1994 'Why Japanese need their comics', March 21, p. 8.

REFERENCES

Japan Update 1988 'Weekly Magazines: Keys to Information Society', Spring, p. 9–10.

Jenkins, Henry 1992 *Textual Poachers: television fans and participatory culture*, London: Routledge.

Kasza, Gregory 1988 *The State and The Mass Media in Japan 1918–1945*, Berkeley and Los Angeles: University of California Press.

—— 1995 *The Conscription Society: administered mass organisations*, London: Yale University Press.

Katō, Hidetoshi (ed.) 1959 *Japanese Popular Culture*, Tokyo: Tuttle.

—— 1974 *Japanese Research on Mass Communications: selected abstracts*, Honolulu: Hawaii University Press.

——, Powers, Richard and Stronach, Bruce 1988 *A Handbook of Japanese Popular Culture*, New York: Greenwood Press.

Kelly, William 1993 'Finding a Place in Metropolitan Japan: ideologies, institutions, and everyday life', in A. Gordon (ed.) *Japan as Post-war History*, Berkeley and Los Angeles: University of California Press, pp. 189–238.

Kimindo, Kusaku 1995 'The demise of the Japanese Salaryman' *Japan Echo*, Spring, pp. 50–55.

Kinsella, Sharon 1995 'Cuties in Japan', in L.Skov and B.Moeran (eds.) *Women, Media and Comsumption in Japan*, London: Curzon Press, pp. 220–254.

—— 1996 'Editors, Artists and the Changing Status of Manga in Japanese Society, 1986–95', unpublished D.Phil. thesis, Oxford University.

—— 1998 'Japanization: Babe Power Goes West', in C. Branizagli (ed.) *Nightwave 1997*, Milan: Costa & Nolan (Italian version), pp. 95–103.

Kiridoshi, Risaku 1995 *Omae ga Sekai o Koroshitai Nara* (If You Want to Destroy the World), Tokyo: Film Art Sha.

Kogawa, Tetsuo 1988 'New Trends in Japanese Popular Culture', in G. McCormack and Y. Sugimoto (eds) *The Japanese Trajectory: modernisation and beyond*, Cambridge: Cambridge University Press.

Kosaka, Kenji 1994 *Social Stratification in Contemporary Japan*, London: KPI.

Krauss, Ellin 1974 *Japanese Radicals Revisited*, Berkeley and Los Angeles: University of California Press.

Kure, Tomofusa 1990 [1986] *Gendai Manga no Zentai Zō* (Contemporary Manga: The Complete Picture), Tokyo: Shiki Shuppan.

—— 1991 'Kanji kana majiri bun ni yoku taeta kimben naru nihonjin' (The Japanese genius of combining Chinese characters with syllabary), in *Geijitsu Shinchō* , August.

Kurihara, Akira 1982 *Kanri Shakai to Minshū Risei: Nichijō Ishiki no Seiji Shakaigaku* (Managed Society and Democratic Reason: a political sociology of everyday consciousness), Tokyo: Shinyōsha.

Lane, Michael and Booth, J. 1980 *Books and Publishers: commerce against culture in post-war Britain*, Cambridge, Mass.: Lexington Books.

Le Monde 1998 'Le négationnisme japonais s'affiche dans le publications populaires', January 31, p. 26.

Lent, John 1989 'Japanese Comics', in H. Katō and R. Powers and B. Stronach (eds.) *A Handbook of Japanese Popular Culture*, New York: Greeenwood Press, pp. 221–235.

Mainichi Daily News 1989 'A Place for Manga Lovers', November 17.

—— 1992a 'Submarine Metaphors', February 29.

—— 1992b 'Tezuka museum going ahead despite protest', August 9.

—— 1992c 'Manga Visions of the Floating World', August 15.

Mainichi Shimbun 1993 'Papa, Mama anshin shite ne' (Mum and dad can relax), July 2.

Manga Mania 1993 'Details Details', p. 6.

Manga Japan Tsūshin (Manga Japan News) 1994, October 5.

Maruyama, Akira 1993 *Manga no Kanzume* (Canning Manga), Tokyo: Horupo Shuppan.

Matsui, Midori 1993 'Little girls were little boys: displaced femininity in the representation of homosexuality in Japanese girls' comics', in S. Gunew and A. Yeatman (eds.) *Feminism and the Politics of Difference*, St. Leonards: Allen and Unwin, pp. 177–196.

Miyanaga, Kuniko 1993 *The Creative Edge: individualism in Japan*, New Jersey: Transaction Publishers.

Miyoshi, Masao and Harootunian, H. (eds) 1989 *Postmodernism and Japan*, London: Duke University Press.

—— 1991 *Off Centre: power and cultural relations between Japan and the United States*, Cambridge, Mass.: Harvard University Press.

Moeran, Brian 1989 *Language and Popular Culture in Modern Japan*, Manchester: Manchester University Press.

—— 1991 *Media and Advertising in Japan*, NIAS Report 4.

—— 1993 'The Orient Strikes Back: Advertising and Imagining in Japan', *The University of Hong Hong Supplement to the Gazette*, 40(1), pp. 77–110.

—— 1996 *A Japanese Advertising Agency: an anthropology of media and markets*, Richmond: Curzon Press.

Monbushō Chōsa 1994 (Monbushō Survey) (Detailed survey carried out every year by the Ministry of Education and Culture which records the changing reading habits of youth including those for manga.)

Morioka, Heinz and Sasaki, Miyoko 1990 *Rakugo and the Popular Narrative Art of Japan*, London: Harvard University Press.

Morley, David and Robbins, Kevin 1992 'Techno-Orientalism: Futures, Foreigners, and Phobias', *New Formations* 16, pp. 136–156.

Morris-Suzuki, Tessa 1995 'The Invention and Reinvention of 'Japanese Culture',' *Journal of Asian Studies* 54 (3), August, pp. 759–780.

Munroe, Alexandra 1996 'Pulp Fiction and the Floating World', in *Paintings by Masami Teraoka*, New York: Smithsonian Institute, pp. 33–49.

Murakami, Tomohiko 1991 *It's Only Comics*, Tokyo: Kōsaitō Bunko.

Nagai, Katsuichi 1987 *GARO Henshūchō* (Editor of GARO), Tokyo: Chikuma Bunko.

REFERENCES

Nagatani, Kunio 1994 *Nippon Mangaka Meikan* (Japanese Manga Artists Directory), Tokyo: Data House.

Nakane, Chie 1984 *Japanese Society*, London: Penguin Books Ltd.

Nakano, Haruyuki 1993 *Tezuka Osamu to Rojiura no Mangatachi* (Tezuka Osamu and the 'Rojiura' Manga), Tokyo: Chikuma Shobō

Napier, Susan 1996 'Panic Sites: the Japanese imagination of disaster from *Godzilla* to *Akira*', in J.W. Treat (ed.) *Contemporary Japan and Popular Culture*, pp. 235–262.

Natsume, Fusanosuke 1995 *Tezuka Osamu no Bōken* (The Adventures of Tezuka Osamu), Tokyo: Chikuma Shobō

—— 1996 *Tezuka Osamu wa Doko ni Iru* (Where is Tezuka Osamu?), Tokyo: Chikuma Bunko.

NAYD Japan, introductory booklet in the English language.

Nihon Keizai Shimbun 1993 'Shōjo Manga de Katsuyaku no Shakaiin' (Active Citizenship Through Girls' Manga), in the regular column 'Tokyo wa Shiawase desu ka?' (Happy in Tokyo?), August 13.

—— 1994 'Manga PR ni Ichiyaku' (A part to play in manga PR) May 10.

Nikkei Business 1993 'Manga Industry Special Report', September 13, pp. 115–119.

Nikkei Weekly 1992 'Comic Book Problem is Sexism not Sex' September 9.

Nippon Tsūshin 1995 'Usagi to Kaeru' (Rabbits and Frogs), January, pp. 22–23.

Nishimura, Shigeo 1994 *Saraba Waga Seishun no Shōnen Jump* (My Youth and Jump), Tokyo: Asukasha.

Noguchi, Y. 1933 *The Ukiyoe Primitives*, London Agents: Kegan Paul Trench Trubner and Co. Ltd.

Noma, Seiji 1934 *The Nine Magazines of Kodansha*, London: Methuen.

Nosaka, Akiyuki 1979 'Kashihon manga: No Return', p. 114–7 in *Bungei Shunju Deluxe*, September, pp. 114–117.

Ohizumi, Shitsunari 1996 *Kieta Mangaka* (Manga Artists that Dissappeared) Tokyo: Ohta Shuppan

Ohtsuka, Eiji 1989 'M. Kun no Naka no Watashi, Watashi no Naka no M. Kun' (The Miyazaki in Me, The Me in Miyazaki), p. 438–44, in *Chūō Kōron*, October, pp. 438–444.

—— 1994 *Sengo Manga no Hyōgen Kūkan* (The Expressive Space of Post-war Manga), Tokyo: Hōzōkan.

Okada, Toshio 1996 *Otakugaku Nyūmon* (An Introduction to *Otaku*ology) Tokyo: Ohta Shuppan

—— *et al.* 1997 *Otaku Amigos* Tokyo: Soft Bank.

Okonogi, Keigo 1978 'The Age of Moratorium People', *Japan Echo* 5 (1) pp. 17–39.

Ono, Kosei 1983 'Disney and the Japanese', *Look Japan*, July 10, pp. 6–12.

—— 1993 *Asia no Manga* (Asia's Manga), Tokyo: Taishūkan Shoten.

Osakafu Seishōnen Kenzenikisei Kenkyūshukai Hōkokusho (Public Statement of the Osaka Prefecture Branch of the National Assembly for Youth Development) 1991, (Printed by the same organization.), October.

Ozawa, Ichiro 1994 *Blueprint for a New Japan: the rethinking of a nation* (Nihon Kaizō Keikaku), Tokyo: Kodansha International.

Penley, Constance 1991 'Brownian Motion: women, tactics, and technology' in Penley, C and Ross, A eds. *Technoculture*, Minneapolis: University of Minnesota Press.

Read Shuppan 1989 *Mangaka no Yumei 500 Nin* (500 Famous Manga Artists) Tokyo: Read Shuppan, 1989.

Richie, Donald 1982 *The Japanese Film: art and industry*, Princeton: Princeton University Press

Robertson, Jennifer 1998 *Takarazuka: sexual politics and popular culture in modern Japan*, London: University of California Press.

Rofuto Books Editorial 1997 *Kyōkasho ga Oshienai Kobayashi Yoshinori* (What the textbooks don't teach you about Kobayashi Yoshinori) Tokyo: Rofuto Books.

Rohlen, Thomas 1977 'Is Japanese Education Becoming Less Egalitarian?', *Journal of Japanese Studies* 3 (1).

Sabin, Richard 1993 *Adult Comics: an introduction*, London: Routledge.

Satō, Takao 1970 'Afterword', in S. Tsurumi (ed.) *Manga Sengo Shi I* (Post-war Manga Volume I), Tokyo: Chikuma Shobo.

—— 1973 *Nihon no Manga* (Japan's Manga), Tokyo: Hyōronsha.

—— 1996 'Popular Culture in Modern Japan', *Japan Review of International Affairs*, Spring, pp. 141–158.

Schodt, Frederick 1996 *Dreamland Japan: writings on modern manga*, Berkeley, California: Stone Bridge Press.

—— 1988 *Manga! manga!: an introduction to the world of Japanese comics*, Tokyo: Kodansha International.

Segal, Lynne and MacIntosh, Mary (eds) 1992 *Sex Exposed: sexuality and the pornography debate*, London: Virago Press Ltd.

Seymour, Christopher 1992 'Alienated Zombie Computer Nerds', *Tokyo Journal*, May, pp. 26–31.

Shimizu, Isao 1989 Manga Shōnen to Akabon Manga (*Manga Boy* and *akabon* manga) Tokyo: Tōsui Shobō

—— 1991 *Manga no Rekishi* (The History of Manga), Tokyo: Iwanami Shoten.

—— 1993 'Japan's Rich Tradition of Cartoons and Comics', *Echoes of Peace*, January, pp. 13–15.

Shinoyama, Kishin 1991 *Santa Fe*, Tokyo: Asahi Shuppan.

Shōkun! 1994 'Innocent na anarchism de happō yabure no teikō' (Fighting Back Against the Curtailment of Innocent Anarchism), July, PP. 272–273.

Shūkan Bunshun 1989A 'Miyazaki Tsutomu ga Mayoikonda Tōsaku no Mori' (The Forest Where Miyazaki Tsutomu Lost his Way), September 7, pp. 37–40.

—— 1989b 'Miyazaki Tsutomu no Chi to Niku Himitsu' (Miyazaki Tsutomu's Secret of Blood and Flesh), August 31, pp. 35–38.

Shūkan Post 1989a 'Otaku-zoku' (Otaku tribes), September 25, pp. 32–42.

—— 1989b 'Yōjigazō' (Pictures of Infants), October 1, pp. 39–42.

REFERENCES

Shūkan Shinchō 1992 'Seizaikai na Gekiga no Hakuryoku' (The Power of Political Economic *gekiga*), October 15, pp. 139–143.

Shuppan Geppō (Publishers' Month Report) March 1994, March 1997, April 1997, September 1997 issues. Produced by the *Shuppan Ryōgaku Kenkyūjō* (Publishing Research Centre).

Shuppan Kai no Jishū Kisei ni Tsuite 1994 (Automatic Regulation within the Publishing Industry) in the February 1994 report of the *Shuppan Rinri Kyōgikai* (Publishing Ethics Committee), obtained from *Nihon Shuppan Kyōkai* (Japan Publisher's Association).

Shuppan Nenpō (Publishers' Annual Report) 1979, 1980, 1981, 1983, 1994, 1996, 1997 issues.

Skinner, Kenneth 1979 'Salaryman Comics in Japan', *Journal of Popular Culture*, Summer, pp. 141–160.

Skov, Lisa and Moeran, Brian (eds. 1995 *Media, Women and Consumption in Japan*, London: Curzon Press.

Smalley, Martha Lund 1997 *American Missionary Eyewitnesses to the Nanking Massacre*, New Haven, Connecticut: Yale Divinity School Library.

Smith, T. 1993 *Japanese Book News*, The Japan Foundation – 2(2).

Soeda, Yoshio 1983 *Manga Bunka* (Manga Culture), Tokyo: Kinokuniya Shoten.

Sontag, Susan [1964] 'Notes on Camp' pp 108–9, in 1983 *A Susan Sontag Reader*, London: Penguin Books.

Stefánsson, Halldór 1993 'Nordic Mythology and Icelandic Sagas in Japan: The Academics and the Cartoonists'. Unpublished paper, Oxford University: St. Antony's College.

Sunday Mainichi (colour supplement) 1995 'SF, Anime to Aum' (Science fiction, animation and Aum religion), June 3.

Sutherland, John 1995 *Victorian Fiction: writers, publishers and readers*, Basingstoke: Macmillan.

Swann, Peter 1958 *An Introduction to the Arts of Japan*, Oxford: Bruno Cassiner.

Takarajima 1989 *Otaku no Hon* (The Nerd Book), Tokyo.

Takekuma, Kentaro 1995 *Watashi to Armagedon: otaku shukyō to shite no Aumu Shinrikyō* (Me and Armagedon: Aum supreme truth cult as an *otaku* religion), Tokyo: Ohta Shuppan.

Takeuchi Osamu 1992 *Tezuka Osamu Ron* (Thoughts on Tezuka Osamu), Tokyo: Heibonsha.

——1994 'The Japanese Children and Comics', *Child Welfare: quarterly news from Japan* 15 (1), June, pp. 2–9.

——1995 *Sengo Manga 50 Nenshi* (Fifty Years of Post-war Manga), Tokyo: Chikuma Library.

Taku, Hachiro 1992 *Ikasu! Otaku no Tengoku* (Viva! Otaku Heaven), Tokyo: Ohta Shuppan.

Tanner, Roy 1994 'Toy Robots in America, 1955–75: how Japan really won the war', *Journal of Popular Culture*, 28(3), pp. 125–154.

Tezuka, Osamu 1967 'Kansō no Kotoba' (A Word From the Creator), *COM*, Issue 1, pp. 184–185.

TIME 1985 'Romance Japanese Style: for Millions of Weary Women, Life is a Comic Book', November 11.

Tokyo Journal June 1994 'The Conversation: Kobayashi Yoshinori', pp. 18–20.

Tokyo Post 1992a 'Ninki no Risō Kachō, demo Genjitsu wa ...' (A Fantasy Section Chief is Popular, but in Reality ...), July 16.

—— 1992b 'Manga Geppan, PKO de Mondai Teiki' (Manga Monthly, Suggestions about the PKO problem), July 31.

—— 1993 'Taiwan de Nihon Manga Zasshi ga Zōkan Boom' (New Japanese Manga magazines are Booming in Taiwan), January 30.

Treat, John Whittier 1993 'Yoshimoto Banana Writes Home: *shōjo* culture and the nostalgic subject', in *Journal of Japanese Studies* 19(2), pp. 353–387.

Tsukuru 1991 *Yūgai Comic Mondai wo Kangaeru* (Thoughts about the Danerous Manga Problem), Tokyo: Tsukuru Shuppan.

Tsukuru 1993 *Shigaisen* (Reading Civil War), Tokyo: Tsukuru Shuppan.

Tsurumi, Maia 1997 'Gender and Girls' Comics in Japan', *Bulletin of Concerned Asian Scholars* 29(2), April–June, pp. 46–55.

Tsurumi, Shunsuke 1967 *Genkai Geijitsu Ron* (Border Art), Tokyo: Keisho Shobō.

—— (ed.) 1970 *Manga Sengo Shi I & II* (Post-war Manga Volumes I and II), Tokyo: Chikuma Shobō.

—— 1987 *A Cultural History of Post-war Japan 1945–1980*. London: KPI Publishers.

—— 1991 *Sengo Taishū Bunka Shi 7: manga no dokusha to shite* (Post-war Popular Culture – Volume 7: a manga reader), Tokyo: Chikuma Shoten.

Tsuzuki, Katō (ed.) 1993 *Tokyo Style*, Tokyo: Kyoto Shoin.

Ueda, Atsushi and Eguchi, Miriam (eds) 1994 *The Electric Geisha: exploring Japan's popular culture*, London: Kodansha International.

Ueno, Chizuko 1989 'Kyujū Nendai no Sexual Revolution' (The Sexual Revolution of the Nineties), in Takarajima, *Otaku no Hon,* Tokyo, pp. 131–136.

Vogel, Ezra 1963 *Japan's New Middle Class*, Cambridge: Cambridge University Press.

Wall Street Journal 1987 'Grown Men in Japan Still Read Comics and Have Fantasies', July 27.

Washington Post 1991 'Comic Strip describes 'Office Lady' revolution', August 23.

—— 1992 'Japan's Serial Addiction', April 22.

Watanabe, Kazuhiro 1990 *Otakudama*, Tokyo: Ohta Shuppan.

Whipple, Charles 1993 'The Silencing of the Lambs', *Tokyo Journal*, July, pp. 35–41.

White, Merry 1994 *The Material Child: coming of age in Japan and America*, London: University of California Press.

—— 1995 'The marketing of adolescence in Japan', L. Skov and B. Moeran (eds) *Women, Media and Consumption in Japan*, London: Curzon Press, pp. 255–273.

REFERENCES

Williams, Raymond 1976 *Keywords: a vocabulary of culture and society*, London: Fontana.

—— 1977 *Marxism and Literature*, Oxford: Oxford University Press.

—— 1981 *Culture*, London: Fontana Press.

Witek, Joseph 1989 *Comic Books as History*, University of Mississippi Press.

Yamazaki, Masakazu 1994 *Individualism and the Japanese: an alternative approach to cultural comparison*, Tokyo: Japan Echo Inc.

Yomiuri Shimbun 1992 'Manga Geppyō, Seiji ga Mangateki da to Manga ga Seijiteki ni naru!?' (As Politics becomes more like a Manga Scenario, Manga Stories are becoming more Political!), November 10.

Yomota, Inuhiko 1994 *Manga Genron* (Manga Base Theory) Tokyo: Chikuma Shoten.

Yonezawa, Yoshihiro 1985 *Comiket, Graffiti, Manga, Animation Dōjinshi no Jū Nen* (Ten Years of Comiket, Graffiti, Manga, Animation, and Amateur Manga), Tokyo: Asahi Shuppan Sha.

—— 1989 'Comiket: sekai saidai no manga saiten' (Comiket: the world's biggest comic festival), in Takarajima, *Otaku no Hon*, Tokyo, pp. 75–88.

—— (ed.) 1991 *Bessatsu Taiyō Shōjo Manga no Sekai* (The World of Girls' Manga), Tokyo: Heibonsha.

—— (ed.) 1996 *Bessatsu Taiyō Shōnen Manga no Sekai I* (The World of Boys' Manga I), Tokyo: Heibonsha.

Yoshino, Kosaku 1992 *Cultural Nationalism in Contemporary Japan*, London: Routledge.

INDEX

administered mass organisations 156
Adorno, Theodore 5
adult: conceptual category 48–9, 209
adult manga: books 148; labelling
  148–9, 211; magazines 45–9, 162,
  209; new genres 71–8, 202
Agency for Cultural Affairs 95
akabon 27, 102
Akira 13
aniparo 113
amateur manga 4, 11, 102–39, 183,
  204–5; response of professional
  publishers 133–6, 184
AMPO 31–4, 78, 87, 185–6
Angouleme 193
anti-manga movement 143–7, 150,
  153, 156; lobbying in National diet
  146
Aoki Yūji (Osaka Way of Finance) 83,
  172, 174
Arai Hideki 141
arbitaryness, problems of 184
artist/editor relationship 9, 55–8, 180,
  183, 188, 199
art-work 61–2, 64–5
Association to Stop Racism Against
  Blacks 143
Aum Shinri Kyō 89, 208
avant garde 37–9, 188, 198, 202

Balu, Herve 193

BCCI bank fraud 173
Benjamin, Walter 5
bishōnen-ai 117
blacklisting 142, 147, 158, 164, 202,
  211
BLUE 149–50
boys' manga 10, 113, 120
Bourdieu, Pierre 110
British Cultural Studies 210
Bulletin of the Reader's Civil War 158
business manga 71, 163

camp 120–1, 211
Captain Tsubasa 113, 125
censorship 22–3, 89, 129, 132–3,
  139–161, 164, 200, 202; technical
  evasion of 141; self-censorship
  149–152, 159; the role of editors
  164
Chen Uen 193–5
chief editors 17
circulation figures 20–2, 30–1, 41–4,
  180; decline of 44, 181
citizen's organisations 145, 153,
  155–6, 203
Cold War 1, 207
COM 54, 103–4
comfort women 89
Comic Box 109, 121
Comic Market 106–13, 117, 119,
  126–7, 131–5

comic: strips 20, 23, 200; industries in
    Europe 43
computer games 4, 44
conservative 166, 207; political
    lexicon 148–9, 158–9, 212
Constitution (1946) 140, 142
contract editors 163, 196–9; different
    social experience 197–9; salary
    199
copyrights 55; infringement by
    foreign publishers 160, 211–2
corporate: communications 71–5,
    77–8, 179–80, 202–4; space
    162–3, 179–80
cosplay 113
cultural: capital 110, 168; citizenship
    202; institutions 92–7, 202–3;
    similarity 124–6
cute 28, 112, 122, 182, 184

Dentsu 161
Disney 28–9, 111
distribution networks 67–9
division of labour 50–1
dōjinshi 105–6, 109, 111–2, 125, 127,
    132–3
dōjinshi artists 109–113, 128–32,
    134, 137–8

early postwar period 24–30, 59–60
editors 7–9, 16–8, 164, 180;
    consciousness 186–8, 198–9, 204;
    creative work 162–201, 205–6;
    cultural tastes 168–9; ideas 172–4,
    178, 180, 183, 197, 199–200, 206;
    innovation 188–196, 205–6;
    management track 167–8; social
    class 166–9; university education
    166–9, 175, 197–8
editorial: meetings 9, 172–3;
    production 51, 103
education 6, 10, 29, 32, 63, 71, 78–9,
    97, 110–1, 166–7, 169–72, 174,
    176, 200–1
emotional expression 6–7
Environment White Paper in Manga
    95–6

Equal Employment Opportunity Law
    (EEOL) 178
ex-radicals 105

fantasy 127–8, 180
fanzine networks 105, 110; Anglo-
    American 124–6, 210
feminism 145
film 41–2, 174, 175
foreign: artists 163, 180, 193–196;
    cultural experts 92–3; press 92
Fukumoto Yōji 189, 192–3

Garnham, Nicholas 209
GARO 31, 37, 40, 45, 68, 73, 103–4,
    117, 152, 188–9; GAROtique 189
gender disjuncture 123–4, 137–8
gekiga 17, 25–9, 31–4, 37, 46, 54, 73,
    90, 92, 102–3, 112, 128, 133, 136,
    143, 152, 188–9, 207; assimilation
    202; erotic gekiga magazines 105,
    143, 151
Ginnansha 185, 197–9
girls': culture 138, 150; manga 37, 45,
    48, 111–5, 117, 138, 152, 178, 202
government agencies 10, 13, 70, 136,
    139, 152–8, 140, 142–3, 148, 152,
    154, 202
Gulf War 87, 206

'harmful' manga 141–4, 147–54, 211
Hatanaka Jun 141, 183
Hata Tsutomu 83
heroes 82, 84, 173, 178, 181, 186
hippies 37, 129
Hirokane Kenshi 17, 82–5, 93, 172,
    176–7, 207
history teaching 73, 76, 77, 89, 143–4
homoerotica 117–8, 122, 124–5, 210
homosexuality 124
hungry, conceptually 185, 199

Indecency Act 140–1
'indecent' manga 139–141
individualism 37, 137–8, 169, 182,
    199, 204
industrial reproduction 61–2

information manga 11, 70–8, 161, 164, 174–7, 202
intellectual balance of power 12, 180, 199, 205–6
internet 44, 105
Ishinomori Shotaro 34, 36, 70, 78, 91–2, 95, 103–4, 113, 157–8, 161, 174
Iwaaki Hitoshi 189–90

Jamie Bulger 11, 128
Japanimation 125
Japan Inc. 70–2, 161, 164, 174, 203
Japan Publisher's Association 148, 151

Kaji Ryūsuke's Principles 81, 84–6, 171, 174, 176–7, 179, 207
kamishibai: see picture card shows
kashihon: see rental manga
Kawaguchi Kaiji 17, 86–7, 113, 134, 172, 176, 186, 196
Kobayashi Yoshinori *(Arrogance Manifesto)* 87–90, 150, 152, 171–2,180–1, 210
Kōdansha 14–8, 40, 48, 165–7, 178
konjō manga 184–9
Kurihara Akira 5

Lane, Micheal 164, 169
Left-wing 12, 31–7, 87, 90, 98, 185–6, 198, 200, 207; assimilation 204
Liberal Democratic Party (LDP) 84, 86, 91, 146, 156–7, 186, 2–3
local government 139, 142–3, 151–2, 154–5, 203
Lolita complex *(Lolicom)* manga 11, 46, 109, 121–4, 128, 134–5, 152, 184, 202; publishing 134–5, 149; Lolita-ization 122
love-comedy 143, 149

Made in Japan 73–5, 77–8
manga: competitions 52, 54, 189; circles and clubs 106–8, 134;

conventions 106–8, 170; criticism 92–101, 104, 162, 164; classics 77; exhibitions 13,93–5; hand-written 104; international marketing 12–3, 160–1; price 30, 77; promotion 161, 164, 202–3, 205; as a form of public relations 78–9; retail 69; theory 100–1; secondary meaning 29; system of valuation 136
manga artists: assistants 51–2, 58–9, 189, 193; associations 22–3, 55, 112, 157–161; 'canning' 18, 56; contracts 54–5; female 109, 111–2, 114–5, 173; geniuses 178, 181–2; image of 133; income 55, 103–4; lack of ideas 182–3, 206; newcomers *(shinjin)* 56, 181–4, 188–9; numbers of 52; personality 178; role in manga production 163, 176, 199; role in society 159–161; social class 169–171; social experience 178–80, 183–4, 188, 196; studio production system 51–2, 55
Manga Boy 28, 52
Manga History of Japan 73, 76, 77, 161, 174, 200
Manga Japan 153, 159–61
Manga Studies 95, 97–101
Mangaism 104
Marxism 22, 104, 185
masculinity 83, 121, 124, 145, 179
masturbation 69, 182, 184
middle class 9, 10, 110, 169, 200–1
mini communications 104–5, 111
Ministry of Education and Culture 70, 73, 203
Miuchi Sakue 113–5
Miyazaki Tsutomu 11, 126–30
Miyazawa Rie 140
Modern Manga Library 94
Monbushō: see Ministry of Education and Culture
moral panic 11, 126, 129, 131, 138
Morizono Milk 134, 150–1, 160, 202
Morning 15–16, 133, 171–9, 182,

188, 193, 198, 200, 207;
international project 14, 193–6

Nanking massacre 89, 210
Narita airport 186
Narita Akira 17
National Assembly for Youth
Development (NAYD) 153–6, 164,
203
national: culture 92–4, 164–5, 202,
204; identity 91–4, 96–7, 126
National Olympic Memorial Youth
Centre (NYC) 153
neo-conservative 10, 70, 87–9
nerd 128, 112, 128–38, 184, 199;
nerdish 134–5, 182, 188
New Frontier Party 204
new politics 203, 206–7
newspapers 6, 11, 70, 73, 79, 90, 97,
121, 144, 164, 166, 174, 200
NGOs (domestic) 140, 152–8
nostalgia for the Sixties and Seventies
184–8

offset printing 104–5, 136
original manga 117, 119
originality 119–20, 181
otaku 128, 112, 128–38, 184, 199;
otakuppoi 134–5, 182, 188
Otaku Studies 131
over-particularism 133, 182–4
Ozawa Ichiro 86, 204

paper 63, 69;
paper shortage 23, 26
parody manga 113, 116–21, 124, 205
passion 162–3, 165, 173, 183–8, 199;
lack of 178, 180–2, 184–5, 196;
compensation for 188–99
Peter-pan syndrome 137
photography 175–7
picture card shows 24–5
Playstation 44, 66
police activity 146, 149, 151–2
political and economic manga 79–81,
176–7, 202, 206–7
political censorship 152, 202;

centralization 203; correctness
145, 203, 206
pop music 4
pornography 45–7, 133, 140–5, 148–9
printing plants 62–6
pro-establishment pop-culture 207
professional activist housewives 156
profits 7, 40–1, 181
Parent Teacher Association (PTA) 34,
136, 139, 151–2, 154, 156
pubic hair 140–1
Puff 108–9, 134
'pure literature' 116
Publishing Ethics Committee 148–9
Publisher's Union 157

racism 143
rave 4, 110
readers 43, age of 48–9; categorization of 44–9, 182, 186, 204–5
Red Army 32, 173, 186
regulation of manga 144–7, 157,
202–3; regulated series 149–152;
self–regulation 147–9, 162
rental manga 24–30, 50–1, 102, 188
respectable 11, 159–60, 163–6,
172–3, 200, 205
responsible 158–60, 164–6, 71, 207
realism in manga 72–84, 90, 163,
166, 171, 175–6, 179–80, 201, 207
retro culture 188–193, 207
Right-wing 87, 89
Royal wedding, parody of 152

Satonaka Machiko 157–9
Scientific Thought Group 97–8, 101,
210
script writer 58, 178, 209
Section Chief Shima Kōsaku 79–83,
171, 179, 207
serial child murder 126–8, 130
Seventies (1970s) 37–9, 108–9
sexual images 144–5, 148, 202
shadow cultural economies 110–1
Shirato Sanpei 24, 26–7, 31–2, 77,
103–4, 143, 185
shōjo 122, 124

shop keepers' children 170
Silent Service 79, 85–7, 113, 116,
    171, 175–6, 207
Sixties 9, 10, 11, 30–7, 48, 102–4,
    106, 111, 119, 127, 134, 139,
    180–1
slash 125, 211
social: direction 162–3, 181, 184–5,
    196; élites 90, 111, 163, 166–9,
    172, 200; fragmentation 137–8,
    182, 204–5
Society for the Freedom of
    Expression in Manga 156–161;
    'Appeal' to readers 158
Society for the Protection of Children
    from Manga Books 145, 154
specialist information in manga
    174–6; field-trips 176; informants
    174–5; objectification of manga
    175
sports manga 184–5
Star Trek 125
story manga 4, 28–9
subculture: control of 135–6; genres
    112–121; industries 108–9, 132
subjectivity 7, 175, 182, 188, 193,
    205
surveillance 139

tachiyomi 43
Taku Hachiro 89, 130–1
'tasteless' *(gehin)* manga 5, 11,
    141–2, 149, 168, 200
team production 175
television 3, 6, 30–1, 40–1, 44, 174–5,
    186, 200
tenkō 207
Tezuka Osamu 27–9, 51, 54, 94–5,
    99–100, 103, 111–2, 143–4, 159
Thirties (1930s) 22–3
Tokyo Metropolitan Government
    (TMG) 142, 155
Tokyo Metropolitan Police 132, 155
Tokyo Mothers' Society 145, 155–6
Tokyo Museum of Modern Art 92, 95,
    203

Tokyo Style 211
Tomorrow's Joe 32, 35, 143, 185,
    187–8
Tsuge Yoshiharu 25, 37, 40, 77, 104,
    189, 208
Tsurumi Shunsuke 5, 25, 97–8, 170
Twenties 1920s, 9, 20–2,
typesetting 59–60, 62

uchiawase 55–6
Uchida Masaru 31, 159, 185
ukiyoe 19–20, 93
underground 37–9, 102–3, 106
United Nations 87, 176
unsold stock 68–9
unuseable artists 162–201, 205;
    'useless' artists 163

violence 34, 133, 143–6, 196

wartime 22–4, 29, 37, 89, 92, 98, 143
Waseda University 2, 32, 167, 173,
    198
weekly manga magazines 30–6, 43,
    51–2; production cycle 57–61,
    102–3
Williams, Raymond 206
working class 5, 6, 9, 12, 110,
    169–71, 200–1

Yagyō 104
Yahagi Takako 118, 131
yaoi 113, 116–8, 124–5, 137, 184,
    202
Yokoo Tadanori 37–9
Young Womens Christian Association
    (YWCA) 153, 155
youth magazines 45–9, 209
Youth Affairs Office 153
Youth Ordinance *(seishonen jōrei)*
    141–2, 146, 148–9
Youth Policy Unit 142, 147–8, 164
Youth Volunteers 153–4

Zengakuren 32, 185, 200